INDIE AUTHOR CONFIDENTIAL

SECRETS NO ONE WILL TELL YOU ABOUT BEING A WRITER, VOL. 8-11

M.L. RONN

CONTENTS

VOLUME 8

VOLUME 9

VOLUME 10

BECOME A TECHNOLOGY AND DATA-DRIVEN
WRITER

LOOKING FORWARD

VOLUME 8

INDIE AUTHOR CONFIDENTIAL

Secrets No One Will Tell
You About Being a Writer

VOL. 8

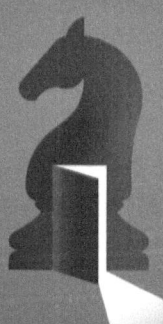

M.L. RONN

INTRODUCTION

I always love starting a new year. The first quarter is always a power quarter for me. I often get more done in the first quarter than other quarters combined. There's something about the winter that inspires me to work faster. It's probably my go-to combination of tea and moody jazz, which is always a more effective combo when it's cold and depressing outside. They help me think deeper. Winter is often my most intellectually creative season for this reason.

2022 promises to be just as crazy of a year as 2020 and 2021. There's still so much uncertainty about the COVID-19 pandemic and how it is going to end, but there are some positive signs that the virus is weakening. Hopefully, that's true for all of our sakes. This disease is driving people nuts, literally and figuratively.

2022 also represents a clean slate for my writing business because I've streamlined my strategy to three strategic pillars instead of five. As a result, I have fewer goals to achieve, which gives me more clarity and focus as I target the most important tactical objectives.

My Core Strategic Priorities

As a refresher, my mission is to create content that entertains and/or educates my audience, preferably both, and to remain nimble in an ever-changing industry. I do this by focusing on three strategic priorities:

- Become a world-class content creator
- Become a technology and data-driven writer
- Become the writer of the future (looking forward)

I believe these three priorities are most important for me to have a long-term, sustainable career.

I have updated the format of this book moving forward. There will only be three sections—one for each strategic pillar—and you can expect approximately 10 chapters in each (down from 12).

By streamlining future volumes of *Indie Author Confidential*, I will free up more time to write fiction, which has always been my focus. But you can still expect the same quality of content in this series.

What's in This Volume

This volume is the most diverse volume I have written yet.

In the World-Class Content Creator section, I discuss lessons learned from getting COVID a second time, an important lesson I learned from studying Dean Koontz this quarter, and a new approach I took to managing my intellectual property that is already paying off massive dividends. I also talk about my exploration into creating my first large print edition.

In the Technology and Data-Driven Writer section, I discuss why I finally made the leap to purchase 1000 ISBNs.

This was a big deal for me, and it opens up so many capabilities that I didn't have before. I also talk about experiments with AI-assisted software for writing my books and why it's a cornerstone of my production process moving forward. I also discuss a colossal success in Q3 2021 that turned out to be a colossal failure. Funny how things change in just six months.

In the Looking Forward (formerly Become the Writer of the Future) section, I talk about the dizzying number of technologies that will be coming in the near future, how I dealt with a recent bout of overwhelm, the continued rise of cover design costs, and what I would do if I were starting my writing business again today in 2022. I am calling this section Looking Forward because I will use it to discuss the future of writing, but also other topics that don't neatly fit into the other categories.

Like I said, I cover a lot of ground in this volume, and I hope it makes for intriguing reading.

Enjoy this volume.

M.L. Ronn
February 1, 2022
Des Moines, Iowa

BECOME A WORLD-CLASS
CONTENT CREATOR

DEALING WITH COVID (AGAIN)

In January 2022, I tested positive for COVID-19. I'm fairly certain it was the Omicron strain.

At the time, I was fully vaccinated and boosted. I had cold-like symptoms and a sore throat for several days. Fortunately, I was fine with no long-lasting symptoms or long COVID.

The illness took me away from writing for a week because my entire family caught it.

My then manuscript-in-progress went untouched. My emails piled up. I had to postpone a speaking event. I missed a week of work.

Yet, something miraculous happened.

My books kept selling,

I landed a speaking engagement.

My business bills remained paid.

When I recovered and sat down at my computer to write, I picked up where I left off. After two days, I was caught up.

Having COVID helped me slow down and reflect on what is most important. It also helped me think about the future of my writing business. That was a blessing.

In the grand scheme of my lifetime, one week is nothing.

The week after COVID, I wrote 20,000 words, which more than made up for the week I lost. The law of averages is always in my favor.

Don't beat yourself up if you have to take time away from your writing. It'll all work out in the end. What matters most is that you sit back down and resume when you're recovered.

A REMINDER THAT TABLES OF CONTENTS ARE UNDERRATED

While researching for my book, *The Author Estate Handbook*, I wanted to find some good resources.

I was browsing for legal books on the topic. Wills. Trusts. Estate planning basics. Executor guides. I had a lot of choices.

The experience was a powerful reminder of how important tables of contents are for nonfiction. Out of the 12 or so books I browsed, one of them had an amazingly granular table of contents. It was much more detailed than the other books, whose contents had an air of sameness about them. It didn't just have a chapter on wills—it had several subchapters, each one exploring a different legal problem with wills. It did this for every chapter.

After reading the table of contents, I felt like the book had so much more to offer, even though it was the same length and in the same price range as the other books. I bought it without hesitation.

It was a reminder to me that tables of contents are prime real estate in my nonfiction books. If you can show value in the table of contents by being more thorough than comparable books, you'll stand out.

I took that lesson to heart again when I wrote *The Author Estate Handbook.*

DEAN KOONTZ PATTERN INTERRUPTS

I was reading *Odd Thomas* by Dean Koontz. I had a bad experience with Dean Koontz in the early 2000s—I read *Watchers* and didn't like it. I thought I wasn't a Dean Koontz fan until I read *Odd Thomas*. Now he's one of my favorites. Funny how one book can distort your perception. It's easy to forget that authors evolve, and that one book isn't truly representative of an author's aesthetic.

As I was reading the book, section after section captivated me. I wondered how Koontz did it.

After I finished reading, I went back to a few of the sections that I enjoyed and tried to dissect them to see if there was anything I could learn.

To say that I learned a lot was an understatement. Studying Koontz was like walking through the doorway to another world.

I could talk about many techniques that Koontz uses that I will soon be incorporating into my own work, but the one that resonated with me most was his pattern interrupts.

I wrote a book called *The Writing Craft Playbook*, and it is a recap of a few techniques that mega-bestsellers use to keep readers hooked. In that book, I talk about the concept of fiction as fabric. Let me explain this before I dig into Koontz's technique.

A few years ago, my wife and I visited an outlet mall. This outlet mall has stores by many designer brand names. You can often buy clothes at this outlet mall for much cheaper than you could, say, on the coasts.

But there is just one problem with this mall: sometimes the clothes have defects. I once bought a shirt where the seams were crooked. I've learned to be careful when shopping here, so I inspect my clothes thoroughly before I buy them.

During this shopping trip, I happened to buy some dress shirts, and I specifically remember checking the seams due to my last bad experience.

After buying my shirts, I followed my wife around one of the women's clothing stores. Normally, on a trip like this, I like to find a couch or a bench and write on my phone or read a novel while my wife shops. This outlet mall doesn't have anywhere to sit—I'm convinced it's by design to get people to shop or leave.

Anyway, I had to stand around while my wife shopped, and I happened to be reading *Jurassic Park* by Michael Crichton at the time.

As I was reading, I noticed that Crichton writes in 400-to-500-word sections, followed by a "turn of thought," which is a sentence that transitions the story. For example, he'll write 400 words from the perspective of the viewpoint character about a scientific concept, and then the phone will ring, launching them into a conversation. The phone ringing is the turn of thought. The turn of thought acts as the "seam" that holds the two pieces together.

If you read Crichton's work, it's just a patchwork of little sections. The turns of thought happen like clockwork. Once you see this, you can't unsee it. It's true of almost all the mega-best-sellers.

This is where Koontz comes in. He helped me take the concept further. If you break a 400-word section into two pieces, there's another divider: a pattern interrupt.

A pattern interrupt is a change in focus. It guides the reader's eye, much like a cut in a television show or a movie. That's the best way to think about it.

Here's what I observed in one of Koontz's chapters:

- It begins with approximately 100 words of setting.
- A pattern interrupt shifts the narrative focus to the character taking an action (walking down the street). This is just one sentence.
- The narrative returns to the setting, capping it with a photographic turn of thought (the character looking up at the stars).
- Whereas the turn of thought is at the story level, the pattern interrupt is at the narrative level. The author uses them to switch cleanly between different narrative styles like setting, character voice, action, and dialogue.

This was an "a-ha" moment for me because what it really means is that a novel is just a series of 100–200-word sections. You can write 100-200 words in a few minutes. Write them, ensure that they're appropriate, finish nicely with a pattern interrupt, and every other pattern interrupt, use a turn of thought.

It's so simple! But man, simple ain't easy.

To reiterate that, here's what it looks like on the page:

- 100-200 words of a narrative choice (action, dialogue, setting, character voice, and so on)
- Pattern interrupt that uses another narrative element
- 100-200 words of a narrative choice (perhaps the same as you started with)
- Turn of thought that finishes the section cleanly
- Repeat

I know this makes fiction sound formulaic, but that's not what I'm suggesting. If you did this over and over in your novels, then it probably wouldn't turn out well.

I am suggesting that if you look at the works of mega-best-sellers, you'll see this pattern. It's one of many variations they use. You may even be doing this yourself and don't realize it.

It's an unconscious thing. I don't think authors do it on purpose. But it's perhaps the closest thing I can find to perfect form.

That's an important lesson that Dean Koontz taught me.

QR CODES IN A PAPERBACK

A reader emailed me with some questions. One of them was what I thought about putting QR codes in a paperback that take readers to a certain place.

I've heard of this over the years, but I never really considered it. QR codes are mainstream, but they never really took off the way people thought they would. Android users are familiar with them because QR codes are built into the Android operating system, but Apple dislikes them. They make you take a bunch of steps to scan a code.

That said, I still think it's a great idea. It got me thinking about what a proper execution would look like if I ever wanted to do it.

You can create QR codes on many websites for free with an account. You can route people to a website link or a document. It just takes a few seconds.

Let's take the following use case: in one of my paperbacks, I want to include a QR code that routes people to my next book. I could send them to the book's sales page on my website, or I could route them to a service like Books2Read where they can choose where to purchase the book right away.

I only have a few concerns. What if QR scanners become obsolete? That would be a problem.

That's why I keep coming back to just using a simple link. As much as I like the idea, I think QR codes are more work than necessary. I do like the idea, and using them lends a certain professionalism to your marketing, but it's more to manage and maintain.

OVERVIEW OF MY MASTER PUBLISHING FILE

Last quarter, I wrote a book called *Keep Your Books Selling: How to Manage Your Book Portfolio and Make More Money*. The book gathered the lessons I learned while cleaning up my book files and sales pages.

I learned that running an organized, logical publishing business is more difficult than it seems. I also learned that no matter how organized I am, none of it will matter if I don't leave written documentation.

I began the process by asking, "What do I need to know about my books?"

I remembered reading a book by M.L. Buchman called *Planning Your Author Estate*. In that book, he gave away a free "master publishing file" template that helped you gather all the metadata for your books. It's an ingenious tool. I used that as a foundation. Many hours later, I had my own master publishing file, and boy, is it powerful.

I'll quickly cover what I capture on the spreadsheet.

- Series and series number
- Title, subtitle, and any previous titles

- Author name
- Year written
- Book type (novel, writing book, short story collection, and so on)
- Genre and subgenre
- Publisher
- Publishing style (traditional or indie-published)
- Word count
- Print page count
- Book formats published (e-book, trade paperback, audio, and so on)
- ISBNs
- Unique store identifiers (such as ASINs)
- Price per format
- Original publication date
- Date copyright registered
- Copyright registration number
- Links for the major retailers
- Distributors that carry the book (like Draft2Digital and PublishDrive)
- Book Funnel link
- Cover designer and year designed
- Cover design cost
- Whether I have font and image licenses on file for the cover
- Whether I have model releases on file for the cover
- Whether I have the cover source files and draft materials on file
- Prior designer information
- Current version published
- The date that version was uploaded
- The date the book passed EPUB validation

- The date I checked all internal and external links in the book
- File formats I have saved the book in
- Book description version and date published
- Editor information and dates edited
- Editing cost
- Whether I have the edits on file
- Trade paperback trim size, interior color, and page color
- Hardcover trim size, interior color, and page color
- Audiobook publication date, narrator, and ACX contract terms
- Whether I have the audiobook MP3s on file

That's not all of the fields, but it's most of them. I did this exercise for every single book I published. To say it was tedious and painstaking is an understatement.

But this process helped me create a system that I can replicate for every new book that I publish. A few days after I publish a book, I simply fill out the spreadsheet. All the data is captured once and forever.

Even better, I can use the master publishing file to run pivot tables. Earlier this quarter, I decided that I wanted to jump into hardcovers all-in. I've dabbled with them, but now I'm ready to run. However, KDP Print and IngramSpark have minimum and maximum page counts for hardcover books. I needed to know quickly which of my books fell outside the boundaries. In just a few seconds, I created a pivot table that gave me a list of books that I could not publish in hardcover. Everything else was eligible.

This exercise also helped me spot gaps in my catalog. For example, I discovered that I had accidentally left the price of one of my books at $0.99! I also realized that my pricing strategies needed some work. I was able to see the prices of all my books in one place, and that helped me determine a better strategy.

The exercise also prompted me to review my pricing strategy in international currencies. I wasn't always consistent with how I priced a book in England, for example. Now all of that is fixed.

I also discovered, to my embarrassment, that I had published a Book 1 in a series with a 6x9 trim, but the sequels were 5.25 x 8. Oops!

These things happen, especially if you don't have a system. Fortunately, they can all be fixed. This exercise helped me clean up my portfolio, make more money, and increase the value of my portfolio overall. I believe having a well-managed portfolio of intellectual property is important, especially when you have as many books as I do.

I'm so glad I took the time to do this project. It took a lot of time, effort, and money, but it has already paid for itself. I have more peace of mind than I ever had in my early years of publishing when I only had a few books. I'm never more than a few clicks away from knowing what's going on with all my books. That's something every author should strive for.

THE AUTHOR HEIR HANDBOOK: AN INTELLECTUAL SWING AND MISS?

This quarter, I finished a book called *The Author Heir Handbook*, which is a follow-up to *The Author Estate Handbook*. It's the heir's guide to understanding and managing a literary estate. My master plan with the book was to recommend it at the back of *The Author Estate Handbook* as a must-buy for authors to give to their heirs. I envisioned it as a perfect stocking stuffer or something to slip into a safe deposit box for an heir to read when an author passes away.

I thought it would be a good idea to write a book for author heirs because, to my knowledge, there are no books on the market for them. Trust me when I say they are going to need a lot of help. I predict there will be a cottage industry of free-lancers who exclusively work with author estates in ten to twenty years once many prominent self-published authors start dying.

I like to establish thought leadership for opportunities like this. I tend to be ahead of my time when it comes to these types of books, but the investment will pay for itself in the long term.

I decided to write the book and jumped in without thinking too much more about it. As I wrote the book, something didn't feel right. I didn't like the "tone" of the book. It felt like I was just giving orders, and I didn't think that's appropriate given the fact that many heirs' situations will be different. With authors, I feel more comfortable doing that because, well, I'm an author!

I scrapped the book. I *never* do that. I commit to a book, write it with every inch of my soul, publish it, and then forget about it. But I took a few days to rethink this book because something about it bothered me.

What I realized (and should have known) was that this book is technically for a different target audience. It's not for authors; it's for heirs. And, if my hunch about heirs is correct, they won't have any understanding of the publishing industry. I couldn't use jargon; I'd have to use plain English. I would have to explain the writing life in ways that I haven't explained it before, and I would have to do it for an audience whose background would be far more diverse than my typical author audience. An heir could be twenty years old or seventy; they could live in any country in the world; they could be tech-savvy or barely use a computer; and most importantly, they could all be inheriting vastly different estates. An heir whose author followed my *Author Estate Handbook* would be in a much better position to manage the estate than an author who did no estate planning at all.

I'll admit that this realization disoriented me. If I was going to approach the book again, I'd have to do it with a softer touch and a different angle.

I tried again.

Here's how I did it.

First, I committed to plain English. I don't know if I succeeded, but I tried. I really did. In retrospect, I think writing a calculus book would have been much easier than trying to explain the publishing industry to non-publishing people.

Second, I kept the paragraphs short. I hit the Return key more than I usually do. I kept the sentences short too. And most importantly, I capped almost all the chapters at around 1500 words, which I think is a nice bite-sized length. Many were less than that. Smaller chapters are easier to consume.

Third, I defined all terms. I never assumed that the heir knew what a term meant. Much of the book is defining terms and explaining them with simple examples.

Fourth, I took the approach of giving the heir awareness rather than explaining in detail *how* to do something. I used the chapters to explain a problem, give examples of how one *might* solve the problem, and then mention the names of sites or resources the heir can look up to find more information. This is a double-edged sword because some readers will definitely want more hand-holding. But as I pointed out, this is impossible to do that because every reader is starting from a different place. I had to keep the book high-level, which goes against my nature given that *The Author Estate Handbook* was the most detailed book I've ever written. There was no way around this.

Fifth, I had to omit some topics. I completely stayed away from any legal or financial topics, again because I didn't know where the reader would be coming from.

The result was a 30,000-word nonfiction book that I hope will give heirs a foundation of what they need to know about running an author estate. It walks them through securing the estate, organizing the estate, and managing the estate. I teach them how to create an inventory of the author's books (using a streamlined version of a master publishing file), how to update books on retailers, and how to refresh books over time with new covers, new book descriptions, and more. There's also a chapter on marketing.

Will the book be successful? I have no idea. It was the most difficult book I've written since *The Indie Author Bestiary*.

Do I care if the book is successful? Not really. I committed to the idea, saw it through, and now it's in the world.

There are only three possible futures for a book:

- it will perform poorly, selling a few copies every now and again (but still increasing my income over time)
- it will sell as well as my other titles
- it will outperform everything and change the trajectory of my writing business as I know it

You never know what will happen until you publish. *The Author Heir Handbook* was an interesting intellectual challenge, and it taught me some valuable lessons that I will apply to future books.

LESSONS FROM CREATING MY FIRST LARGE PRINT EDITION

I finally broke down and bought ISBNs. That's a huge deal for me because I've been so resistant to doing it in the past. I'll talk about that later.

But now that I have ISBNs, I can create additional formats for my books. One of the first items on my list is large print editions.

This was especially on my mind as I created *The Author Estate Handbook*. The content lends itself to a large print edition.

I spent a weekend educating myself on the format and how to create it.

The target audience for large print editions is seniors and the visually impaired. Therefore, large print editions must follow certain rules to be considered large print. Some publishers only publish large print editions, which I found fascinating.

I'll recap what I learned about creating this format and the steps I took to successfully create my first edition.

. . .

Formatting Considerations

First, I had heard that Vellum can create large print editions. I create all of my other editions in it, so I figured I'd try it. While Vellum can create large print editions, it misses some key elements of the format. I found myself shaking my head as I created my large print edition in Vellum.

Atticus handles large print editions much better. It's still not my main formatting app yet because I believe it still needs some work, but in the future, I may consider moving my large print editions to it.

Large print editions will always have more pages than a trade paperback because the font size is bigger. The recommended font size is 18 points with 1.25 or 1.5 line spacing. The margins in a large print book are wider too. All of this will increase your printing costs considerably, so indie authors should use the biggest trim size they can to keep the costs down. That size is 6.14 x 9.21, but you could also do 6 x 9.

It is also recommended that the body font in a large print edition be a sans serif font to increase readability. (Vellum only offers serif fonts—one of the reasons why I shook my head.)

You cannot have smaller fonts in the book than your body. This means that if you have images with captions, you have to remove the captions and make them part of the body text. You also must put footnotes at the end of a chapter and make them big enough to read.

You should use block paragraphs instead of indentations, and the text should be left-justified (ragged right). Hyphenation at the end of a line is a big no-no.

You should also avoid large blocks of capital letters, particularly in chapter headings. Unfortunately, this is something I cannot avoid at this time.

Images should be aligned to the left to improve readability, which is something Atticus can do (but Vellum cannot).

Another important element of large print editions is to avoid italics. I'm guilty of using italics a lot in my nonfiction. I'll be rectifying that moving forward. It is recommended that you replace italicized text with bold text instead.

Cream pages are the best recommendation to help with contrast. Fortunately, all my books are in cream anyway.

So, if I look at the requirements for a large print edition, I can meet all of them except:

- sans serif font
- no large blocks of capital letters in the chapter headings

Complaints about Vellum aside, that's not bad. It's not perfect, but it's not enough to hold back creating an edition. I believe that the Vellum developers will eventually get this right, and when they do, I can regenerate titles and reupload them as needed.

Marketing Considerations

It's critical to differentiate a large print edition from the regular trade paperback. Otherwise, you'll have some disappointed readers.

For this reason, it's a good idea to include the words "Large Print Edition" in the book title when you publish it. KDP Print and IngramSpark also let you designate a title as a large print edition.

You should also put a button on the cover with the words

"large print" on them. This will make it easy for readers to see that it's a special edition.

I would also recommend putting the words "large print" on the title and copyright pages of the book just to cover all of your bases. This way, no one can give you a bad review claiming they didn't know what they were buying. If they do, it's clear that they can't read.

Make sure you don't forget the back cover. It should also be in a sans serif font in a big font. I suspect many people are missing this one.

You've also got to think about a pricing strategy. If your trade paperback is priced at $14.99, you might want to price the large print at $16.99 or $18.99, depending on the printing economics. Whatever you do, you should have a strategy so your large print pricing is uniform across titles.

(Oh, and I forgot to mention that you can create hardcover large print editions too! Libraries prefer large prints hardcovers because they last longer.)

The main goal is to get the large print edition to show up next to the trade paperback on the striker's sales page. This makes the book look more professional.

In researching this, I noticed that a lot of authors weren't doing this. In fact, the large print edition was the only edition of the print book on the sales page. I believe the reason for this is that there is a data issue between Amazon and Ingram, and it's easier for authors to create a large print edition as the only edition.

From what I could tell, the proper way to handle this is to create all your paperbacks on Ingram and don't use KDP Print. Otherwise, Amazon may suppress the Ingram versions. I don't know any of this for sure; these are just observations. But in my opinion, it doesn't make sense to only have a large print edition as the paperback unless your target audience is seniors or the visually impaired.

There's another key issue that I believe is preventing more authors from creating large print editions: retailers don't really like them. Amazon is biased against them. You have no idea if a book is a large print edition until you click on it. It shows up as "paperback" on the sales page. You have to click into additional formats to see the large print edition, but even then, you won't see it unless the author put the words large print in the title. You'd think Amazon would be better about this.

So, the burden is on the author to let readers know large prints exist. You could do this by putting a line at the top of the book description that says "Now available in e-book, paperback, audio, and large print!"

You should also consider putting this on your website, with a direct link to the large print edition. Otherwise, readers won't know that it exists.

As I said, there's a lot to consider, and a lot of steps to follow if you want to do this correctly. I observed several self-published authors on Amazon who are not publishing large print editions correctly, and I think that's going to come back to bite all of us if retailers ever decide to start enforcing rules.

I believe we are in the early days of self-published large print editions. At some point, retailers will make it easier to publish them and easier for readers to find them.

My strategy moving forward is to publish large print editions on day one. It's just a few extra steps for me in the publication process, and the design cost is minimal.

The real question is how I plan to handle my backlist. At some point, I would like to enable large print editions for my backlist, but that will require a considerable time and money investment that may not provide a profitable return for a long time. I'll probably create large print editions for a few titles per year and whenever I refresh covers.

MAXIMIZING MY PORTFOLIO

In a previous chapter, I talked about creating my master publishing file. It allows me to know what's going on with my books.

It also helps me spot opportunities and fill in gaps. A question I've started asking is "What can I do this month to maximize my portfolio?"

What if I could wave a magic wand and make my portfolio the best it could be? What would that look like?

For starters, I would have:

- All of my books available in e-book, trade paperback, hardcover (dust jacket), audiobook, AI audiobook, and large print editions.
- All of my books at all possible retailers and distributors that are willing to carry them, with bookstores and libraries able to buy any book in my catalog.

I can do all of this now, whereas I couldn't necessarily do it a few months ago before I purchased ISBNs.

Since I have fewer goals for 2022, I've decided to spend a few hours each month maximizing the portfolio. In reviewing the first quarter, I identified the following opportunities with just my 2014 titles alone:

- I can create an audiobook edition of my book, *Muse Poems*. The audiobook would be less than an hour and cheap to produce. While I probably wouldn't make much from this edition, it would fill in a gap.
- Remove an early audiobook from sale. I did this on a royalty-share on ACX. I need to pull the book down because it no longer fits in my portfolio. This will require me to buy out the narrator on ACX.
- Create a new cover for my short story collection *Reconciled People*. It's the oldest cover in the portfolio and it desperately needs a refresh.
- Expand my distribution to StreetLib, which is a European book distributor that distributes to many retailers around the globe that I can't reach with my current distribution partners.
- Republish all my paperbacks with a new ISBN and distribute them on IngramSpark. This will make them available for bookstores and libraries.

Which one should I do? There's no wrong answer. I'll probably do several of them this year, prioritizing the ones that will bring me the most income first.

Tending to a book portfolio is like tending to a garden. There's always something to do, and if you want a nice garden, you have to spend more time than anyone else is willing to spend.

I'm excited about this new way of thinking about my books,

and I know that it is going to pay dividends over the next decade.

CORRECTING A MISTAKE FROM THE PAST

The first year of any author's publishing career is probably riddled with mistakes. I am no exception. I made almost every mistake you can imagine in 2014.

I was learning how to write fiction and dealing with all the struggles that go along with being new to the craft.

I was learning book formatting, and while my e-books looked okay, my paperbacks looked awful.

I spent a fortune to buy a trademark, which I ended up abandoning because I quickly realized my mistake.

I spent money on marketing in all the wrong places.

My early covers were awful.

And that's just scratching the surface. Perhaps one of my biggest mistakes in 2014 was engaging in royalty-shares with audiobook narrators. It sounded like such a great idea at the time—pay nothing upfront, get a great-sounding audiobook, and then share royalties with a narrator!

Except that the royalty-share is in perpetuity. There is no time limit on it. Almost all the early titles I produced did not sell a single copy. As a result, I can't do anything with the format. I can't pull it down and create a new edition because I signed a perpetual contract. Again, colossal mistake. If I knew what I know now, I wouldn't have done it.

That said, the narrators I worked with were fantastic people and they all did a great job.

I reviewed the ACX contract and determined that there is a way out of the royalty-share agreement: buying out the narrator. I have heard of authors doing this.

I decided to see if I could reduce the number of royalty-share titles in my catalog to maximize the number of rights I have. One of those was for my book *Eaten: The Complete First Season*, which I ultimately rebranded, rewrote, and republished as *Food City*. The audiobook is just floating out there. It hasn't sold a single copy since 2015.

I offered to pay the narrator a generous sum that accounted for what I would have paid them plus what the title could have earned over the next seven years. The narrator accepted the offer, we signed a contract that I drafted, and we contacted Audible to have the title removed. Once they did, I paid the narrator and rested easy knowing that I could pull the title down and not have any encumbrances on it moving forward.

I take full responsibility for the title. It was unfair to the narrator to create a title that didn't do well, and I view it as my responsibility to do something about it. This was an expensive mistake but one that I'm thankful I can correct. Over the next few years, I'll work with my narrators to dissolve royalty-share agreements that didn't turn out the way we both hoped. But I have to do this while ACX allows it, and while the narrators are still alive. Otherwise, if a narrator passes away, I am literally stuck in a perpetual agreement, and I have no idea if the narrator has heirs who will even receive their share of the income. My only option at that point will be to use copyright termination, and I'm not so sure that it would work because I would still own the copyright—I would have just given away perpetual distribution rights.

Yep, this is what happens when you don't think ahead. But as I said, most mistakes in this new world of publishing are fixable. At least I didn't give away the copyright or lose the rights to the work, or worse, all my works. It's just a constant reminder that there are always consequences to everything you do.

HOSPITALITY WOES

I traveled recently and stayed at a hotel. My wife and I like this particular hotel franchise because it is family-friendly. We have stayed at this hotel many times, but this was the first time we stayed there since the pandemic began.

The hotel had completely changed.

The lobby was dirty.

The two front desk attendants carried on a long conversation as if we weren't standing there waiting to check in.

The room was barely clean and didn't feel fresh.

The breakfast and happy hour were pathetic, with old food, watered-down beer, poorly mixed drinks, and employees who seemed to hate their lives.

And don't even get me started on the swimming pool—I'm convinced the water was carrying legionella. I did *not* swim in the pool.

I couldn't believe how far the hotel had fallen. It wasn't just one thing—the entire experience was bad. Even my seven-year-old daughter kept complaining, and she's normally a chipper kid who sees the best in every situation.

The pandemic hadn't been kind to the hotel. I learned that

they suffered from staffing shortages because they laid off much of their staff during the early days of the pandemic and couldn't find anyone to replace the original staff when the economy came back. They were also struggling to keep their occupancy rates high, which meant they had to drop the room rates...which explains why our stay was so cheap.

If that's not a death spiral, I don't know what is. I don't expect the hotel to remain under the current owners for long. They have two to three years max, and that's being generous. I felt bad for the establishment.

Later that month, I needed to schedule my car for routine maintenance at my local dealership. I generally reserve curse words for auto dealers, but I like my current dealer a lot. They were very fair with me when I bought my first car, and they have a package where you can get an oil change, tire rotation, and a car wash for very cheap. The technicians have always been honest with me. They've never put pressure on me to make a repair or pulled any funny business that dealers are notorious for. And trust me, I've dealt with a lot of crooked mechanics.

This dealer's service was impeccable. They had a shuttle service that I used whenever I had to drop my car off during a weekday. I got to know the shuttle drivers, who were great guys. In the early days of the pandemic, the shuttle drivers would come to my house to pick up my car so I could stay home. They did it for no charge.

And then, something happened. I usually schedule my appointments online, but I noticed that the website calendar wasn't working. I sent the dealer an email letting them know that the site was broken. I didn't receive a reply.

A few days later, I tried again with no luck. This time, I used the online chat feature—the representative didn't even bother to help me.

I called the dealer and told them about the issue on their website. I left a message. My voice mail went unreturned.

I called again and had to schedule an appointment over the phone with an employee who had terrible phone skills. I told them about the website issue and she said they'd look into it.

Three months later, they're just now getting around to fixing it...I can't imagine how much business they lost during that time. I'm a patient guy. I bet the average person would have just called someone else.

My appointment didn't go well. The technician seemed rushed, and he overcharged me. When I caught the billing error, he promptly corrected it, but the damage had been done. It was clear that I needed to find another shop.

I learned that the dealer was acquired during the pandemic by another, larger dealer conglomerate from out of state. This conglomerate, clearly incompetent, didn't like how the dealership was run, and when they tried to implement new cost-cutting rules, the staff walked out. This explained everything. I bet the dealer is hemorrhaging customers.

My point in telling you both of these stories is that the pandemic has wreaked havoc everywhere. The institutions we know are no longer the same.

The hotel I had fond memories of is now just a memory. The dealer I could trust can no longer be trusted. Now I have to find new service providers in many areas of my life. It is requiring a lot of time and effort.

Excellent customer service is almost impossible to come by right now. I can't think of the last time I had a pleasant experience calling a company since the pandemic began. People are stressed out and they have realized that their employers don't care about them. Many employers acted shamefully during the pandemic, and they got away with it.

At an employer like that, why should employees care? Especially at a call center, which was probably hell on Earth *before* the pandemic? I don't blame the employees for feeling or performing the way they do, though it is inconvenient for me. I especially don't blame them for quitting and leaving a staffing shortage.

Out of this vacuum will come opportunities. Companies who treat their people well *and* who manage to maintain superior services and products despite the devastation of the pandemic will do very well.

Some hotels found ways to weather the pandemic, and those are the ones that will survive. Same with auto dealers. But, in all cases, I would bet that they were well run before 2020.

That got me thinking about authors. The pandemic has hurt the publishing industry, authors included.

Has the pandemic blunted your customer service? Are there parts of your platform that need to be refreshed, such as parts of your website, contact forms, or other reader-facing items? This is a good time to check all your touch points with readers.

The last thing you want readers thinking right now is that you don't care.

Readers, like me, are experiencing terrible customer service everywhere too. Don't add to it. If you can strive to be a positive example, then you'll be fine.

My customer service commitment has always been to respond to emails quickly. While my response times did get slightly longer during the worst early days of the pandemic, I still respond to emails very quickly.

I keep my website up-to-date and my contact form operational. I added direct sales functionality in 2020. I'm exploring cryptocurrency functionality now. I'm always looking for ways to remain relevant and provide great service to my fans.

I keep publishing books at a regular pace. I keep trying to help people whenever I can. I hope that my stock is growing during the pandemic. I know that many authors have slowed down during these times, maybe even stopped writing altogether.

But here I am, and I plan to keep going, business as usual. Several years from now, I believe that is going to make a big difference.

BECOME A TECHNOLOGY
AND DATA-DRIVEN WRITER

WHY I FINALLY TOOK THE LEAP ON ISBNS

I finally bought my own ISBNs. After spending $1500, I am the (not-so-proud) owner of 1000 ISBNs.

I bought the block of 1000 because I have 74 books at the time of this writing, and my plan is for all my books to be available in e-book, trade paperback, hardcover, audiobook, and large print. That's at least 370 ISBNs that are spoken for. That leaves 630. If I publish books in five formats moving forward, this block will last me for 126 books. It took me about 10 years to write 100 books, so if I keep my same pace, I estimate that this block of ISBNs will last me at least that long.

The *only* reason I bought them was that I had a windfall of income near the end of 2021 and I need to make a big expense to defray the tax consequences. Seriously. That's the only reason I bought them.

Will this block of ISBNs earn me more than $1500? I think so. It will allow me to open up to new sales channels that I haven't been in before, like bookstores and libraries.

The next questions I had after buying the ISBNs were:

- How do I clean up the mess I've made for the last eight years by *not* having them?
- Do I need to republish my books to use a new ISBN?

I definitely created a mess, and there's no way around it. When you publish an e-book, you have one opportunity to enter an ISBN. If you don't, the retailer assigns a free one for you. The only exception is Amazon, which only uses ISBNs for documentation purposes. You can update an ISBN there after you publish a book.

You also lock in a free ISBN when you publish a paperback title. The only way to undo this is to unpublish the paperback and republish it with a new ISBN.

Therefore, I've decided that the best course of action is to update my ISBNs whenever I refresh titles. For example, I'll be republishing my *Good Necromancer* series with new covers and interiors sometime in 2022. I'll also be putting them under my Michael La Ronn pen name. Since I'll have to unpublish the titles anyway, I'll just use new ISBNs at that time.

At some point, I'm also going to refresh my short story collection *Reconciled People*. While I don't need to unpublish it, I'll probably do so just so I can put a new ISBN on it.

Over time, as I refresh my books, they'll all eventually get new ISBNs. This way, I'm only doing a few titles at a time and it will minimize disruption.

When you publish a new book, you have to update your website with new links, which makes this a pain. But there is definitely a benefit to having all official ISBNs on all titles in my catalog.

What if, one day, one of my books takes off and sells millions of copies? What if bookstores and libraries suddenly want more of my titles? They'll be able to buy them if I have official ISBNs. If my portfolio is a patchwork of official and unofficial ISBNs, it will hurt my professionalism.

So yes, that's the price I've paid for the last eight years. Was it worth it? Yes, I think so. I've said for a long time that I can use $1500 way more efficiently than purchasing ISBNs, and that has been true.

Now that I have this capability, I'll use it and see where it leads me.

SUDOWRITE

I've started experimenting with AI-assisted writing tools. The one I like and have been using is Sudowrite.

Sudowrite is built on the GPT-3 AI engine. It reads the text you've written and then recommends a block of 100 to 200 words as a jumping-off point.

When you have written at least 200 or so words, you can use a feature called "The Wormhole," which generates text for you. You have several options to choose from. You can import the suggested text exactly as-is, modify it, or not use it at all.

Sudowrite doesn't write your story for you, but it offers alternative directions you can take the text that you didn't consider. Sometimes the suggestions make no sense, but more often than not, they're interesting and cogent. I find this feature endlessly fascinating.

I don't think AI-assisted writing tools will replace writers anytime soon. But I do think they should be part of your author toolbox.

Another way I've been using Sudowrite is with dictation. I use it in Chrome for Windows along with the Dragon extension so I can dictate my words directly into the browser. After about

30 seconds of dictating, I hit the wormhole and see where it takes me.

I haven't used Sudowrite to write full books yet. So far, I've just been experimenting with it here and there—not enough to put a disclaimer in my books.

In Q2, I will incorporate Sudowrite into a new fiction series to see what happens. I'll click the wormhole every 500 words or so. I'm curious to see what would happen if I did this for an entire novel, or even an entire series.

If you use a tool like this that much, then I believe you should disclaim it on the copyright page so you're transparent with readers. The tool does generate text for you, so, in a way, it's a shortcut.

There are also problems with these tools, though. First, you have to be careful that you don't lose your author voice. Just because a tool recommends text, it's still not smart enough to identify what makes you YOU.

Also, these tools are often used out-of-context. If you don't use them consistently, it doesn't know what came before and it won't know what comes after. This is still a major problem with artificial intelligence and natural language processing. You're using it to generate text for the moment, which is problematic when you're telling a long-form story.

I actually think these are good things. It keeps you in control of your stories.

Oh, and by the way, I wrote this chapter with Sudowrite (but you probably knew I was going to say that). This chapter is approximately 600 words, and Sudowrite generated around 200 of those words.

If you extrapolate this throughout a novel, then it's possible that for a 50,000-word novel, then Sudowrite would generate around 16,500 words, or 33 percent.

Would this enable you to write fiction faster? Or would you

have to spend more time in revision? It's a fascinating question that I look forward to answering in the next volume of *Indie Author Confidential*.

LESSONS IN TWO-FACTOR AUTHENTICATION

While on my estate-planning journey, I learned a lot about two-factor authentication (2FA). 2FA has been around for a few years, but it's still not widely adopted. The average person has no clue how it works or why it can be detrimental to your heirs if you pass away suddenly without a plan.

I thought I would share a chapter from *The Author Estate Handbook* that covers 2FA. You may find it useful.

———

At the time of this writing, two-factor authentication (also known as 2FA, two-step verification, multifactor authentication, or MFA) is a relatively new security feature that requires a user to enter a second proof of identification to access an account.

With traditional logins, you have to enter a username and password to access an account. With two-factor authentication, you have to enter your username and password *and* verify that you are the owner using an additional method. Usually, that method is a one-time passcode that is sent via text message or email. The code is time-sensitive.

Many banks require 2FA as an additional security measure, but most companies do not require it. At the time of this writing, you usually have to opt-in for it.

I strongly recommend that you use 2FA to secure your accounts to give yourself added security while you're alive. It is designed to be foolproof, and with a few exceptions, it is. You may be using 2FA on some of your accounts already.

Another potential danger you should be aware of is identity theft after death. Cyber thieves troll obituaries and death records to look for easy prey. They can file tax returns under your name, open bank accounts, and wreak all sorts of havoc that your heirs will have to clean up. If you don't follow cyber best practices while you're alive, you will be defenseless after you're dead.

Consider that, as an author, you're a public figure, and if you've achieved some success, there may be some publicity about your death so that people can pay tribute to you. That's a prime opportunity for a thief to look for accounts to hack into—no one's going to be paying attention because they'll be busy grieving, after all. 2FA keeps you protected.

However, if you do use 2FA in any capacity, be very careful. If not, your heirs will be locked out of your accounts even if they have your usernames and passwords.

That's why 2FA is a Silver Bullet of Doom. You may be required to use it already on some sites, and more sites may require it in the future. You will not be able to get around this problem.

Most people right now are using their phones for 2FA, which is dangerous in several non-obvious ways. I bet you have received those text message passcodes again and again and never once thought about how screwed your heirs could be if they don't have access to your phone. If something happens to your phone while you're alive, you'll be locked out of your accounts until you can buy a replacement. If you die and your heirs disconnect your phone without understanding 2FA, they'll be locked out of your accounts forever.

At this juncture, you have a critical question to answer: are you using 2FA today in any capacity?

If the answer is no, the next critical question is whether you should. If you choose not to, fine.

If the answer is yes, then you may have an existential threat to both your personal and author estates. You must read this chapter and you must make sure you understand it. 2FA is not difficult, but some people may find it a little too technical and "techy." I won't deny that.

If 2FA doesn't make sense after reading this chapter, I recorded two short videos so you can see it in action. I'll link to them at the end of this chapter.

Please note that failure to take steps to address the 2FA problem may doom your author legacy. If I sound overly alarmist, it's because I don't believe enough authors understand how much danger 2FA is to their estates. I predict that too many people are going to learn the hard way. This chapter will open your eyes to just how problematic 2FA can be, and how you can address the problem safely.

Now that I've rung the alarm bells enough, let's turn them off and talk about the different types of two-factor authentication methods.

TEXT MESSAGE (SMS) AUTHENTICATION

. . .

With text message authentication, the company sends you a text message with a one-time passcode that you must enter after inputting your password. This is also known as SMS authentication. To validate your account, you must have your phone nearby. Your phone serves as your key.

SMS 2FA is the most common verification method, but it is the least secure because of an attack hackers can use called "SIM swapping." In a SIM swap attack, a hacker calls your cell phone provider and pretends to be you. They convince your provider to switch your phone number to a different SIM card. Then, when they log in to your accounts with your username and password, they receive the one-time passcode to their phone.

The chances of a SIM swapping attack are rare for most people, but it could happen.

There's another better reason not to use your phone for two-factor authentication that I mentioned previously: if something happens to your phone, you won't be able to receive text messages until you find a replacement. When you die, your phone number will eventually be terminated. What happens, for instance, if you die and your heirs disconnect your phone without realizing that they need it to authenticate your accounts? Uh oh.

Even if your heirs keep your phone active for a time, they're going to have to cancel it at some point. That's why SMS authentication is a bad idea. Yet, at the time of this writing, many companies *only* offer SMS authentication, which makes the issue more difficult. Cyber security professionals have been urging companies to move away from SMS authentication for the reasons I mentioned in this section, but companies are reluctant to do so.

. . .

MOBILE PROMPT AUTHENTICATION

Some companies such as Google rely on an app that already exists on your phone to authenticate your account.

For example, at the time of this writing, Google will ask you to open a Google app on your phone such as YouTube. When you do, a code will appear in the YouTube app and you have to match that to the code in the account where you are trying to log in.

These types of prompts are tied to your phone number. As with SMS authentication, if your phone is lost, you can't authenticate, which will lock your heirs out of your accounts.

EMAIL AUTHENTICATION

Instead of an SMS notification, you can elect to have your one-time passcode sent to your email address, which is much safer, but not 100 percent secure if your email accounts are ever breached.

However, email authentication is much better than SMS because if something happens to your phone, you can access your email from any device that has an internet connection. If you secure your email address with a strong password and two-factor authentication (for your email account itself), then it is a safe way to authenticate your accounts. Logging in to your email may be less convenient than receiving a text message, but it's still a good way to protect yourself.

Also, it's worth pointing out that if your heirs don't have access to your email accounts, then you're relegating them to doom because they'll never be able to pass 2FA for any other account you have.

APP AUTHENTICATION

You can also authenticate your account using a dedicated authenticator app. Examples include Google Authenticator, Authy, and Microsoft Authenticator. I use and recommend Authy.

All authenticator apps are free and they work the same way: they generate one-time passcodes for your accounts and change them every 30 seconds. You log in to your desired account with your username and password, open your authenticator app, grab the code, and you're in.

At first glance, authenticator apps usually scare people off because they look way too complicated, but they're not. They're not immediately intuitive, though.

To set up any authenticator app, the steps are the same:

- Go to your account dashboard, enable two-factor authentication, and then select the authenticator app option. You will see a QR code appear on the screen.
- Open your authenticator app, select "Add Account," and that will activate your QR scanner. Scan the code.
- In your authenticator app, you will then be given a one-time passcode that expires in 30 seconds. Enter the code in your desired account to complete the authentication.

- The next time you log in and are asked for the code, open your authenticator app to get it.

The major benefit of authenticator apps is that they can be used on *both* desktop and mobile devices. This means that if you pick the right one, you won't be married to your phone for codes.

Some password managers such as 1Password also allow you to generate one-time passcodes within the app. You'll see it next to your password. However convenient this is, this is less secure, because if someone hacks your password manager, they can get your codes too. It's probably safer to use a separate authenticator app.

The authenticator app I recommend is Authy. Authy works on both your desktop and phone, and it allows you to sync your account between devices. This means that if anything were to happen to your phone, you can still get the one-time passcode on a computer. Your codes are stored in the cloud, which could be a concern for some, but they are encrypted on your computer before they're sent to the cloud, so you have pretty good security.

Security experts don't recommend using cloud backups for 2FA, but the small tradeoff in security is worth it for one important reason: your heirs can install Authy on their computer, link your account, and start getting the codes right away. It's very, very useful, and it will get heirs around this Silver Bullet of Doom.

I recommend an authenticator app as your primary or secondary 2FA method.

PHYSICAL SECURITY KEY AUTHENTICATION

. . .

If you want the best security of all, you can buy a physical USB security key. After you enter your username and password, you insert your security key into a USB port on your computer or the charging port on your phone. Some sensors require you to tap the key or scan your fingerprint to authenticate your account.

This is a YubiKey 5C NFC. You insert this into a USB-C slot and then tap the gold button on the key to authenticate. It fits easily on a necklace or a key ring too.

Physical security keys are considered to be the safest authentication method because hackers can't fool them. They also can't replicate them digitally. A hacker would have to hack your accounts *and* steal your security key, which is next to impossible.

There's another good reason to use a security key. Some-times, hackers can use a trick called "spoofing." With a spoofing attack, the hackers create fake websites that look eerily similar to the real ones, such as a bank's website. They lure you to the website by sending you an email or text pretending to be the company you trust. If you enter your credentials, they'll steal your login info. A security key can detect spoofs because it scans the website domain. It will only work on the real version of the website, therefore frustrating hackers and alerting you to the fact that you were fooled. You can then immediately change your password and report the attack.

You can also take security keys with you everywhere you go. They're small enough to fit on a keychain, in a wallet, or on a necklace.

I recommend the YubiKey brand. There are many models to suit your needs, but most IT and cybersecurity professionals agree that these are the best security keys on the market. Another prominent security key model is Google Titan.

On a desktop or laptop, you can leave your security key in a USB port so that you don't have to insert it every time you need to authenticate your accounts. As long as the key is in the port, you'll enjoy near-automatic authentication.

On a phone, security keys are a little more cumbersome, but not very. You will have to insert the security key into your charging port every time authentication is needed. However, some keys support near-field communication (the same technology that powers Apple Pay and Google Pay), and you can tap the key on the back of the phone to authenticate, which is much more convenient.

I paid around $50 for each of my security keys. New models are coming out all the time, so research the one that is best for you.

If you buy a security key, buy at least two: one as your primary, and another as a backup that you keep in a fire-resistant safe or safe deposit box. You can link both to your accounts. Most places that accept security keys allow you to link an unlimited number of keys to your account. This way, your heirs can use *any* of your keys.

Security keys aren't well-supported right now, but I expect that to change in the future.

BACKUP CODES

Some providers give you one-time backup codes to use in case you are locked out of your account. These are the option of last resort, but useful if you ever need them.

If a company gives you backup codes, store them in a safe place. Write them down or put them in a password-protected file. Don't be the person who doesn't write them down and then needs them someday!

SECURING TWO-FACTOR AUTHENTICATION FOR YOUR HEIRS

At the time of this writing, not every website supports 2FA. Not every site supports it equally either.

Most banks don't support authenticator apps or hardware keys yet, so you're forced to use SMS.

Some sites like Adobe only allow SMS and email authentication.

Other sites, like Google, Facebook, and Amazon allow for all authentication methods.

As a result, if you use 2FA, you're likely using a patchwork of different methods, which is the biggest drawback right now.

My 2FA strategy is to use physical security keys as my primary method wherever and whenever possible, and an authenticator app as my secondary method. If absolutely necessary, I will use email authentication. I disable SMS at any place that will let me. I'm betting on authenticator apps and security keys enjoying better support in the future. I may be wrong, but at least I know I'm taking the best steps to secure my accounts.

Your strategy could look like mine, or it could be more conservative, with you enabling as many 2FA methods as possible to maximize your heirs' chances of recovering your accounts. It's up to you.

It's not enough just to use 2FA while you're alive. You must also be thoughtful about how your heirs will get your passcodes.

WHERE TO START

It doesn't matter whether you like 2FA and use it regularly or if you actively avoid it. Chances are high that you're using it *somewhere*, and you need to document where. Otherwise, your heirs will be locked out of your accounts.

Use a site like the 2FA Directory to determine which sites support 2FA. Go through the list slowly and write down the websites where you have accounts. Don't rely solely on your memory; you may forget one or two websites and that could be troublesome for your heirs. Some password managers like 1Password can also alert you to which companies support 2FA.

Also, go through your favorite bookmarks to see if there are any additional sites where you use 2FA.

Create a password-protected spreadsheet that records how you're addressing 2FA. I've created a template for you at www.authorlevelup.com/2FAtemplate. Modify it as you see fit. I also have an Estate Plan Organizer Excel sheet that I'll share at the end of this book that also includes a tab for 2FA.

Next, go to each website and determine which 2FA methods they support, and which ones you are willing to use. Record the website and mark which methods you are using on the spreadsheet. If the service offers backup codes, create a separate tab on the worksheet and paste your codes there.

As an obvious reminder, you'll also need to update the spreadsheet any time you create a new account that supports 2FA.

Next, password-protect the spreadsheet and store the password both in your password manager and in your fire-resistant safe or safe deposit box.

Creating this spreadsheet will be a pain, but it's the best way of getting your heirs around the two-factor authentication problem that I can think of. Otherwise, you're forcing them to guess where you've used 2FA and you're increasing the chances that they won't be able to find your codes.

Also, consider imparting some strong words to your heirs: *Under no circumstances* should your phone line be disconnected until all 2FA websites have authentication disabled or have been updated with a new phone number that your heirs will have access to. Otherwise, they could be cutting themselves off from your accounts.

FINAL THOUGHTS

When used with a password manager, two-factor authentication will maximize your security with:
- secure passwords that are difficult for hackers to guess
- passcodes that hackers won't have access to

2FA isn't the most convenient thing in the world to use, but it's critical. Many experts say that you should enable it on your email accounts, bank accounts, and other sensitive financial or health accounts at a minimum. I recommend adding it to any account you have that provides it, especially your writing-related accounts.

Two-factor authentication is a must-have in today's digital world. Not every website supports it, and most that do allow it to be optional. As cyberattacks continue, more websites will change their stance. Try if you want, but you won't be able to get around this problem even if you actively avoid 2FA.

At the time of this writing, few writing-related websites even offer it. Amazon and Draft2Digital are the first that come to mind. Expect more retailers to offer it in the coming years, either as a result of a security breach or because of user demand.

If you still need help understanding how 2FA works, I've created two short videos to help you see it visually:

•Two-Factor Authentication Explained in Three Minutes
•How to Set Up an Authenticator App in Three Minutes

You can watch the videos at www.authorlevelup.com/2FAvideos.

＝

If you're interested in *The Author Estate Handbook*, you can grab it at www.authorlevelup.com/estatehandbook.

AMAZON KDP PRINT WOES

I feel like I was the only person in the self-publishing space that had serious troubles with KDP Print last year.

Usually, I can rely on KDP Print to be my most trusted retailer channel when it comes to publishing and updating books. The paperback versions of my books are almost always available before the e-books. The same goes for any changes that I make to my books.

But in Q4 of 2021, KDP Print had major problems. A site-wide bug afflicted their servers, and it prevented changes from getting through.

I know this because it coincided with my book portfolio refresh that I covered in *Keep Your Books Selling*. Almost all of my 70+ books were updated in some form during this project.

I didn't have any problems until around book 50. Then, I noticed that the changes I requested weren't going through.

When I built my master publishing file, I implemented a versioning system on my book interiors. You can find them on the copyright page of any book I publish. You'll see "Version X.X." This helps me know which version of the book is for sale. I implemented a versioning system across all of my books exactly for the problem I'm about to describe. It's unobtrusive for the reader and helps me stay organized.

Most people would publish an update and not think about it ever again. But what happens if the retailer doesn't accept the update? You'll never know about it.

If you publish a book with some minor changes to the interior, how will you know if those changes were made? You could check the sample, but if the changes you made were past the sample, then you don't really know for sure.

That's why a versioning system helps. I keep a change log on my computer that describes the changes I made in each version of the book. Then I put the version number on the copyright page. After I upload the book, I set a calendar reminder to check the sales pages of the book across all retailers in 48 hours. If the sample on the retail page shows the correct version number, then I know the change went through. If it doesn't, then I know either to wait or to check for an error on the dashboard.

I was making changes to my paperback editions on KDP Print and the correct versions weren't showing up in the sample after a week. I emailed the KDP Print support team, and they informed me about the bug. They also assured me that the correct version would be printed if a reader purchased the book (but I don't know about that).

After the new year, I resubmitted the changes and everything appears to be fixed.

That's why you should develop a system for quality-checking your books. If you don't, then little things like this will slip past you. They'll add up over the years. The impacts could range from minor issues in the case of a few typos, or major issues in the case of broken links that should have been repaired, incorrect calls to action at the back of the book, or major plot holes that you fixed at the last minute and didn't want readers to see.

I am now organized enough that I know when a change doesn't make it through a retailer, and that's a beautiful thing. I'm in a much better place than I was a year ago.

THE THREE-MINUTE CHALLENGE

I went to my local UPS store where I have a mailbox. I stuck the key in the lock and it didn't work. I asked the store employee what happened and they asked who I was. I gave them my name, and they said I wasn't in their system.

They gave my mailbox to someone else and didn't even tell me!

I spoke to the manager and he apologized and promised to get to the bottom of it. He asked me to produce documentation for the mailbox.

I whipped out my phone and, within three minutes, I had a copy of the mailbox agreement, my most recent renewal, and a confirmation email from the store confirming that my registration was valid.

Thank God I am fairly organized. I had just restructured all my bookkeeping folders the week prior as part of a cleanup project (which I'll discuss later). I took a lot of time structuring that folder in particular so that expenses would be very easy to find. That little bit of foresight paid off big time.

Lo and behold, I got my box back, but imagine what a pain

in the ass it would have been if I had to spend hours looking for documentation (if any existed).

As I was in the store hammering out this problem, I came up with a little game that I am going to hold myself to moving forward.

The game is this: any time I am presented with the task of finding anything related to my writing business, I must find it in three minutes or less. If I do, I win. If not, then it's a failure and I have to rework things so that I can find it in the future quickly.

When I made it home, I did some "drills" to test how organized I was. I passed most of the time.

Let me give you four simple (but not necessarily easy) challenges and see if YOU can pass them.

If you can pass all these challenges, you are on the right track with your writing business. Remember, you have to be able to find the answer in three minutes or less.

- Challenge #1: Write all businesses expenses that you made on this day, two years ago. Bonus points if you can find the receipts for those expenses before time is up.
- Challenge #2: Generate a list of all services that you currently pay a subscription for your writing business (hint: domains, email marketing, and so on).
- Challenge #3: Write down the total amount of your business expenses for the current year. No "going from memory." It needs to be as exact as possible.
- Challenge #4: Write down how much money you made on all book retailers last year. If you're exclusive to Amazon, your challenge is to write down how much money you made per format (e-

books, paper, audio). No need to itemize this by
book—just the amounts.

Can you find the answers to the challenges above in three
minutes or less?

I can. Sure, I cherry-picked the examples, but the point
stands.

Here's why these challenges are important.

Challenge #1: Knowing your expenses is important. If you
have a service like QuickBooks, then you can nail this one.
Being able to find a single expense at any time, anywhere
quickly is critically important. What happens if you get audited
at tax time and receive a bunch of questions about a particular
expense? What if you have to settle a dispute, as I did with my
mailbox?

Challenge #2: If you got hit by a bus tomorrow and your
heirs needed to stop credit card payments for certain services,
where would they start? For example, if I die, I don't need Photoshop anymore. That subscription needs to be canceled on day
one. Otherwise, my bank account will leak money that my heirs
could be enjoying.

Challenge #3: Again, you can nail this one if you use Quick-
Books or a similar service. Knowing your expenses is critical. It's
also critical for your heirs to know your expenses and income for
at least three years prior, as you can still be audited even when
you're dead.

Challenge #4: Knowing how much you make at each
retailer in a given month is soooo nice. It's not easy to do,
though. There are tools such as Scribecount that are making
sales tracking easier, but I don't believe in tying myself into a
paid ecosystem to glean data that I should already know. But a
service like this would be wonderful for heirs.

Think about it: every minute you spend trying to find something is a minute you can't spend writing. That adds up. Not to mention the stress from not being able to find something when you need it.

The next level of thinking here is, could your heirs pass these challenges in three minutes or less? If so, wow. Congratulations.

Every minute your heirs spend finding something is robbing them of their own passions and obligations too. Getting organized is really being kind to them after you're gone.

USING AI FOR AUDIOBOOK PROOFING

I recently spoke with a company called Pozotron, which aims to use artificial intelligence for an unlikely task: proofing audiobooks.

In a previous volume of this series, I wrote about the importance of audiobook proofing. I committed to hiring an audiobook proofer, as there is a cottage industry of people who provide this service now.

I never considered that AI can help with this.

The software works by scanning your text and comparing it to your audio. It marks any discrepancy between the two.

You (or an audiobook proofer) can review the discrepancies and approve or reject them. When you're done, you generate a list of timestamps that need to be corrected along with a summary of what needs to change. You give this to your narrator and they make the necessary corrections.

Authors can use audiobook proofing software to help them proof. It's slow-going, tedious work, and I think many authors would welcome the assistance.

Audiobook proofers can use this software to enhance the

value of the services they provide. It ensures they will catch even more errors.

I see it as a win-win and an elegant solution to an existing problem.

MY WRITING APP DATABASE: A LESSON IN FAILURE

In the previous volume of this series, I wrote about my book *The Writing App Handbook.*

I developed a database of writing apps to help writers find the perfect match.

I hired a developer who created a well-designed and easy-to-use database. I loved it, and early users in my community did too.

I committed to maintaining the database. When I priced it, I set aside a percentage of the development costs each year for maintenance because I knew that WordPress updates would facilitate maintenance.

What I failed to realize, however, was just how frequently I would have to update the database. I thought it would be a once-a-year occurrence. Boy, was I wrong!

I deployed the database in June 2021. In September, it was broken. Other than updating WordPress and plugins, I didn't make *any* updates to my website or do anything that would've broken the database. And trust me, I was very careful to avoid breaking the database.

My developer fixed the problem quickly and we got the database up and running again.

Then, in January, it broke again. At this point, I exceeded my maintenance budget. It wasn't worth it if I had to hire someone every 90 days to fix the database, especially since it is not monetized.

So I did the math and decided to retire the WordPress database. I'm not going to spend any more money on it. Did I hire the wrong developer? Maybe, but I like to think I vetted them pretty thoroughly.

I replaced the database with a Google Sheets spreadsheet. It's not nearly as elegant, but it still gets the job done.

This was a failure, and an expensive one given that I have nothing to show for it. But I did learn a lot about website development and just how expensive it can be.

URBAN FANTASY DATA AND
ANALYTICS IN 2022

Every year, I purchase a K-Lytics Report on the status of the Urban Fantasy and Paranormal Romance market. Since it's my main fiction genre, I like to keep track of how the genre is evolving. I've bought the report every year since 2017. My, how the genre has changed, and my, how it has stayed the same.

Out of the top 300 titles, 66 percent of the books have female protagonists. This has been the case for as long as I can remember. About 10 percent of the books feature male protagonists, 8 percent feature a couple or team, and 12 percent feature a symbol.

I write primarily male protagonist urban fantasy. I'm still in the minority.

Google search interest in Google fantasy peaked in 2012 and reached its lowest point in 2017. Search interest is back to 2014ish levels, but it has been on somewhat of a downturn.

On average, there are approximately 40 to 60 new urban fantasy and paranormal romance titles released each month on Amazon. Most of those are in Kindle Unlimited.

Out of all analyzed books on Amazon, the most common price point was $4.99, which indicates that authors can get away with higher price points than the basic $2.99. This is useful to know because I have been pricing my Book 1s at $2.99.

Ninety-five percent of the top 20 sellers in urban fantasy and paranormal romance are in Kindle Unlimited, which is crazy. If you look at all books in the genre, around 60 percent are in Kindle Unlimited. I'm willing to bet that closer to 80 percent of those titles that are self-published are in Kindle Unlimited, but that's just a guess. Given that Kindle Unlimited is predominantly in the United States, this means that 60 percent of urban fantasy and paranormal romance cannot be found anywhere other than Amazon.

Short reads (books less than 100 pages) only account for 7 percent of sales.

The average book length is around 328 pages.

Those are just some of the key data points from the report.

I'm always careful not to put too much stock in a report that only captures data at one retailer. There are also some data problems inherent to Amazon, like the fact that categories don't actually match the content of a book. Authors abuse the category system and get away with murder. So, you don't really know how a true subgenre is performing without doing more digging. However, K-Lytics offers a useful starting point.

Some things that were very clear to me after reviewing the report:

- Male-driven urban fantasy represents a long-term opportunity. It's a smaller pool, which means I can make a name for myself in it.
- Male-driven urban fantasy represents a long-term opportunity for retailers outside of Amazon because all the bestsellers are in Kindle Unlimited.

- I need to write more titles with male protagonists until I have a hefty number. It will give my brand more staying power.
- I need to develop a marketing strategy for retailers outside of Amazon. No one will be doing this, so it will be a good idea to gain an advantage for myself.
- The genre seems on the verge of another breakout a la *Twilight*. Interest is rising again, and it's probably just a matter of time before we see another mega title.

Most importantly, this data is a reaffirmation to keep writing and to keep moving in the same direction. As a genre hopper, I used to say that I couldn't find a genre I could settle down in. I always struggle to find a niche. I think I've found one now, so I just need to keep at it.

MY INITIAL THOUGHTS ON CRYPTOCURRENCIES AND BLOCKCHAIN

I've been watching cryptocurrency and blockchain closely. I still haven't taken any action, but I'm fascinated by how the technology is evolving.

A few years ago, I would have put cryptocurrencies into a "hype" category. There are a lot of people pushing it who clearly just want to make money.

There are a lot of things I like about crypto and a lot of things I don't like.

Let's start with what I like.

I like the anonymity that crypto provides. Being able to purchase things privately is one of my biggest selling points. Not that I am buying things that should be secret—I just like having some privacy from peering eyes on the Internet who will use my purchases against me in the form of advertising.

I also like the fact that cryptocurrency will enable micropayments. I see many opportunities for licensing and copyrights.

I also like that cryptocurrency seems a lot like gold. It has a place in your investment portfolio and that's a great thing.

Now, let me start with what I don't like about crypto.

I don't like the learning curve. I don't care who you are—

crypto is not friendly to the uninitiated. I consider myself to be fairly tech-savvy, and I still have a hard time wrapping my head around some of the concepts. I don't think this can work for the average consumer without a facelift.

I don't like the fact that crypto security is so unstable. The fact that crypto can be stolen on an exchange or the fact that if you lose your wallet seed phrases, you lose all of your money forever is way too scary. Sure, this is true to a certain extent with cash, but crypto just seems scarier, especially when you consider that cyber burglars are way savvier at this than you will ever be. My biggest concern with cash is getting punched in the face at an ATM. The thought of waking up one morning with all your money stolen is a heavy burden.

And if that's not true and I'm wrong, then crypto has a perception problem.

That leads me to the final problem—decentralization. I actually like the decentralization concept, but the problem is the execution. If everything is decentralized and unregulated, that means no one will help you. You're completely on your own, and if something happens to you, it's your fault and there's no way to get justice. I don't like that.

Imagine a completely decentralized world and you can see where I am going with this. I'm not crazy about our current corporate overlords, but at least there's *some* oversight and regulation.

That's why, as I'll discuss later in this book, I believe that investing in cybersecurity will be important for writers in the future.

There has been a lot of talk about smart contracts and how they have the power to disintermediate industries. I believe this to a certain extent, but if you study smart contracts, you'll realize that they're not actual contracts. They're code.

A smart contract will execute no matter what, and when it

does, a third party could find a vulnerability in the code and use it to exploit the contract.

In the real world, that would never happen with a traditional contract because third parties don't know about the existence of a contract. Therefore, if smart contracts take off, we'll live in a future where contracts will have to be defended after deployment, which will require a mixture of a lawyer and a programmer, a profession that doesn't quite exist yet.

And again, when you factor in decentralization, you're on your own and you have to trust that you're dealing with an honest actor when you hire out a smart contract, which puts you back at square one as far as contracts go.

Those are just some of the thoughts I've had about cryptocurrency over the last few weeks. I still don't think we have seen the technology evolve into what it will ultimately be yet, and that's exciting.

In many ways, it reminds me of the early 2000s Internet. It's so foreign a concept that we can't yet see how it will impact society. I don't think anyone would have realized in 2003 the impact that the Internet would have on just the next decade, let alone human civilization.

DECENTRALIZED SOCIAL MEDIA

While researching cryptocurrencies, I stumbled across a service called Bitclout, which is one of the first decentralized social media platforms (known as DESO).

Social media platforms today are centralized. This means that one company (or in the case of Facebook, one person) controls the rules, what you see, and what you can and cannot say.

The social media apps of the future will be decentralized. This means that the community will decide what is and isn't acceptable, and if you don't like it, you can find another community that acts in accordance with your values. There will be many, many decentralized social media apps.

Bitclout aims to be the first of these decentralized social media platforms, and it has interesting ideas.

The platform was originally founded by a mysterious person, which is always suspect to me. However, that person eventually revealed their identity.

Bitclout is similar to Twitter in that it has a newsfeed and it encourages short but thoughtful posts from creators. However, the major difference is that every creator has their own "coin." If

I signed up, I would have a "Michael La Ronn" coin, which is its own cryptocurrency. As I build more clout on the platform, more people can buy my coin. The more follows, likes, and shares I receive, the more my coin grows in value. If I do something stupid (like committing sexual harassment), or piss people off in the community, my coin value goes down.

In many ways, Bitclout is Twitter meets the stock market, where your reputation is your currency. That's incredibly profound.

If users like my content, they can send me micropayments of $0.04, $4, $40, or $400, so my content is technically monetized. That is also profound. Today on Twitter, nobody sends me any money when I make a killer post...

Honestly, when I first discovered Bitclout, I was beyond impressed with the idea. It's probably one of the best ideas for a social media platform I've ever heard.

There are problems, though.

The biggest problem is that the "coins" can't be redeemed for anything. So even if I have a "Michael La Ronn" coin, I can't cash it out. The same goes for any micropayments sent to me on the platform.

Another problem is that the company committed a ballsy marketing tactic that I think was in poor taste. They imported the top 15,000 Twitter profiles onto the platform and gave them their own coins, which sounds great, but they didn't tell the users about it! At the time of this writing, Elon Musk has the most expensive coin on the platform, and he's not a user.

If the company was really serious about recruiting influencers, why couldn't they have approached, say, the top 100 Twitter users over six months, got them on board, and then used them as a marketing tool? The entire scheme just smells funny to me.

Finally, there are many allegations that the service is a scam.

I won't go into the reasons, but I do think the criticisms are valid.

Will Bitclout amount to anything? I don't know. But it demonstrates a proof of concept that I believe *will* catch hold in the near future—creator reputations linked to cryptocurrency.

Bitclout won't be the last decentralized social media platform. Someone is going to take the lessons learned and apply them to a new platform, and then we'll see this platform hit the mainstream.

People are disillusioned with social media companies right now, and many are looking for ways to give them the middle finger. If a decentralized social media platform came along that offered similar functionality to existing apps (which is what attracted people in the first place) but with greater privacy, no newsfeed or algorithms that manipulate you, and ethical development that isn't designed to maximize your time on the platform, while also giving people free speech, freedom, and the ability to create communities around shared beliefs, I think people will be extremely receptive to it, especially if they can monetize their social interactions. This is a solution that people don't know they want yet.

That said, these services could also fan the flames of racism, xenophobia, and all the wrong values in our society, but that's one of the prices you pay for decentralization. If you support it, you have to support the beautiful and the ugly. But I believe the days of everyone being on the same social media platform and consuming the same content in their newsfeed are dead no matter how you slice it.

LOOKING FORWARD

IF I WERE STARTING AGAIN TODAY

I thought it would be fun to start the inaugural "Looking Forward" section by looking back.

If I were starting my publishing business over today, what would I do differently knowing what I know now?

It's such an interesting question. 2014 was much different from 2022.

In 2014:

- Self-publishing was just maturing.
- There was a lot of information for authors, but not all of it was as helpful as it is today. Today, you can find answers to almost every problem you have.
- There weren't nearly as many distributors and book retailers as there are today.
- Audiobooks as we know them were in their infancy.
- We didn't have nearly as many publishing tools as we have today.

The biggest difference is the amount of knowledge you can find.

If I were to start my career today, here's how I would do it.

First, I would write my first book as quickly as possible without letting myself get stuck in cycles of self-doubt. My goal would be to get it published as quickly as possible. If I had taken half the time it took me to write my first novel, I would have published my first book in the middle of 2013, and maybe I would have been able to see some of the original "Kindle gold rush."

That first book is critical, and I'd write it as quickly as possible, ship it to a copyeditor and a proofreader, and call it good.

I would invest in learning how to do my own covers. This would ensure that my early covers would be bad, but I would be okay with that because I know that it's going to take a while to build an audience anyway.

Learning to create my own covers would help me save costs and avoid being tied to the whims of cover designer prices, which I discussed earlier.

I would take the money I could have spent on covers and buy a block of 1000 ISBNs. Yes, you read that correctly. Like I said, I wouldn't waste money this time around.

I would finish my first book (which would be a series), and then I would write the next two books in the series. I would publish them all at the same time, and I would publish them in e-book, paperback, hardcover, and large print. It would be too early for audio. I would publish the books in KDP Select for the first year to maximize my income.

Once the first three books were published, I would run some Amazon Ads on the first book to see how it performs with readers. Then, I would book some other little promos here and there to see what happens. This would be mainly to learn the ins and outs of pay-per-click advertising, not to goose sales.

But most importantly, I would be writing my next books. I wouldn't jump into marketing with any real force until I had at least ten books, preferably in the same series and genre. This would maximize my marketing dollars.

I would invest my money in writing craft workshops.

I would build an author website and also build a mailing list, using the back of my books to do so.

I would invest in technology like Book Funnel to deliver direct sales to my readers.

I suppose this chapter is saying that I would do most everything the same except for my big mistakes. I would use technology and data to their full extent, as a lot of tools weren't available when I started. I wouldn't have been so afraid of Microsoft Excel in the early years either.

I am writing this chapter because I *know* that the answer to this question will be radically different in ten years. I'm very curious what my answer will be then!

OVERWHELMED AND DISORGANIZED: HOW I CLIMBED OUT OF A RUT

In the third quarter of 2021, I found myself disorganized. I had just finished my annual Beast Mode challenge, and for the first time in five years, I didn't have to worry about law school classes.

It should have been a time for celebration, yet I felt overwhelmed.

My email inbox was cascading with emails, some that hadn't been replied to in weeks. I had so many emails that I had no idea who was emailing me. I stayed on top of fan-mail, but I had let everything else go. Just thinking about my email gave me anxiety.

I made several errors in publishing some of my Beast Mode books, and those errors were now manifesting themselves. Things like publishing at the wrong price, misplacing files, rushed book descriptions, and more. It was hurting my income.

My tax situation was a disaster. I had gotten negligent in cataloging my expenses and income.

And, to top it all off, my personal affairs weren't in great shape either.

I hit rock bottom one day. I decided that I had to fix this problem not now, but once and for all.

I am a productive person. I get more done before breakfast than some people do in an entire day. I am programmed to think in systems. But sometimes systems break. What happened was that Beast Mode broke my systems. I knew this was going to happen to a certain extent because it happened last year too, but this year was worse. Fortunately, this is a once-a-year problem, but I realized that there were many areas in my writing business where I could have been more organized, to begin with.

If I were to start my career today, knowing what I know now, how would I organize my writing operations?

I made a list of everything in my writing business and committed to organizing it logically. This took several months.

Here are some of the items I cleaned up.

Cloud storage services. My folders had gotten a little messy over the years, so I spent an afternoon organizing folders and deleting files and folders that I no longer needed.

My book files. Did I have all the necessary files for each of my books, like covers, source files, contracts with designers, and so on? I spent several weeks combing through my book files to determine whether I had everything. After that experience, I wrote a book called *Keep Your Books Selling,* which captured my lessons learned. It taught me a lot about what it means to be organized. I found a lot of gaps. For example, for one of my books, I forgot to secure a license for a font on the cover. I bought it, but I didn't save it. I had to hunt it down. It was a lot of little stuff like that, but all the little stuff added up. By the end of the experience, I was supremely organized. The time I spent doing this will keep me up-to-date for at least the next decade.

My sales pages. I reviewed my books on all retailers and corrected errors in pricing, book descriptions, keywords, categories, and so on. This was a lot of work. I also developed a system to track all of my books.

My computer hard drive. I deleted applications that I was no longer using. I also updated all existing apps on my machine to improve performance. I also invested in software that helped me clean up my computer and improve its performance.

My external hard drives. They needed some cleaning up and maintenance too.

My online account passwords. I had become lax in my passwords over the last few years. It was time to update them, record passwords that I didn't track, and do some general account maintenance. I also invested in a new password manager that helped me keep everything organized. I also took this opportunity to enable two-factor authentication on as many accounts as possible. I learned how to use an authenticator app, and I purchased a few hardware security keys. Now my accounts are as secure as possible.

My tax documents. I gathered all of my expenses for the year and organized them. I came up with a better system for tracking my expenses. I finally broke down and started using QuickBooks.

My notes. I keep a digital notebook in Evernote of ideas that I come up with. I have many, many notes. But I don't like Evernote, so I migrated my notes to Bear. In the process, I cleaned up my notebooks and organized them a little more logically so I can find things better.

My Kindle collections. My e-book collection was a mess, so I cleaned that up and cataloged my books.

My website. I swept my websites and cleaned up broken links, typos, and outdated content.

Email addresses. I cleaned up my email folders and

simplified my emails. I also deleted mountains of emails that I no longer needed, reducing my email storage footprint.

My safe deposit box. I have a lot of stuff in my safe deposit box, so I took a trip to the bank and reviewed the contents.

My storage room. I have a room in my basement with a bunch of books and old stuff. I took a weekend and sorted through it, giving things away, listing things on Facebook for locals to buy, and throwing some things in the garbage. I have fewer things now, and that's a beautiful thing!

Existing work. I have a dozen or so short stories that have been sitting on my computer for years. They're finished and should be published in a collection, but I haven't gotten around to it yet. Shame on me. I plan to address this in 2022.

Those are just a few of the items I cleaned up and organized. Then, I climbed out of my existing rut. It was important to me to clean everything up first before addressing my current problem. This ensured that once I cleaned up and got everything up-to-date, that I would stay up-to-date for a long time. I started this project in the third quarter of 2021 but didn't finish it until the first quarter of 2022.

Running a publishing business is a lot of work. You don't always get it right in the beginning. You can always go back and fix mistakes. You can always clean up your act!

THE COSTS OF COVER DESIGN CONTINUE TO RISE

The costs of cover design continue to rise. The beginning of a new year is always the time you'll see rates increase, so I benchmarked a few designers who I've been following closely to see where they are at the beginning of 2022.

- Designer A raised their rates from $350 to $450, which is a 28 percent increase.
- Designer B raised their rates from $400 to $750, which is an 87 percent increase.
- Designer C raised their rates from $300 to $600, which is a 100 percent increase.

The costs keep rising, and I'm shocked that more authors aren't raising hell about it. I've only heard one major podcast mention it, and that was in passing.

Why are designers raising rates?

First, the common reason is that they are receiving more work and need to price their time accordingly. They may also need to hire virtual assistants to help them. They may also be paying increased prices for storage devices, technology to create their artwork, and art supplies. Those are acceptable and under-standable reasons.

But are they the only reasons?

What about the pandemic? What if a spouse was laid off or sick?

What about inflation and the fact that everything costs more? What about where the designer lives? Wouldn't it stand to reason that a designer in rural Iowa would potentially charge less than a designer in Malibu because their overhead is less?

I don't know the answer, and I am not saying designers shouldn't raise their rates. I *am* saying that this type of year-over-year change is unsustainable, and it will dampen many indie authors' output, or worse, put them out of business. There's no regulation on what designers should charge, and the amount they charge is specific to each designer's situation.

In the designers I benchmarked, the average cost of a cover increased from $350 to $600, which is an average increase of 72 percent year-over-year. In 2025, the cost of these three cover designers will be over $2000 on average. Even if I'm too high in my estimate, the average cost will almost certainly be over $1000. If you think I'm exaggerating, write me in three years.

In the meantime, I'll be designing my own covers. I'll be writing about this in Q2.

LESSONS IN LICENSING: WHERE IN THE WORLD IS CARMEN SANDIEGO?

Recently, I was feeling nostalgic and searched for the *Where in the World is Carmen Sandiego* franchise. I had many fond memories of playing the computer games, reading the books, and watching the game show in the nineties.

When I was writing *The Author Heir Handbook*, I used the franchise as an excellent example of how copyright licensing works. However, I decided that it would be better to use a book example so I used the *Harry Potter* series instead.

I kept the text that I originally wrote and decided to put it here because I learned a lot about how the series has been licensed over the years.

━━

The *Where in the World is Carmen Sandiego* franchise started as a computer game in the late eighties. It was about a globetrotting, cunning supervillain. It merged geographic education with detective novel elements. The series was created to cultivate and inspire children to take an interest in geography.

The *Carmen Sandiego* series began as a series of hit

computer games—*Where in the World is Carmen Sandiego?*, *Where in Time is Carmen Sandiego?*, and *Where in the USA is Carmen Sandiego?*, just to name a few.

Then, in the nineties, something happened that would completely change the franchise forever—the creators turned the idea into a hit game show for kids in the United States and Canada. Every kid in the nineties wanted to be a contestant on that show. The sales of the video games and other associated products exploded.

Anyone who remembers the game show remembers the catchy acapella theme song too—the creators also created a soundtrack for the show that they sold on CDs.

The franchise expanded to include console video games, many series of novels, merchandise, activity books for children, and most recently, a television show on Netflix.

All of this because of one idea: the original video game.

Just to reiterate, what could have been just one video game became many different intellectual properties.

And here's where the magic of copyright lies: the creators of the franchise didn't sell their copyrights. They "licensed" them. When you sell something, it becomes the property of another person or company. When you license it, you only license part of the copyright to someone else, and you keep the rest. So, when the creators of Carmen Sandiego licensed the television show, they kept the rights to everything else. This is how they were able to capitalize on the brand, spinning off product after product. They licensed the game show to two public television stations, a series of novels to a major publisher, a television show to Netflix, and so on. But at the end of the day, the creators never sold the franchise. All of the products they licensed became streams of income that flowed back to the company, which allowed them to create even more products.

That's the beauty of copyright when done properly: you

license it, not sell it. If you remember that copyright is an infinite bundle of rights, then anything is possible!

ESTATE PLANNING CONSULTATIONS WITH ATTORNEYS

In researching *The Author Estate Handbook*, I consulted with several different estate planning attorneys to talk about my family and author situation. Two of the consultations in particular were worth sharing. One was with an estate planning attorney; the other was with an estate planning attorney who specialized in copyright and author estates.

Both attorneys and I had good conversations about steps I can take now to preserve the legacy of my books and how to keep them in a position of earning income for my family after I'm gone. Most importantly, the attorneys gave me advice on how to avoid leaving a mess.

This chapter is a loose, cleaned-up summary of my notes. Do with this information what you will. None of this is legal advice, but merely info to get you thinking about this.

When you die, an estate is opened in your name to transfer your assets.

When you die, your executor has to create a reporting inventory that contains a list of all your assets and their value. That includes any books or copyrights you may own. How do you value your copyrights? No one really knows for sure, and every situation is different.

In many states, the reporting inventory is public record (which is a little scary if you think about it). Do you want everyone in the world knowing what your books are worth after you die? What if one of your books hits it really big and attracts a film studio? Do you want them to know how a court valued the book as they're preparing to make your family an offer?

You must value your inventory so that you can value the estate. Valuation is also for taxes. When you die, the government is entitled to a portion of your estate.

If you're not careful, if your book IP is worth more than your estate, then your heirs will have to file for bankruptcy.

The value you place on your IP is completely different from what a court will. Courts don't care about your feelings, and they won't buy an author's excuse that a book isn't worth much. It's worth whatever they say it's worth. And your heirs may not like the end result.

There are a few different taxes the government can assess.

In the United States, there are estate taxes (also known as death taxes). At the federal level, this tax applies to multimillionaire estates. At the state level, the thresholds are lower.

There are also estate income taxes, which are taxes on income generated by your estate after you die.

And finally, there is an inheritance tax, which is paid by your heirs upon receiving your estate.

You won't have to pay all the taxes I listed above. In some states, you will pay no tax on your estate after death. In some states, you will pay an inheritance tax but not an estate tax. It depends on where you live.

Every attorney will recommend a will, a power of attorney, and if applicable, a trust.

Wills are common knowledge and I won't explain them here. Trusts are worth discussing, however.

The main reason to set up a trust is that, by doing so, your reporting inventory is no longer public record. Therefore, you maintain some privacy. Also, you can transfer your copyrights into a trust and have your family (trustees) manage them (more on this later). This also applies to your book income. This way, you can control how, who, what, when, where and so on when it comes to the money. You can also ensure that your heirs won't sell your copyrights on a whim because they need to pay rent (known as squandering). However, setting up a trust incorrectly and not following legal guidelines can be just as bad as dying without a will and making your family go through probate.

On average, an attorney will take on average two percent of the value of the estate, so it pays to keep the value of your estate down!

Quotes I received from a few different attorneys to do wills and a trust was about $500 for a will and $1500 for wills and a trust. Not cheap by any means, but it can save your family in probate costs, which are very, very expensive and can easily land in the thousands, minimum.

Here's what I learned from the copyright attorney.

What are the pros and cons of putting your copyrights into a will versus a trust versus a publishing corporation you own?

If you leave your copyrights to someone via a will, the copyrights will go through probate, thus creating many of the problems I mentioned above.

If you leave your copyrights to a trust while you're alive, you'll avoid probate, but there's the problem of copyright termination. Under copyright termination (in the United States), you can revert your rights after 35 years. It's designed to protect authors from bad contracts they sign early in their careers. The termination right also passes to your heirs after death. If you have dishonest heirs, they can invoke copyright termination, pull your copyrights out of the trust, and then squander them. They cannot do this if you leave copyrights through a will. You can leave your copyrights to a trust via your will through what's called a pour-over provision. This may help to prevent the copyrights from going through probate.

If you leave your copyrights to your publishing corporation while you're alive, the same issues remain with copyright termination.

Leaving your copyrights to a trust or a company also has tax considerations. Trusts have some of the highest tax rates in the United States. It may be more favorable tax-wise to leave your copyrights to your publishing company, but it depends on your situation.

I can't guarantee that any of the information above will be helpful for your situation, but it's a reminder that there's a big world out there. You may be focused on just finishing your first book, and that's the smartest thing to do. The writing life is hard enough without having to think about all this stuff, trust me— and I know that better than anyone.

But at some point, you have to pull your head out of your manuscript and learn the business side of things. If you don't, you could be damaging the legacy you want to leave as an author.

ESTATE PLANNING LESSONS

Estate planning was a focus for me this quarter. I wanted to document some more lessons I learned while writing *The Author Estate Handbook.*

Estate planning just isn't discussed in the indie community. It's not sexy and it doesn't create income. But if you don't plan for what will happen to your books after you die, your books will die with you.

To make the problem worse, there's a lack of information on estate planning for writers. You can find many resources on estate planning for regular people, but sometimes that advice is bad for authors.

In reviewing my will, I discovered the unpleasant reality of this. My attorney really screwed me in my will, and I had no idea until I did my research. I document how in *The Author Estate Handbook,* but if I had relied on this attorney's advice, I would have wrecked my estate.

I learned that there are so many pitfalls with wills for writers. Unless you get some help from a copyright attorney, a traditional estate attorney can really mess your will up. This is because they don't always understand copyright. Yet, I suspect that most authors will rely on what their attorney tells them without question. Read my section on wills in the book and you will see how scary this can be.

I learned about the power of trusts and how amazing they can be as estate planning tools. I promptly set up a revocable living trust for my family.

I learned just how critical usernames and passwords are. Sure, I knew this before, but my research showed me first-hand scenarios about how deadly not leaving passwords can be. Your heirs won't have a fighting chance.

I also learned about two-factor authentication and how dangerous it is as well. I don't know if many people are using two-factor authentication properly. If they died tomorrow, I am convinced that most heirs would not have access to the author's codes. I talk about why in the book. My learnings in two-factor authentication were perhaps the most eye-opening in my research. It scared the crap out of me, because if your heirs can't get your two-factor passcodes, they can't get into your account, even if they have your username and password. Read that last sentence again.

I learned a lot about banks and how they treat accounts when a customer dies. That was also eye-opening and scary. I realized I wasn't taking the proper steps to ensure that my family has access to my business funds after my death. I quickly corrected that.

I also learned about how retailers and distributors treat your publishing accounts when you die. This is a tricky, complicated topic. The short answer is the terms of service control what happens. Some retailers require your heir to create a new account and republish your titles. Others allow the heir to keep the existing account, but they must take several steps to get the account changed. If they don't have the username and password, they're SOL.

My research also took me down paths I didn't expect, like how my heirs will be targets for scams, how to treat posthumous work, or how I want my estate to communicate with my readers after my death.

The Author Estate Handbook is perhaps the most detailed nonfiction book I have written. I cover a lot of ground and spend a lot of time in minutia, but I hope it will be as helpful for writers as it was for me to write it.

If you'd like to check out the book, you can buy it at www. authorlevelup.com/estatehandbook.

WEB 3.0 TRENDS

It's time for me to create a new website in the next few years. I keep saying that I am going to do it, but then I don't because I realize that web technology is evolving and I want to make sure that the next version of my website is built on a stable footing.

Besides, any changes I make to the website at this point would be cosmetic and technical. It's not an urgent need.

I've been researching Web 3.0 to see where the future of the internet is going. If I can figure out what author websites will look like in ten years, I can start designing my vision of what it will look like now.

In a previous volume of this series, I outlined the features that my new website needs to have:

- better design
- more sales-driven functionality to get the right book to the right reader at the right time
- up-to-date with all the latest web standards and best practices
- Web 3.0 ready, even if that functionality is not needed at the moment

Some of the research I've been finding on Web 3.0 is...interesting, to say the least. I think Web 3.0 is weird, and I say that as someone who came of age around the advent of Web 2.0.

I used to work for a web development company that specialized in bringing businesses from Web 1.0 to Web 2.0.

Web 1.0 was the original Internet, with flat, poorly designed web pages. It was known as the "read-only" Internet.

Web 2.0 connected people to each other and facilitated the interaction between websites. Social media, search engines as we know them today, application programming interfaces (APIs)—that's all Web 2.0. I was drafting Web 2.0 proposals for businesses as early as 2008.

Now we are moving into Web 3.0, which is built on artificial intelligence and the blockchain. Web 3.0 is about connecting the Internet of Things (IoT), artificial intelligence, blockchain, machine learning, virtual and augmented reality, cryptocurrencies, and other emerging technology to each other. Whereas Web 2.0 was about connecting people, Web 3.0 is about connecting things so that it makes our lives less labor-intensive.

That's just the beginning. I don't think we truly know what Web 3.0 will bring. Here were some of the things I found in my research that indicate what could be coming.

The Semantic Web. Current web technology uses keywords and categories to determine what content is. Search engines can't "read" or analyze content effectively. The semantic web will use machine learning and artificial intelligence to analyze content and make recommendations to users based on what they are looking for at the time. While companies like Google and Amazon can do this today to a limited extent, in the future, all websites will be connected. You won't receive just the benefit of Google's expertise—everyone will leverage each other's knowledge through machine learning to create hyper-accurate results, and it will be decentralized. It's intriguing to think that the walled gardens we have today (Amazon, Google, and so on) will be broken down.

I see a few opportunities for authors in this technology. First, if keywords and categories are eliminated, it's possible that books could breed their own metadata. Many in the industry have been advocating for this for years. Wouldn't it be nice if a retailer could scan your book and recommend it to people based on the actual content of the books? This would eliminate the rampant category abuse on places like Amazon, and it would revolutionize the BISAC system that the book industry uses for categorizing books.

I also see this as a cure for the discoverability problem. When someone searches for a certain genre, they'll get hyper-accurate recommendations based on their history, preferences, and dislikes. Therefore, search engines and retailers can start recommending books that historically have been on the long tail to readers. Books that were making coffee money could suddenly become popular because the content will matter. This could radically shift the balance of power and bring books into the fray that have been there all along but ignored. This is one of the reasons why I keep saying that the authors with the biggest backlists will win.

Three-dimensional websites. I played around with a few 3D websites and they were weird. But imagine a website where the content exists on a plane where you can navigate it with a character or avatar. One website I explored was a map of a 17th-century French town. You could click around and explore it. It reminded me of a gimmicky Flash website from the early 2000s, but much slicker. This technology could make it easier for authors to create interactive experiences with their books. I'm still convinced this part of Web 3.0 is a gimmick. It's the first thing people talk about. I believe it will be more than this.

Users owning and monetizing their data. Today, when you use Facebook, you don't get paid for it. Tomorrow, when you use the social media apps of the future, you will. People can send you money in cryptocurrencies, and if the company uses your data to create a product or service, it will automatically send money to your wallet.

The metaverse. You will be able to use virtual and augmented reality to visit virtual locations and connect with people in person instead of by text on a website, such as a comment. Take a site like YouTube. When you watch a video and want to comment, you interact with other users by typing comments. In the future, you might log in to the metaverse, watch the video in a virtual room, and then chat with other avatars who were also watching the video. Or, you might be able to hear conversations about a video a la Clubhouse and *watch* people get into arguments rather than read them. Now, imagine people doing this on a book review page. Every book's review section could become a book club (or a fight club). This could take the concept of "building a community around a book" to a completely new level.

Decentralization. People are getting fed up with big tech companies abusing their data and manipulating them. Many people are going to support decentralized apps (dApps) which will perform many of the same functions as big tech apps, but without the data and privacy issues. What if there was a decentralized book retailer who used the semantic web as a way for readers to find books? And what if this retailer allowed authors to publish books on it? It could be a mixture of Amazon and Goodreads, with authors being compensated every time someone purchases a book. It could even facilitate micropayments, with the author getting paid by pages read. Everyone who uses the app receives a share in how the website is run, meaning that the website serves as a co-op of sorts. Will it be as sophisticated as Amazon? Absolutely not, but it would be an interesting mashup of Amazon, Kindle Unlimited, Goodreads, blockchain, cryptocurrencies, and an e-reading app.

I'm just getting started, and I'm still exploring Web 3.0, but those were the features that stood out to me. Based on my initial research, I believe the following action items are clear:

- Think of your author website as an experience, not a website.
- Spend less time focusing on categories and keywords and cataloging your content in the future and more time understanding what content looks and feels like in a given genre. Today, we focus on copying the style of other authors as a way to signal to readers what our books are about. We need to start focusing on what authors are doing within the pages of their books, which will require deeper concentration and more research. Eventually, tools will be able to help us with this.
- The future belongs to authors who specialize in genres. The further down you can niche your writing and understand competitive books, the more you will be able to write works that will be recommended by future Web 3.0 algorithms.
- Accepting and paying in cryptocurrencies is a must. While the technology doesn't quite exist yet and there are many, many cryptocurrencies, the websites of the future will need some way to accept crypto from users (and even pay users in crypto). This will need to be right next to your standard retailer links.
- Beware of fads. There will be a lot of them as Web 3.0 gets started.

- Application programming interfaces will continue to be important with Web 3.0 because they will connect websites and services to each other. I predict that APIs will become easier to use and more websites will use them.
- Understanding cybersecurity in a Web 3.0 world will be more important than ever, and you can start that today.

I'm excited to see where Web 3.0 takes us, though I'm not necessarily looking forward to the time and energy it will take to develop a new website for it.

CYBERSECURITY FOR AUTHORS IS
THE FUTURE

In 2020, I created a course called *Writing in Hard Times*. I recorded it during the COVID-19 lockdown and released it for free to the community at the time. The course is about identifying threats to your writing business, developing contingency plans, and learning about future threats.

When I put the course for sale, it promptly died. Only one person has purchased it. I believe it is one of the most important pieces of content in my catalog. In it, I talked about cybersecurity and how it is a growing threat for authors.

When most people think of cybersecurity risk, they think of big companies getting hacked. It seems like every week there is a news article about a company suffering a cyberattack or a ransom attack.

However, if you look at the statistics, the most common targets for cyberattacks are small businesses. One of the growing sectors of targeted businesses is contractors, and if you think about it, it makes a lot of sense. Many contractors don't necessarily have technological sophistication. That's not a knock on contractors. They are easy targets.

Authors are small businesses too. It's just a matter of time before someone realizes we're easy targets.

Think about it. Do authors use cybersecurity best practices to protect their data? Probably not, because they don't think they are targets.

If you were hit with a cyberattack tomorrow, what would you do? What would you do if a hacker locked your computer and demanded $1000 in Bitcoin? Would you pay it? Who would you even call to get tech help?

What if your reader's information was stolen, like credit card information or email addresses? Would you be required to report it to the government?

These are important questions that we as a community are unprepared for.

You can purchase cyber insurance for this type of exposure. It used to be relatively cheap, but the cost is increasing because cyberattacks have been rampant since the COVID-19 pandemic.

In this volume, I've spent a lot of time talking about emerging technology like cryptocurrencies, blockchain, and decentralization. Soon, cybersecurity is going to become even more important and your most valuable data is going to be at even more risk than it is today.

Therefore, cybersecurity needs to be a focus for writers of the future.

What does that look like? I'm not sure yet. But I think authors need to be extremely careful. We're heading into uncharted waters as far as security goes, and it's hard to know what types of technology and tools will exist to help us protect our identities, currency, and data. This is an area of concern for me and something I will be paying more attention to in the coming years.

SOME THOUGHTS ON THE PACE OF TECHNOLOGY

As I documented my opinions and lessons learned in this quarter's volume, I realized that this volume has perhaps the widest range of topics of the entire series.

There are chapters on writing craft, productivity, large print editions, publishing data and analytics, book distribution, artificial intelligence, blockchain applications, cryptocurrencies, Web 3.0, ISBNs, copyright licensing, automation, estate planning, and more!

Wow, what a dizzying list!

This range of topics is remarkable for a few reasons.

I've found myself unable to focus on just one technology lately. It's not because I have difficulty focusing—it's because so much technology is dependent on each other. I don't see that changing in the future. I believe it will make sense to think holistically about the writing business because everything will matter.

I am also getting the sense that we're on the cusp of another technological wave that will completely change the way we do business. I've said this over the last three years, but I especially believe it will be true within the next five years.

In this section alone, I've discussed several factors that I believe will change the author profession. In the next section, I'll discuss more.

I missed the last wave that transformed the author business (self-publishing). I was too young to capitalize on the early days of self-publishing from 2009 to 2013. I joined in 2014, and I've always felt I was late to the party (which couldn't be further from the truth, but I still feel like it).

I've always promised myself that I won't miss the next wave, but the next wave isn't going to look anything like the one that hit in 2009.

I predict that the next wave is going to put a lot of authors out of business. It's going to take them by surprise, and the technological advancement is going to leave a lot of people behind.

In the early days of the self-publishing revolution, the pioneers were the authors who:

- dared to publish their work without a publisher
- were traditionally-published but reverted the rights to their work so they could self-publish it

People mocked self-published authors. It was still a stigma back then. (It still is now, but it's more commonly accepted).

The people who especially mocked indie authors were those who romanticized the old way of doing business—traditional publishing. Many of those authors either came to their senses or were left behind, their careers strangled by draconian publishing contracts and hefty doses of self-doubt and self-sabotage.

As I look at the next ten years, I see a convergence of many technologies:

- the reduction of the importance of smartphones and devices
- cryptocurrencies and blockchain technologies such as smart contracts
- Web 3.0
- virtual reality, augmented reality, and the metaverse
- rapid decentralization across many sectors
- artificial intelligence, machine learning, and automation
- and more

Navigating each of these will require skill sets that we do not have yet.

Also, many of these technologies are not as immediately intuitive as tech in the early 2000s and early 2010s.

For example, I can explain the technology behind an EPUB to even the least tech-savvy of writers, and they will get it. Even if they don't, they can use a simple application to help them achieve industry-standard e-books.

As a counterpoint, I *cannot* yet explain the blockchain to someone without them looking at me sideways. And if someone wanted to use a blockchain application, they would have no idea where to start. Whether you're initiated or not, it's complicated.

And that's the problem. The average self-published author today is used to preparing e-books and paperbacks, uploading them to retailers, and using tools like Book Funnel or Payhip as an added technology layer. While we claim to be a technology-driven industry, we are not. Almost everything we do is manual, though we do benefit from some automation.

Will people still want to read books in the future? Will the concept of a book change?

What happens if reader preferences do change? Will indie authors adapt? Really, though—will they? Or will they do exactly what many did at the beginning of the self-publishing revolution, which is romanticize the way they do business?

Given the impending future that is on the way (and in some respects, here now), it'd be awfully easy to want to protect the status quo of publishing. There's something simple and quaint about writing books, uploading them, doing some marketing, and enjoying the benefit of your hard work. Why mess around with blockchains, AI, Web 3.0, and other technology that has a deep learning curve and requires a skill set that many authors currently do not have?

That's what I think will happen. It's human nature. Therefore, I must resist that nature and try to see the potential in any new technology despite criticisms, however valid those criticisms are.

I believe 2022 is the last full year to get my fundamentals in order. Change is coming, and I want to be ready when it arrives so I can take advantage of it...repeatedly. When December 31st, 2022 arrives, I will stand ready to finally become the writer of the future—the result of several years of planning.

What are the fundamentals?

- Sound business fundamentals and a good tax strategy.
- Being a writing machine, writing more books than the average author per year with less effort.
- Creating manuscripts with fewer errors than the average author's.
- Turning the art of publishing into a science by creating high-quality, well-packaged books on day one.
- Maximized distribution, meaning the books are available to buy everywhere humanly possible.

- Maximized formats, meaning the books are available in as many formats as I can manage.
- A reliable and sizable community of people willing to buy my books on day one.
- A good, up-to-date website that gets the right book to the right reader at the right time.
- The ability to track expenses using automation.
- The ability to track book sales using automation.
- The ability to use data to make informed decisions about the business.
- Reducing costs wherever possible to keep the business lean and ready for anything. This means learning to do your own covers.
- Supreme organization skills.
- An estate plan that takes care of your family.
- Chaining all of these elements together with technology to increase my efficiency and deliver more value to my readers.

Those are the fundamentals, and after this year, I'll have put those behind me. I may still need to make some improvements, but all of my fundamentals will be working together harmoniously.

Then, in 2023, I'm going to be entering a new world, developing new skill sets, and venturing down new routes.

It's a little scary to think about, but if I do this now, I'll be in a much better position to capitalize on the next wave of technology that is sure to arrive soon.

If I fail to get my fundamentals in order, as I believe many authors will fail to do, then I won't have the capacity, time, or money to invest in new technology, which means I will get left behind. I don't plan on getting left behind, so this is going to be a fun year!

Q1 2022 PROGRESS REPORT

2022 is a fresh year for me because I've streamlined my goals. It feels good to have fewer targets to aim for.

BECOME A WORLD-CLASS CONTENT CREATOR

To achieve my goal of becoming a world-class content creator, I will focus on the following tactical priorities:

- Demonstrate a commitment to learning the craft of storytelling and teaching
- Demonstrate a commitment to outstanding quality AND quantity

Examples of day-to-day activities that will help me carry out my tactical priorities include:

- Keep learning through online courses and workshops taught by professional writers who are further down the path I want to walk
- Reading
- Developing mentorships
- Finding new ways to increase my daily word counts
- Mastering different writing methods
- Documenting my process of becoming a successful writer in the *Indie Author Confidential* series
- Cleaning up my platform to ensure a consistent quality reader experience

What did I do to become a world-class content creator during Q1 2022?

- I have taken approximately 15 workshops from Dean Wesley Smith and Kristine Kathryn Rusch on writing craft.
- I have read (and studied the craft in) 12 books so far this year.
- I am on track to publish 100 books by the end of 2023.
- I adopted Sudowrite into my writing routine, helping to increase my writing sessions by an average of 200-500 words per session.
- I bought 1000 ISBNs and expanded my potential distribution into bookstores and libraries by publishing with IngramSpark.
- I expanded my distribution into StreetLib, giving me access to new international markets. I'll complete the process of listing all of my books with them by the end of 2022.

- I expanded my day one publication process to include hardcovers and large print editions.
- I have returned to making regular weekly YouTube content.
- I organized all areas of my writing platform to be more productive and efficient in creating new work.

BECOME A TECHNOLOGY AND DATA-DRIVEN WRITER

To achieve my goal of becoming a technology and data-driven writer, I will focus on the following tactical priorities:

- Use technology to make the business more efficient
- Use data to get insights

Examples of day-to-day activities that will help me carry out my tactical priorities include:

- Developing a tax plan
- Developing an estate plan assisted with technology
- Learning how to design my own covers
- Hiring a personal assistant for small tasks where it makes sense
- Developing a metadata database for my work
- Improving my readers' experience on my website
- Implementing direct sales for my fiction

What did I do to become a more technology and data-driven writer during Q1 2022?

- I developed a solid tax strategy for 2022 that will minimize my tax liability, with a longer-term plan for the next three to five years that will further shrink the amount of taxes I owe to the government...legally.
- I created my estate plan to ensure that I will leave a legacy as well as income for my family after I'm gone. This included an updated will, a revocable living trust, and helpful documents my heirs can use to run my publishing business.
- I created a master publishing file for my books that gives me insights into how my books are listed as well as potential opportunities to maximize the portfolio. I am now extremely organized and able to manage my book portfolio with the same skill and ease as someone who only has a few books.
- I've started researching the possibilities of cryptocurrencies and blockchain and how I can utilize them to move into the future.

I'm off to a great start for 2022. Next quarter, my focus will shift to learning the basics of cover design and maximizing the value of my book portfolio.

As I said in a previous chapter, 2022 is the final year for me to get my fundamentals right. I'm excited about that, and I'm looking forward to what the next quarter brings.

CONTENT CREATED WHILE
WRITING THIS BOOK

This section recaps the books I've published and media I've created during the quarter. To keep the book evergreen, I will not include links to podcasts or magazine articles because sometimes links break over time, especially with podcasts if the hosts stop podcasting. You can easily search for them to see if they're still active at the time you're reading this book. If they are, enjoy! If not, please accept my apologies.

Books

Keep Your Books Selling

M.L. Ronn covers the process he followed to organize his book portfolio and make more money. If you've ever wanted to get more organized and know what's going on with your books across all retailers, this book will help. It will help you keep your books selling.

Buy at www.authorlevelup.com/selling.

. . .

The Author Estate Handbook

This book will help you plan for what will eventually happen to your books after you die. Organize your affairs and leave a legacy that you will be proud of. More importantly, leave a portfolio of books that mints money for your heirs long after you're gone.

Buy at www.authorlevelup.com/estatehandbook.

The Author Heir Handbook

The book for overwhelmed heirs who need help managing an author estate. The perfect book to buy for your heirs while you're still alive. This concise book is written in plain English with many examples to help them understand publishing, business, and marketing.

Buy at www.authorlevelup.com/heirhandbook.

Magazine Articles

"How Law School Made Me a More Business-Savvy Writer." *Writer's Digest*, January/February 2022 Edition.

In this article, Michael shares his major learnings from law school and how he applied them to his writing business.

Podcast/Video Appearances

"Interview with Michael La Ronn" on the Ken and G Podcast.

In this interview, Michael talks about beating writer's block and how to be more productive.

.   .   .

"Masayuki Uemura Tribute" on the Ken and G Podcast.

In this interview, which is a complete 180 from what he normally does, Michael discusses his top 5 Super Nintendo games.

"Interview with Michael La Ronn" at Valley of Writers.

In this interview, Michael shares productivity tips and his process for writing quickly and efficiently.

"Writing App Speed-Dating." *Writer's Digest* Virtual Novel Writing Conference 2022 (available to purchase).

In this talk, Michael discusses the hottest new writing apps and the technologies powering them. You'll learn major trends in writing apps and features you didn't know existed. You might even find a new perfect match!

VOLUME 9

INDIE AUTHOR CONFIDENTIAL

Secrets No One Will Tell You About Being a Writer

VOL. 9

M.L. RONN

INTRODUCTION

2022 is shaping up to be a good year for my writing. The second quarter is usually a steadfast quarter—I don't accomplish as much as I do in the first quarter, but the victories are still meaningful. I chalk up the lower productivity to the fact that it's getting nicer outside...and no, I'm not one who spends a lot of time outside. I just produce better when it's cold and depressing.

Spring is always an interesting season because the first half of the quarter is still technically winter; it's cold but slowly getting nicer outside. I lament the change of the season...

Joking aside, I had some personal issues this quarter that slowed me down too—my wife battling long COVID and a family member dealing with cancer. I also dealt with a kidney stone. Yet, somehow, I managed to have a great quarter.

This is the second quarter operating under my streamlined strategic priorities, and I am seeing a big difference. It has helped me to focus more intently on content creation, technology, and data.

My Core Strategic Priorities

As a refresher, my mission is to create content that entertains and/or educates my audience, preferably both, and to remain nimble in an ever-changing industry. I do this by focusing on three strategic priorities:

- •Become a world-class content creator
- •Become a technology and data-driven writer
- •Become the writer of the future (looking forward)

What's in This Volume

In the World-Class Content Creator section, I discuss the value of *The Indie Author Confidential* series, thoughts about the dreaded one-third mark of novels and how to beat it, my experience in rebranding my Good Necromancer and Chicago Rat Shifter series and retiring the M.L. McKnight pen name, and crazy experiments with voice recorder dictation and transcription that exploded my daily word counts and improved my dictation accuracy to around 99 percent.

In the Technology and Data-Driven Writer section, I discuss my first lessons in learning how to design my own book covers, lessons learned in creating large print editions, and my experience with a service that provides helpful market snapshots on the urban fantasy genre. I also discuss issues around pricing books internationally.

In the Looking Forward section, I analyze the 2022 Future Today Institute Trends Report, which outlines major trends that will impact every area of our lives. I also look back at previous volumes of this series to see what was on my mind one and two years ago during this same time. I also discuss a concerning trend with copyright trolls that could impact authors.

Enjoy this volume.

—*M.L. Ronn*
April 15, 2022
Des Moines, Iowa

BECOME A WORLD-CLASS
CONTENT CREATOR

ASSESSING THE VALUE OF THE INDIE AUTHOR CONFIDENTIAL SERIES

Someone recently asked me why I write this series. These books don't necessarily have actionable advice, they're not focused on any single topic, and, to some people, they might be perceived as vain.

I write this series for several reasons.

First, I write it for myself because by doing so, I am more likely to retain the information I learn. If I can articulate concepts simply in 500 to 1,000 words, then I've grasped them.

Next, I wrote this series because of great advice I heard from Gary Vaynerchuk a long time ago. He recommends that influencers and entrepreneurs should "document" their progress and use marketing tools as practitioners of those tools. People will follow you because they're interested in the process and the steps you're taking. That has been insanely true for my writing business.

This series will continue to build in value with every volume I create. Every four volumes (which represents a year, except for the first year), the series quadruples in value. I keep reminding myself of just how powerful a series like this can be ten years from now, or when my career really takes off.

I don't know of a single mega-bestselling author who documents their day-to-day experience like I am doing. For example, I believe it would be immensely valuable to know what Dean Koontz was learning early in his career, especially events that shaped his writing. People would pay a lot of money for that.

Therefore, if I start documenting my progress now while I'm a relative nobody, and I keep it up even when it's not financially lucrative to do so, and if I write honestly, thoughtfully, and intentionally, there's no telling what could happen with this series.

At the time of this writing, each volume of the series is worth $4.99. Every year, I add approximately $10 in value to the series. I do have an anthology collection that pulls all the quarterly volumes together, so I would expect a reader to buy that over the individual volumes.

With the current number of volumes I have published, if a reader bought the entire series, that would gross around $20 if they bought the anthologies (which would net me $14), and $40 if they bought the individual volumes (which would net me $28). That's *per person*, for just the early volumes in this series.

If 1,000 people bought this series in its entirety, that would make me between $20,000 and $40,000.

Traditional publishers would laugh you out of the room if you told them you were only going to sell 1,000 copies of a series. Successful indie authors would laugh you out of the room if you told them you were only going to sell 1,000 copies too.

But here's where they completely miss the point: this is just one series. And sales of this series could help to improve sales of my other titles too.

If I become a bestselling author with a lucrative career, I'll be making way more than $20,000 or $40,000, so this series just adds to my profit. Hell, that money is the equivalent of many people's salaries. Ten years from now, I'll have way more books in this series, and the average value per reader will be over $200.

If I do the same math but ten years from now, if I sell just 1,000 copies of this series, that will between $200,000 and $400,000.

Again, for just one series. For just 1,000 people. I'm assuming that this series will not be a bestseller. If it becomes one, the math changes.

Funny how the numbers add up like that.

Are these numbers delusional? No. Ambitious? Yes. But if I've learned anything over the last decade, it's always to bet on yourself and that success happens in ways that you least expect.

THE PROBLEMATIC ONE-THIRD
MARK OF NOVELS

I wrote a blog post this quarter that resonated with my audience. It had to do with the one-third mark of novels, which is often a graveyard for writers. Here's what I wrote, lightly edited for your pleasure.

I wrote 2,000 words today. I'm approximately at the one-third mark of this novel, which is around 16,000 words.

Oh, the one-third mark...it's a serial killer. So many novels die during this patch somewhere between the 25 and 33 percent mark.

I write about the one-third mark in my book *The Pocket Guide to Pantsing*. It's a strange phenomenon that I can't explain other than to say it exists and it rears its ugly head in almost every novel I write. I'm not the only one who experiences it.

The one-third mark is the first point in the novel where you have literally no idea what is going to happen next. You've been on a sugar rush from the time you started the book, and now your sugar levels have crashed. You lose momentum and every word feels like a struggle.

I have a theory for why this happens.

First, many writers would agree that you want to introduce all the key players and stakes within the first 25 percent of the book. All heroes, supporting characters, and villains (to an extent) should at least be introduced so the reader is aware of them. The first quarter of the book, in a way, is about setting up all of this so you can develop the story and characters.

Once you've set the table, so to speak, now all your character and plot lines are converging—hero, supporting heroes, villains, settings, A plots, B plots, and so on. It's like a giant traffic jam and you have to figure out how to unclog the road so that everyone has their lane. Again, for most novels, this hits right around the 25 to 35 percent mark, sometimes sooner. It hits with varying degrees too—some novels (like the one I'm writing) only have small traffic jams. Others have massive ones.

While your subconscious is figuring all this out, it pumps the brakes and your writing output slows down somewhat. Not completely, but enough to where you notice that you can't "see" what happens next as easily. You may have zero idea what to write next and lose confidence in yourself and/or the story.

The novel I am working on now my 37th novel, so fortunately, I've developed some tools to deal with this.

Tool #1 is to write the next sentence, even if you don't know what it is. Follow your fingers. Easier said than done, but it works.

Tool #2 is to take frequent inspiration breaks, such as walking your dog, taking naps, getting away from the writing keyboard and exposing yourself to new people and situations, watching movies and television, and so on. The trick is to look for a "spark," that one thing that your subconscious needs to smooth out the traffic jam and get going again. Find the spark, and the novel will ignite.

Tool #3 is to remember some basic tenets of writing;

1. When the going gets rough, throw a man with a gun in the scene. It works like magic.

2. If the words aren't coming well, write quickly through the current scenes. Not sloppy, but quickly. Don't overthink them—it's very easy to fall into the trap of overthinking. The secret is, when you return in editing (or looping), most of the time, the scene will read better than you felt it did when you were writing it. Always assume your mind is playing tricks on you. When you think something's good, it may not be. When you think something is bad, it also may not be. The best thing you can do is get to the finish line, hire editors, and let readers decide. Readers will often surprise you.

3. Keep momentum every day. Even just a few hundred words is okay. The one-third mark only lasts a few thousand words or so.

The experience I dealt with went like this: I knew exactly what was going to happen for the next three to five chapters, but I found myself in an immediate scene where I didn't know what would get the hero to the next scene.

In other words, I knew what would happen in Chapter A, C, and D, but not B. Chapter B was the trouble.

I followed the tips above and I moved past B into C, and all is clear now. The words are coming back in full force.

Again, don't be sloppy. But don't overthink your writing either.

MAKING CHANGES TO CONTENT WITH SPEED AND EFFICIENCY

I've talked before about the benefits of thinking about your books as a portfolio. I've documented my efforts in managing my book portfolio extensively in this series. In short, I believe it is critical to know what is going on across your portfolio at all times so that you are never caught off-guard. It is important to be able to make changes quickly because speed and efficiency are one of the key advantages that indie authors have over traditional publishers.

I got to test my preparedness and new workflows with the acquisition of Smashwords by Draft2Digital.

At the time of this writing, I distribute my books through both Draft2Digital and Smashwords. Draft2Digital is a top vendor for me; Smashwords is near the bottom, but I do have readers there.

I've had some gripes with Smashwords over the years. Their interface has always been terrible; even recent changes didn't improve it appreciably in my opinion. For the last few years, I wrestled with turning off the platform entirely for my distribution. Almost all of the platforms it distributes to are reachable through other distributors like Draft2Digital. However, the Smashwords marketplace is unique and worth being in.

In the fall of 2021 after some frustration with the user interface, I decided to turn off all distribution channels on Smashwords except for the Smashwords marketplace. Approximately 90 days later, Smashwords was acquired and it was announced that all books there would be integrated into Draft2Digital's platform. I'm glad I did that in retrospect.

Immediately, when I received the email about the acquisition one morning, I asked, "What's my exposure here?"

The biggest exposure was a messy data migration. When retailers merge books, weird things happen. My main goal was to be prepared for this and stay vigilant for these types of problems.

I was able to verify that all my titles were delisted from Smashwords except for the marketplace. This should insulate me from the worst of the data migration issues. I also use the same email address at both platforms, so there should be no trouble linking my accounts when the developers start migrating data.

Because I already delisted my titles, I can hopefully avoid the messy data migration issues that are sure to follow once the platform integration begins. By *only* having Smashwords's marketplace enabled, I should be able to avoid major issues and keep my distribution business as usual.

Here's what I hope will happen: I will wake up one morning, discover that my Smashwords account is no longer active, and that the Smashwords marketplace shows up as a distribution point for all my books in Draft2Digital. Then, when I log into Draft2Digital, I'll receive a pop-up window that asks if I want to enable the Smashwords marketplace for all my titles, or, it will tell me that this has already been enabled. That's what I'm hoping anyway. In reality, it probably won't be that simple.

That was the first exposure, which I hope will be shored up by end of the year.

The second exposure was that some of my writing books mention Smashwords. Any references to it risk becoming obsolete. I reviewed my portfolio to find all instances where I mentioned Smashwords. In about 15 minutes, I identified four books that contained a potentially soon-to-be obsolete reference to Smashwords. Approximately 45 minutes later, I had made all the necessary updates to the titles, logged the changes in my change log for each book, and uploaded new versions to all retailers.

By noon that day, all updates were published, preserving the evergreen status of those books. (No book is one hundred percent evergreen—there will always be chinks in the armor at some point.)

Because of the portfolio management process I describe in my book *Keep Your Books Selling*, I was able to identify this issue and implement these changes before most authors could even figure out what it meant for them.

This was a great trial run. It's just another sign that the investments I've been making are paying off.

It helps to be organized.

THE SECOND BOOK IS ALWAYS EASIER

A few times a year, I receive a desperate email from an aspiring writer who tells me that they don't know if they can continue their novel. They've never been through the process, they're stuck on the emotional rollercoaster, and it all just seems too difficult to manage.

I know that aspiring writers read the *Indie Author Confidential* series, so I'd like to share my thoughts around how I typically answer this type of inquiry.

First, most obviously, there is already a problem if someone is coming to me. I'm just a random guy who lives in Iowa. What do I know about the personal problems you face? Sure, I've come a long way, and sure, I know a few things about fear and writer's block. But I can't solve your problems for you.

Anxiety is driving you to feel this way. You need to figure out where the anxiety is coming from. Something I've learned over the years is that there are two types of people in this situation. The first type is able to navigate this strange landscape, connect with their feelings, and address them properly. While the process of writing still remains a problem for this group, they have the ability to arm themselves with new skills and techniques so that the anxiety no longer has power over them.

The second type are incapable of addressing this anxiety. I don't mean that as an insult. I mean that they are physiologically unable to stop the bad movie that plays in the theater of their mind. These people need medical and/or therapeutic help. Again, I don't say that as an insult. I say it because it's true.

These people start writing and they come to a spot where they don't know what is going to happen next. Then, the fear kicks in. They tell themselves they can't do it, that their work is not good enough, and other unproductive self-talk. For this group, the self-talk might as well be reality. Their frustration and lack of progress leads them to seek help, which is admirable. But the help they need is not any help that I can provide. And no advice I (or anyone else) give them ever seems to work, which is unfortunate. It's not their fault. Success begins for this group when they admit that they need true help. That should never be a stigma. Personally, I think it's one of the most honorable things you can do as a writer.

All of this is a preface to my answer to the statement "I don't think I can finish my first novel. Help!"

Here's the answer: everything gets easier once you finish your first novel. It doesn't matter how you finish it; it doesn't matter what methods you use—all that matters is that you finish it. When you finish, you will gain a tremendous amount of insight into yourself and how you operate. This insight is impossible to glean when you are writing your first book. It is magnified if you have done the self-work necessary to minimize the inner critic.

The example I like to use is a math class in high school. As a student, I hated math. It just wasn't the way that I thought about the world. Every semester, I wondered if my next math class would be the one where I took home a failing grade.

But somehow, I always made it through the coursework. At the end of the semester, I would look back on the curriculum with pride and tell myself, "That wasn't so bad."

The next semester, when I would have to draw upon knowledge of statistics or algebra or trigonometry or something that came before, I would remember what I learned, and that knowledge would serve me well.

Writing a first novel is like taking your very first mathematics class. It's a different way of thinking, one that you don't intrinsically understand. Like math, you don't know anything about character development, plot, pacing, setting, productivity, and virtually everything else other than what you've read or what someone else has told you (and let's face it—not all advice is equal). You think you know how it's going to go, but you have no idea.

(And if you're a math person, then humor me...I'm sure there is some subject that you dreaded in school.)

Just like taking a pop quiz, a midterm exam, or final exam, you too will be tested at several points throughout your first novel.

Pop quiz number one: how do you actually write a novel? What does it look like on the page? Are you writing prose that looks like what you read in books?

Pop quiz number two: how do you start a novel? Not as easy as you think if you've never done it before.

Pop quiz number three: you're humming along in your novel and you reach the one-third mark, which is notorious for sinking many aspiring writers. I can't tell you how many writers I know personally who have serious struggles with this part in the novel, which usually takes place somewhere between the 25 and 33 percent mark. This pop quiz alone could make you fail the course.

Midterm exam: you've reached the middle of the novel.

Welcome to the murky middle! How do you slog through a bog that you've never been through before? What happens if you show up wearing socks and tennis shoes when you need a pair of waders instead?

Pop quiz number four: what happens when you run out of gas? You've come so far, but now you just don't know if you can continue. Frequently, this is where many of the writers who reach out to me are.

Final exam: can you finish strong?

Those are just some of the pop quizzes and exams where you will be tested during your first novel.

But remember the universal truth of becoming a writer: once you finish your first novel, the next novel will become infinitely easier. How you get there is up to you. Every writer has a different working style. I could recommend many different tactics, but you have to find the method that will work best for you. Just understand that the finish line is the same for everyone. It doesn't matter how you finish that first novel. What matters is that you do.

When it's time to write your second novel, you'll be better at it. It won't feel like it, but you'll have internalized the process so that it won't scare you as much anymore. And for many writers, that will make all the difference in the world—if they have the courage to keep writing.

FALLING PREY TO PERFECTIONISM

This is a story about how I need to follow my own advice.

I frequently teach about how to avoid the perils of perfectionism. Perfectionism is no stranger to writers, and it strikes us in so many ways throughout the production of our manuscripts. We believe that our stories have to be perfect; we feel that sometimes there isn't enough editing in the world that could make a story match the vision we have in our heads; we tweak the formatting of our books endlessly in pursuit of perfection, and so on.

What I failed to understand for myself was just how multifaceted perfectionism can be. I forgot that we are just as likely to become victims of perfectionism outside of the manuscript production process.

Over the last year, I took a break from my YouTube channel. I did this mainly because the pandemic made it difficult to concentrate. Despite being home *all day with access to my video equipment and the ability to record any time*, I told myself that it wasn't the right time.

Why wasn't it the right time? I asked myself that question one day, but I couldn't come up with a good answer.

"It was the pandemic," I said. But as I said, I had access to my recording equipment all the time.

"My editor moved on to different projects," I said.

Video editors are easy to find. There's always someone looking for work. That wasn't an excuse either.

"My videos just wouldn't be at the same level that my subscribers would expect," I said.

That was the answer.

I was so focused on what people thought about the videos that I stopped making them, forgetting the reason why people watch my videos in the first place: the advice.

When I started my YouTube channel, my videos were well produced. Sure, people commented on the nice graphics and the good editing, but at the end of the day, they stayed for the advice and my personality. Somehow, I forgot that over the years.

I realized that continuing my YouTube channel was as simple as sitting down in front of my camera, turning the camera on, speaking my mind, and hitting the stop button.

I knew this all along, but somehow my brain didn't register that I knew it.

Heck, I've built an entire podcast by doing just this technique. My podcast "The Writer's Journey" was me sitting down in front of a microphone and sharing what was on my mind for an hour. So I knew this—I had internalized this.

But I hadn't yet learned this lesson in the YouTube area of my life.

The moment I realized my mistake, I corrected it. I sat down in front of my camera, said what was on my mind, and hit the stop button. Then I did it again. And again.

I am now back to making videos on YouTube, and it has been a satisfying experience. I gave up all of the stress associated with production values. I stopped paying attention to YouTube analytics. I just focused on being me.

Was the content perfect? Heavens, no. That's okay. It doesn't have to be.

So concludes the story about how I have to follow my own advice, and how the things we learn and carry with us often have to be relearned, but on a deeper level.

HIRING A BOOK FORMATTER

When I purchased Vellum, I thought I would never need to hire a book formatter again.

I'm a big fan of doing things myself, especially when they're easy and don't require much time.

I never liked the idea of hiring a book formatter. When I first started publishing, formatters often nickeled and dimed you for every change you needed to make to a book after publication. Even just a few typo changes could cost you. (The nickel and diming isn't as bad now—many reputable formatters clearly disclose when they will charge you now.)

And don't even get me started on formatters who are no longer around due to change of mind, health issues, or death. They vanished and the authors' manuscripts vanished with them.

I believe that you should have unfettered access to your manuscript to change it whenever you need to. Changes could include typos, cover changes, or call to action changes—it doesn't matter what it is; if you have to make it, you have to make it, and you shouldn't have to pay to do it.

That said, I do understand why formatters charge for interior updates because this is a nuisance on their time. I just choose not to go that route.

Fast forward to Vellum, and I have been a happy customer ever since...until I formatted book interior for *Indie Author Confidential Vols. 4-7*. For the first time ever, Vellum produced a paperback file that did not pass Amazon's print on-demand standards. I believe this was because the book was very large (over 500 pages), and Vellum had issues generating the PDF.

I tried many different options, but I could not generate a Vellum export that passed Amazon QA.

I had no choice to hire a formatter because I didn't want a "format gap" in my portfolio. For instance, I didn't want readers to notice that the first volume was available in paperback and the second volume was not. That's not a good look for your portfolio. It's also the very definition of leaving money on the table.

So I hired a formatter. A week later, I had a paperback file that passed Amazon's quality test.

Did I want to do this? No. Was it worth it? Yes, but again, I didn't want to have to do this.

By hiring a formatter, I gave up some flexibility. If I ever want to make a change to the book, I have to send that change to the formatter. I will likely have to pay to make updates.

I was willing to pay this price to support my portfolio, but I will test Vellum in the future to see if I can generate an acceptable file. The moment I can, I am firing the formatter.

To balance some of the loss of flexibility, I made *very* sure that the interior was not going to change anytime soon. This is why I always hire copyeditors and proofreaders for my books, and I make sure that the front and back matter is as evergreen as possible. This way, any changes I have to make should hopefully be minor in nature. If I have to pay a small fee to get those changes done, so be it.

It just goes to show you that everything in the writing life is a tool in your toolbox, and you'll never know when you'll need it.

REBRANDING THE GOOD NECROMANCER COVERS

I decided to rebrand my *Good Necromancer* series. I learned that creating a second pen name for my fiction was a losing proposition. I decided to retire my M.L. McKnight pen name and bring its titles under my primary Michael La Ronn pen name.

I hadn't been happy with my covers for the series, so in addition to rebranding the series, I also ordered new book covers.

The entire process was expensive, time-consuming, and painful—but worth it.

First, I don't want to talk badly about my original designer. He did a great job, and I take responsibility for not being clear in what I needed and not having a thorough understanding of the urban fantasy genre. At the end of the day, it boils down to how good the covers are, and the covers that I had commissioned were good, but they did not convert into sales. That was my fault, not the designer's.

There were a few reasons for this. First, the model on the cover. It didn't look at all like what readers imagined my main character would look like in their heads. I blame the lack of good

African-American models on stock photos sites. This is one reason why it is so ungodly difficult to put people of color on book covers. The models are never good enough, and when you do find a good one, that model doesn't have enough poses to sustain a long series.

Second, I really struggled with how to visualize necromancy on the cover. This is not a dark series, but necromancy is usually associated with very dark overtones. The tone of my series is serious but not dark. It has some elements of humor. The original covers did not convey that at all. I knew it at the time, but I didn't know how to overcome it. All I knew is that I did not want skulls, graves, or dark imagery on the cover. Those things can get your book sandbagged by retailers.

This time around, I wanted to get this right. I engaged with a new designer and did not tell them that the series had been published already. I didn't want to ruin their frame of reference. Instead, I started fresh.

I drew on an important lesson I learned with previous covers: often, less is more when you're explaining the concept to the designer. I explained that the series was about a necromancer who uses his powers for good. I told the designer that necromancy is usually associated with evil, but I didn't want the cover to convey that. Instead, I wanted to lead with a character that people would be interested in clicking on to learn more about. I told them that my main character Lester was a middle-aged African-American man, the kind of guy you'd want to have a beer with. I gave a few details about the plot of the series, but not too much.

The results were pretty good.

The designer nailed the first cover. I couldn't have asked for a better design. Instead of visualizing necromancy with skulls and dark imagery, they instead used another form of magic: an occult magic circle. The designer put it around the main character and made it look as if he was exiting the spirit world. It gave the cover a serious occult, but inviting vibe.

That's extraordinarily difficult to do with a topic like necromancy. All you have to do is say the term and many readers are going to check out. But the designer did a good job in reimagining the series. I knew I was onto something when I shared the cover on social media and way more people commented on it than normal. This happened for every cover reveal I did for the series.

I also discovered that the process of rebranding a cover is way more technical than I expected.

I redesigned the covers.

I also rewrote the book descriptions.

I redesigned the interiors of the ebooks and paperbacks.

I also updated my website with new covers and links.

I purchased ISBNs for each title.

I prepared new marketing materials for the series, including but not limited to ad copy, ad keywords, ad campaigns, 3D mock-ups, social media posts, and more.

I wrote an email newsletter sequence announcing the rebrand. I also had a separate list for my M.L. McKnight readers that I had to integrate with my Michael La Ronn readers in a way that was compliant with email laws. I even inserted a new autoresponder that promoted the series. I also updated my lead magnet for my mailing list to include Book 1 of the series.

I unpublished the old versions, waited for them to disappear, and then re-uploaded the books and republished them at all the different retailers that carry my books.

I lost all my reviews for the series, so I had to use a service to help me gather ARC readers. It sucked, but there was no way around it.

And so much more.

This was by far the most expensive project I embarked on in

a long time. I don't recommend it. However, it was a great learning experience because every fiction series must undergo a rebrand at some point. Fortunately, I won't have to worry about migrating any more titles over to a new pen name (hopefully).

How will the rebranded series do? I have no idea. However, I am confident that I did myself a big favor by moving these titles over now instead of waiting longer to do it. I also followed the same process with my *Chicago Rat Shifter* series, but I didn't need to get that one redesigned. I just migrated those titles over to Michael La Ronn.

Here's why this project will set me up for success in the long-term: instead of having various urban fantasy titles spread out over to pen names, they are now focused under one pen name with identical branding.

The titles under the Michael La Ronn urban fantasy banner are:

- *Dream Born* (The Dream Mage Book 1)
- *Nightmare Stalkers* (The Dream Mage Book 2)
- *Evil Waking* (The Dream Mage Book 3)
- *Shadow Deal* (The Good Necromancer Book 1)
- *Reaper's Way* (The Good Necromancer Book 1.5)
- *Blood Magic* (The Good Necromancer Book 2)
- *Spirit Chaser* (The Good Necromancer Book 3)
- *Mortal Terms* The Good Necromancer Book 4)
- *Death Moon* The Good Necromancer Book 5)
- *Dead Rat Walking* (The Chicago Rat Shifter Book 1)
- *Rat City* (The Chicago Rat Shifter Book 2)
- *Brother Sister Demon Rat* (The Chicago Rat Shifter Book 3)
- *Magic Souls* (Standalone Novel)

.   .   .

That's 13 titles under one name, overnight. I have never had that level of synergy in my portfolio before.

Generally, my fiction efforts until 2019 were scattered. I wrote some science fiction, some fantasy, and some titles that fell in between. I never committed to a genre. Now, when readers find one of my urban fantasy titles and like it, they have an entire playground to explore. This is something I wish I would have figured out much earlier in my career, but we all learn our lessons in due time.

Now I can advertise to my urban fantasy portfolio with purpose. I don't have to worry about bifurcating titles across pen names. I didn't realize how much energy and money it cost me to have multiple pen names for fiction until I rebranded. Now, I truly understand the mistake for what it was.

The actions I took in this chapter will set me up for more growth in the future. Ten years from now, I'm going to be very glad that I went through this.

PRODUCING AUDIOBOOKS FOR MY ESTATE PLANNING BOOKS

Like many authors, it is my dream to have all of my books produced in audiobook format. It is one expensive dream!

That said, I am always open to publishing books in audio where it makes sense and where I am reasonably certain that I will make a return on my investment. The bigger the audiobook, the more expensive it is, and the more books you have to sell to make back your investment.

When I published *The Author Estate Handbook* and *The Author Heir Handbook*, I knew these books would be good candidates for audio because they fill a niche that is underrepresented. Many authors have thought about estate planning and want to do something about it, but don't know where to start. This type of content lends itself well to commutes, chores, and gym time. It's exactly the type of books I would listen to while doing those things.

So, I put my estate books on my short list of candidates for audio whenever I got around to it.

Around this time, I was approached by the team at Findaway Voices, which is one of the leading audiobook distributors in the world (recently acquired by Spotify). They told me they were launching a new marketplace that connects authors and narrators, and asked if I would be interested in trying it out. They offered to help me find the perfect narrator for the project, free of charge. They also asked me to join them on a livestream to talk about the process in front of their audience.

Naturally, I accepted.

A few days later, the team sent me a short list of very good narrators. They were all professional, had amazing accolades, and if I'm honest, each one could have easily voiced the audiobooks for my estate books.

I chose my top two, and to my surprise, the team at Findaway Voices was able to book those narrators to do a live audition for a sample of my books.

Yes, you read that correctly—the narrators read the text live in front of hundreds of people. Mad props to them for doing that.

Both of the narrators did an amazing job. I had a difficult decision, but I chose the person whose voice felt right to me.

I drafted up a quick contract with the narrator, figured out a few logistics with dates and technical aspects, and a few weeks later, he sent me the first audio files for the book.

Suffice to say that the narrator did a great job. I am very happy with the result.

And now, the inevitable question. The team at Findaway Voices asked me, "Michael, you've narrated your own audiobooks. As much as we want to help you, why did you choose to hire a narrator?"

That is a great question! The answer is that recording my own audiobooks was ambitious—perhaps too ambitious for me. My household is crazy; I have a puppy, chickens, turtle, a seven-year-old, and many obligations to take care of during the day. The only time I can record is between 5 AM and 7 AM during warm months. I can't record during the winter months because that would require me to turn off my furnace, and doing that on a cold winter morning just makes my wife angry.

In short, I don't want to wake up at 5 AM every morning to record audiobooks. I would much rather wake up to write novels. It's a trade-off, but one I'm willing to accept until I am able to go full-time and have a quieter house to work in.

In the meantime, I'm excited to add more titles to my audiobook footprint. I am confident that these titles will perform well. I'll be distributing them on a nonexclusive license to as many places as possible, so I get to play in pools other than Audible, which is always a good thing.

I can't wait for the day that my entire catalog will be available in audio.

EXPERIMENTS WITH VOICE
RECORDER DICTATION

Regular readers of this series know that I am an evangelist for dictation. I wrote an entire book on my methods of dictation called *How to Dictate a Book*, so I won't rehash any of my techniques here.

However, I have been experimenting with new ways to dictate and transcribe, and I am excited about my new dictation setup. I want to chronicle the steps I took to unlock a 5,000-per-day (or better) word count.

First, I've been a dictation junkie for a long time. I started dictating in 2016 with my *Last Dragon Lord* series. Not only did I dictate that series, I wrote it into the dark (without an outline) too! Today, it is one of my more successful fiction series.

Back then, I used Dragon for Mac. Dragon for Mac was always the inferior version, and when it was active, Mac users definitely had the short end of the stick. Fortunately, Dragon for Mac was discontinued shortly after I purchased it. However, the Mac version taught me a lot about dictating. I didn't realize that it was less accurate than the Windows version, so I trained myself to speak differently so that the application could understand me better. This took me approximately two weeks, but it was worth it because it helped me learn the ins and outs of dictation like a pro. In just two weeks, I was able to turn my dictation brain on and off, similar to how I turn my Spanish brain on and off when I speak Spanish. Once I learned it, I never forgot it.

Anyway, Dragon for Mac was discontinued and I didn't have a way to run Windows on my Mac, so I stopped dictating for a while.

In 2019, I purchased an upgraded Mac that allowed me to run Windows. I installed Dragon Professional Individual for Windows, and I have been dictating happily ever since.

My dictation journey began with on-screen dictation. This is the dictation style where you sit directly in front of your computer and dictate into a high-quality microphone. Dragon takes your text and converts it into speech in near real-time. This is how I imagine most people dictate, and it is very effective. The only downside to it is that you have to be in front of your computer for it to work, and, if you're like me, you will find yourself using your fingers, which defeats the purpose of dictating in the first place. Still, there's nothing wrong with this method. I used it exclusively for several years.

Fast forward to 2021. I began using Dragon's transcription feature. I would record text at my computer using my podcasting microphone or on the voice memo application on my phone, then I would upload the audio to Dragon. The results were meh. It depended on my microphone; if the microphone was close to my mouth, then the transcription was better, but it still required substantial cleanup. Fiction was pretty much a nonstarter because Dragon didn't recognize proper nouns consistently. At first, I didn't like this method.

Then, I found myself thinking about this again. I thought about additional ways to improve my transcription. I had one week where I was doing a lot of dishes, and I thought, "Gosh, it would be nice to dictate while I'm doing these dishes and get good quality for a change."

The thought wouldn't leave me. Eventually, I came up with the solution.

I have never heard anyone talk about the methods I am about to describe. You can't do a Google search and find what I'm about to tell you on a blog somewhere. No YouTuber I know has ever talked about this, and I certainly don't recall any podcast episode in the author space talking about improving dictation in this way. At best, you'll hear an argument for why you should dictate, equipment recommendations, and some other tips that are more technical in nature.

None of that was useful for me, because like I said, I had a pretty good handle on dictation from the beginning.

Back to transcription. Transcription is amazing. It is by far the most powerful writing technique I can think of—if you do it correctly. The key is that you must do it correctly.

Here's how I did it in a nutshell:

- address the technical issues
- address the editing issues

Addressing the Technical Issues

I purchased a voice recorder. My reasoning was that voice recorders are relatively inexpensive, but the microphones in them have been specifically engineered to capture the human voice. People look down on voice recorders now because the microphones in smartphones are pretty serviceable these days, but my theory was that a dedicated device would help me improve the accuracy of my transcriptions.

I purchased a Sony UX 570 recorder for $70 on Amazon. It's a compact, lightweight, and affordable voice recorder that does exactly what you need it to do and exactly what you would expect: capture the human voice as accurately as possible. In my early tests, I found that the Dragon accuracy rate with the voice recorder was approximately 98 to 99 percent. When I held the voice recorder directly in front of my mouth, it couldn't be beaten. It produced transcriptions that were more consistently accurate than what my podcast microphone could do.

That was the first step, but that wasn't far enough. There are people all over the world using voice recorders and very good microphones, but they still have the same problem: they dictate, transcribe, and spend a lot of time editing. You should know enough about me by this point to know that those words are anathema. I believe in dictating and transcribing cleanly.

The next step was to figure out how to improve the accuracy of my recordings. The better quality of the recording, the better Dragon's accuracy, but that's not the whole picture.

After many experiments, I came up with a concept that I call "the dictation triangle." It has three parts:

- distance to microphone
- diction/articulation
- acoustic environment

Distance to the microphone. No matter what microphone you use, it will record your voice better and with more fidelity the closer it is to your mouth. That's true of a cheap drugstore microphone as well as an expensive podcasting microphone.

Therefore, you need a reliable way to ensure that your

microphone is always two inches from your mouth (or closer). If you're someone who relies on dictation while multitasking, this is problematic. In the case of a voice recorder, it makes zero sense to walk around or drive holding a voice recorder. It's not productive nor is it safe. I prefer to have both my hands free so that I can do whatever I need to do.

For instance, one of the most effective ways I dictate is while doing my dishes. I can't hold my voice recorder with wet hands! That would damage the recorder and make it impossible to clean my dishes.

If I'm doing laundry, I can't hold a voice recorder while I'm putting clothes in the washer. I especially can't hold a voice recorder while I am folding clothes.

If I'm driving and dictating, I'm damn sure not going to hold a voice recorder with one hand and drive with the other. That is extremely unsafe.

So, I devised two solutions.

The first solution was to purchase a harmonica neck holder. This goes around your neck, and instead of a harmonica, you place the voice recorder inside the tension bar. There are felt pads to protect the case. You slip the harmonica neck holder around your neck and then angle the voice recorder so that it is approximately two inches from your mouth. Then, you can dictate hands-free. No matter how you move your body or how you move your head, the harmonica neck holder will hold the voice recorder in a fixed position. Sure, you're going to look a little funny, but that's okay. The increased word count is worth it.

(When I figured out this trick, my wife and daughter laughed at me constantly for an entire evening. Now, they just roll their eyes every time I put the harmonica neck holder on.) The neck holder cost me $20.

The second solution was to purchase an inexpensive lavalier microphone. I paid $15 for the cheapest, best-reviewed microphone I could find. I clipped the microphone to my lapel, which allowed me to also dictate hands-free. This also looks a little better in public! (But honestly, I would go out with the harmonica neck holder if my wife would let me. It's a more elegant solution and you don't have to worry about cables.)

The biggest problem with the lavalier microphone is – you guessed it – cables. I hate cables.

I am not a fan of lavalier microphones for this reason. When I first started recording videos for my YouTube channel, I used a lavalier microphone. It caused me nothing but trouble because:

- the sound quality was poor.
- I had to fiddle with wires.
- I had to arrange the wires to keep them out of the way.

The results, while decent, aren't nearly as good as the text from the harmonica neck holder. Dragon gave me around an 80 to 85% accuracy rate. I had to do a lot more editing, but I suppose this is a decent trade-off for not looking like a complete weirdo in public.

But seriously, the harmonica neck holder has no rivals. I've tested transcription in many different ways. It is by far the best.

Articulation/diction. This is how clearly you are speaking so that Dragon can understand you. The goal with this side of the triangle is to minimize as many misunderstandings as possible. The fewer times Dragon misunderstands me, the better.

I watched some videos from trained voice actors and singers on articulation and diction. I remembered the legend of the great Greek orator Demosthenes who put pebbles in his mouth to overcome a speech impediment. He went on to become one of the great orators of his day.

I'm not brave enough to swallow rocks, so I substituted those with a cork instead. I put the cork between my teeth and practiced saying difficult tongue twisters. I also watched many YouTube videos from coaches providing advice on how to improve your articulation.

In many ways, you have to relearn how to speak. You have to think about the speed at which you speak, the words that you speak, your pitch, and even the position of your tongue in your mouth. Very difficult to do consciously, but not impossible.

Environment. If you are multitasking, how distracting is the background? What other resources are competing for the microphone's attention?

For example, as I write this very chapter, I am outside walking my dog and speaking into my voice recorder. It is extremely windy. The wind is a factor in my environment that is making it difficult for the microphone to "hear" me, which means that my accuracy could suffer.

The best way to deal with your environment is to avoid bad acoustic environments or compensate for them. For example, talk louder on a windy day and/or put the microphone closer to your mouth. Or, don't record outside if it's too windy. The time you'll spend cleaning up the text won't be worth it.

That's the dictation triangle.

Addressing the Editing

The next problem you have to solve is the editing problem. As I said, I don't like to spend time editing sloppily dictated text. It defeats the purpose.

I came up with an idea one day while doing dishes. My daughter and I had just been watching Pokémon, and I suppose I had Pikachu on the brain. Around this same time, I was also doing some research on audiobook narration, particularly the punch and roll method. The punch and roll method is a narration style that many professional narrators use to save time while recording audiobooks. Whenever they make a mistake in the text, they stop the recording, rewind about five seconds, and then record over the mistake and continue the recording. It's not the easiest method to learn, but when you do, it saves a tremendous amount of time.

I wondered if I could apply that same framework to dictation.

While dictating, I came up with a stop phrase. This phrase was "Pikachu period." This way, in editing, I could easily identify the sentences that needed to be deleted with a simple CTRL+F. The idea worked so well that I called it the Pikachu Method.

The next problem with editing was interruptions. Since I dictate while multitasking and doing things in public, I sometimes have to stop to talk to people, answer my door, tell my dog to stop sniffing or eating something, and so on. Those sorts of things are no good in a transcription.

Again, I had Pokémon on the brain, so I devised another technique. Instead of turning off the voice recorder, which I was normally wont to do, I decided to keep the voice recorder rolling even when I was interrupted. Whenever I got interrupted, I would say the word "Bulbasaur." After that, I would address the interruption, and when I was ready to start dictating again, I would say "Bulbasaur" again. Then, I would dictate like the interruption never happened. This way, in editing, I could also easily identify large sections of the text that needed to be deleted with a CTRL+F. I just had to look for the Bulbasaur.

I called this the Bulbasaur Method.

Next, I hired a developer to create a Microsoft Word macro that does the following:

- look for every instance of the word Pikachu
- delete every sentence containing the phrase Pikachu
- look for the term Bulbasaur
- look for the next instance of the word Bulbasaur
- delete both instances of Bulbasaur and all text between them.

Less than 24 hours later, I had a shiny new Microsoft Word macro that I mapped to a keyboard shortcut (CTRL+D) that accomplished all these steps in seconds as tracked changes in the document. It cleaned up the text instantly.

When you combine all of these factors together, you have a recipe for extremely clean and fast transcription.

It's worth taking a moment to appreciate just how many things have to go right to achieve success with this unique but crazy effective dictation method:

- You must have the fundamentals of dictation down cold.
- You must be able to do dictation speak (I call it Dragonese) and turn it on and off instantly.
- You must be willing to dictate cleanly and commit to recording text correctly the first time.
- You must have the proper equipment.
- You must ensure that the microphone is always two inches or closer to your mouth, no matter what.
- You must learn how to re-speak so that Dragon better understands your articulation and diction.

- You must be aware of your environment at all times and compensate accordingly.
- You must speak in such a way that you can identify sentences with mistakes and interruptions programmatically.

If you follow these steps, you will get results so good that people will think you are cheating.

This isn't easy, though. It requires commitment, dedication, practice, and most of all, hard work.

This method just isn't for some people. There is always going to be a subset of people out there who read everything I just wrote and say, "This is just too much." And that's fine.

But for those who have the ears to hear it, this method is a game-changer.

If you want to improve your word counts, learn dictation. If you want to explode your word counts, master transcription.

That's why voice recorders are the superior way to dictate. Authors like Kevin J. Anderson have clearly figured this out—I'm just late to the party. You can't beat the microphone quality of voice recorders, and if you let the dictation triangle guide you, you'll have unparalleled accuracy. Best of all, you can write anywhere, anytime, while doing anything.

I have a feeling this method is going to explode my word counts.

THOUGHTS ON MY MAGIC BAKERY

I read *The Magic Bakery* by Dean Wesley Smith. I highly recommend that you read the book, but the premise is that you should think of your writing business as a bakery.

A bakery has products: many types of bread, cupcakes, coffee, and more. If you created a bakery that only sold one type of bread, no one would visit. Think about any bakery you've been to; there is a diversity of products. However, it takes time to build a product inventory.

Dean said that, ideally, you want to have around 20 different products before you can expect your bakery to start earning money. That was impactful for me. As someone with over 80 books, I have a hell of a bakery. Or do I?

I inventoried my work to figure out how far along my own bakery is. It turns out I'm not as far along as I'd like to be.

Essentially, I have two bakeries: one for my fiction and one for my nonfiction. You could also argue that I have a third bakery for my poetry, but I'm excluding that for the purposes of this explanation.

My fiction bakery has nearly 40 books. You'd think that it would take off, right? Not quite. I have been a serial genre hopper; I have written science fiction, fantasy, and other genres in between. My fiction bakery is in fact very diverse, but diluted. When I committed to urban fantasy in 2018, that was a step in the right direction, but I don't have enough products in my urban fantasy portion of my bakery. At the time of this writing, I only have 13 titles. I need seven more before I can reasonably expect to see results from my advertising and large portfolio.

My nonfiction bakery is doing quite well. I have over 30 books, YouTube channel with over 300+ videos, two podcast archives, and so much more. But my fiction bakery needs some work.

That's why I am committing to urban fantasy. Moving forward, I am doing my very best to create as many products in this genre as I can. In a few years, I hope my fiction bakery will be thriving. There will be a large concentration of over 20 urban fantasy titles that will bring people in the door. Some of those people will also see my other genres and buy those books as well. There will be an archway in the bakery that opens into my nonfiction wing for those that are interested. Behind the cash register, a television will be playing my YouTube videos and interviews. Okay, I'm taking this analogy way too far, but you get the picture.

Dean discussed much more in the book, like why it is called *The Magic Bakery* and how to think about copyright. Those concepts were helpful too, but the idea of visualizing my work as a bakery was the most impactful for me.

BECOME A TECHNOLOGY AND DATA-DRIVEN WRITER

MY FIRST STEPS IN LEARNING COVER DESIGN

It's not a proper volume of the *Indie Author Confidential* series without me bitching about cover design.

This quarter, I put my money where my mouth is and I started learning the basics of cover design. This chapter will summarize my lessons learned.

First, I took a Photoshop essentials course on LinkedIn Learning. I focused on the basics of Photoshop and learning the ins and outs of every tool. Most important to me was determining when each tool was needed. The course offered an ample number of exercise files that played around with.

I have more confidence every time I open up Photoshop now. That's a good thing in and of itself.

I can't say that I am a master at Photoshop, but if I had to grade myself before I started this course, I would've graded myself at an F in proficiency. If I had to grade myself now, I'd give myself a F+. Still failing—but better. I have a long way to go.

The start of the Russia-Ukraine War also reminded me that I really need to get moving on this. My cover designers are Ukrainian. Fortunately, my designers appear to be okay, but there was a period of two weeks where I had no idea if they would deliver the covers that I ordered. I continue to pray for them and their families because I can't imagine what they are going through. I have no idea how they are able to keep designing covers right now—it's pretty remarkable and admirable.

I had to start thinking about what I would do in the unlikely event I needed to switch cover designers. Could I do some of the work myself? One of the files they sent me needed to be corrected.

Also around this time, I started publishing books on Ingram-Spark. I quickly discovered, as many authors who publish their books on both Ingram and Amazon do, that you have to have two paperback cover PDFs to publish on both platforms: one for KDP and one for Ingram. This requires you to pay your designer for two print on-demand files.

I'm always happy to pay my designers for services I need, but this type of inefficiency is against my religion. I thought, "There has to be a way to convert a KDP file to meet Ingram's standards without paying a designer."

I made a job post on Upwork asking for a designer to sit down with me and help me figure out how to streamline this workflow so that I could take the KDP paperback PSD my designer provides and convert it into an IngramSpark file.

Fortunately, this was easier than I thought. The designer and I jumped on a quick call. She showed me how to use the KDP PSD and adapt it to meet IngramSpark specifications every time. I couldn't believe how easy it was.

Let me show you why this was important. If I did the math on all my 80 books to get them into IngramSpark, and each IngramSpark file cost $30 for my designer to create, I just saved myself $2400. That's math you can believe in!

Seriously though, I couldn't believe how easy it was. There

are no YouTube videos, no blog posts, and no resources from anybody that I could find that cover this topic. Learning this saved me a ton of money and served as a good basic education on how to navigate Photoshop as it pertains to print on-demand files.

The designer also showed me how to resize paperback cover files, which is also not that hard. In short, it is easy to increase a paperback size; decreasing it will still require me to hire someone. That is good to know because it means that I should keep my books as compact as possible—it's easier to put stuff in than take it out. That's useful.

That's the extent of my learning this quarter, but every journey begins with baby steps.

SECRETS OF THE DATA MASTERS

I attended a panel from a reputable consultant firm who studied insurance companies and their mastery of data and analytics. It spotlighted the behaviors of a handful of insurers it dubbed "data masters." In short, insurers who embraced data made higher profits and more breakthroughs in innovation.

According to this study, "data masters" use the following external sources to enhance insights:

- publicly available competitor data
- open data
- proprietary datasets from data aggregators
- analyst/industry reports
- data from hyperscalers (like Google, Amazon, Facebook, etc.)
- data from distributors/partners
- social media data
- data from blogs/product reviews
- supplier data
- consumer usage data
- data from platform providers

- anonymous consumer data

"Data masters" synthesize all of these data sources into valuable insights they can use to make informed business decisions.

"Data masters" control large "data estates." A data estate is all of the data a business owns. That's a fascinating concept.

The analysis got me thinking about the same topic for writers.

I believe that data literacy and the ability to use data to develop insights are key skills that writers of the future will need.

If we applied the lens of data mastery to writing, what would it look like?

Publicly available competitor data. Tools like Publisher Rocket allow you to see how other authors are performing with keywords and sales. K-Lytics and Kindle-Trends provide genre snapshots and data about how top titles are performing.

Open data. If you understand APIs, you have access to mountains of data from services like Google Books, Library-Thing, and Goodreads. My Urban Fantasy Database is also another example. You can use this data to mine insights for your genre.

Proprietary datasets from industry aggregators. We don't have too many of these right now. A notable exception was the Author Earnings Reports, but those have been discontinued.

Analyst/Industry reports. I did a quick web search for "publishing industry data." Most of it was behind a paywall, and it wasn't cheap. The cost of the reports ranged from $468 to almost $5,000, which, in my opinion, is outrageous. I got the sense that most of the reports were high-level industry reports that didn't give you detailed datasets, at least none that would give you deeper insights than you could reasonably guess yourself.

I've always struggled with what to do with publishing industry data reports. Personally, I don't think there is much valuable in statements like:

- the audiobook industry is growing by X percent year over year
- traditional publishers reported X million in profit last quarter
- science fiction is seeing growth after a popular series release on Netflix

The data is too high-level to do anything with.

Data from distributors/partners/platform providers. The best example is monthly sales reports.

Social media data. Objectively, you can build a treasure trove of data about readers through effective pay-per-click social media advertising like Facebook Ads. Subjectively, you can browse social media forums and author groups to get a sense of what techniques are working for authors in a certain genre. You can also do the same with readers to determine their tastes. You can weave all of these sources together into a narrative.

Data from blogs and product reviews. This data is readily available.

Despite seeming the opposite, we have a staggering amount of data at our fingertips. It may not all be useful, but it's a start.

That's why I find myself coming back to the same statement: if you want data, you have to create it yourself. As a small author or publisher, you just won't have access to some of the insights that traditional publishers have. The ironic part is that traditional publishers are sitting on mountains and mountains of data, but I don't think they truly understand it. Worse, I don't believe they have the leadership or internal resources to leverage it. Trust me, I know corporate America. Publishers are no different than other industries.

Are YOU a data master? I believe it's something we should all strive for.

KINDLE TRENDS

I signed up for KindleTrends, which is a data service that provides data on the top Amazon titles per genre and how they are performing. It's a useful service because it aggregates publicly available data and saves you time and effort.

Every week, I receive an email with data and analytics about urban fantasy. The report is structured as follows:

- how many new books are in the Top 100
- a breakdown of how many titles are standalone vs. series, Kindle Unlimited vs. wide, traditionally-published vs. self-published, and how many new titles overall were published in the genre
- a breakdown of authors in the Top 100
- trending topics in the genre
- bestseller rankings
- a cover montage and palette of the Top 100
- word cloud with trending most popular words in the Top 100 book descriptions

- breakdown of how many book descriptions are written in the first- or third- person and how many focus on setting or character
- links to datasets you can download

It's a phenomenal service that gives me far more insights into the genre than I could glean myself. It also includes an interactive dashboard that lets you filter and sort the Top 100 and 300 titles.

One tip that worked well for me was to scan the book descriptions. I can export all the book descriptions into a single Word document. I scan through those documents and look for any descriptions that catch my eye. It's a good way to study copywriting for fiction.

The only problem with KindleTrends is that it's hard to get a sense of how true urban fantasy titles are performing because many of the Top 100 are paranormal romance titles. In fact, I would argue that the urban fantasy and paranormal romance lists are really just two paranormal romance lists. That's not KindleTrends's fault.

That's why I believe the real action in urban fantasy is happening further down the tail where paranormal romance is less prevalent. If you filter the Top 100 to just urban fantasy titles, they are a minority, and they tend to be closer to the bottom of the list.

If someone did a deep dive at the top 1000 titles in urban fantasy, it would give a much more balanced look at the genre. Paranormal romance would still be overrepresented, but you would see what more urban fantasy authors are doing, and you could determine possible trends based on that. But alas, that is not possible at the moment without significant data work. And it would only be a snapshot in time.

That said, we just have to settle for the tools we have, and KindleTrends is a great one.

PROBLEMS WITH CREATING LARGE PRINT EDITIONS

In previous volumes of this series, I discussed my interest in expanding my portfolio to include large print editions. I recently published large print editions of *The Author Estate Handbook* and *The Author Heir Handbook*. Within the first month alone, I started to see sales for these editions. Nothing major, but noticeable.

I am trying to figure out how to operationalize large print editions so that I can create them with minimal effort as part of my existing workflow. However, I ran into some problems that I don't necessarily know the solutions for yet.

First, Vellum allows you to create large print editions (though flawed), but you have to create a separate Vellum file in order to format it properly. You can't click a box and generate a large print edition in addition to your regular paperback. I don't like that.

The point of a program like Vellum is that you should be able to generate as many formats as you need with the click of a button. This is a serious flaw in their program, and I hope they rectify it soon.

Second, there are common conventions that authors use that

are big no-no's with large print editions. For example, large print readers don't like and/or can't read italicized words and phrases, ragged right justification, and sentences or phrases in all capital letters. Therefore, you must change these formatting elements to comply with best practices.

Both Vellum and Atticus provide tools to help you create large print editions, but neither offers a tool to help you *prepare your text formatting* for large print editions easily (and even then, there are issues). The only solution is to maintain two separate versions of your manuscript, and like I said, I can't stand that.

The best solution I have found for the formatting problem is Microsoft Word macros. For example, I created a macro that changes italicized text to bold. It also flags sentences and phrases that are in all capital letters. However, Microsoft Word macros are not perfect at this, and I have not been able to develop a macro that completely changes all bold text, for example. The macros only get me about 75 percent of the way there.

Third, the paperback trim size. Large print editions generally are printed with 6.14 x 9.21 trim sizes. This means that you have to create a separate PSD file and template for your large print edition. Most designers charge a small fee for this. Keep in mind that you will need to create two PSDs: one for KDP Print and a second for IngramSpark.

Fourth, there's the problem of distribution. If you want to do large print editions correctly, you need to have a large print edition on KDP and one on IngramSpark.

KDP only allows you to link one version of your paperback and hardcover to your ebook edition. This means that 1) your large print edition will be out there "floating" on your dashboard, 2) you will have two separate versions of the book, and 3) whichever format you don't link will be difficult for readers to find.

At the time of this writing, Amazon doesn't like large print editions. If a book has an ebook, trade paperback, hardcover, or audiobook edition, you will see them prominently above-the-fold on the sales page. If that same book has a large print edition, you have to click on a button that reveals additional formats. And even then, the large print edition shows up as "paperback." The only way a reader will know if a book is large print is if the author puts the words "large print" in the title, book description, copyright page, and the book cover. Otherwise, they might not notice.

Amazon also doesn't like IngramSpark. If you distribute to Amazon from IngramSpark, it's not uncommon that your title will show as out of stock, or the shipping will take longer. Instead, they prioritize products carried by their own facilities. This is why you must publish large print editions to both Amazon and IngramSpark.

Add all these factors together and you have many head-winds in creating large print editions right now. That's precisely why I am interested in jumping into the format now. This is what things look like before retailers innovate. I'm willing to bet that, several years from now, it will be much easier to create these editions. I'll benefit from having figured all of this out now.

FIXING A CHAPTER TITLE ISSUE

Earlier this quarter, I discovered an embarrassing quality error. This type of error is precisely why I have instituted quality checks for my books. Sadly, my QA process would have missed this error and I only uncovered it out of sheer luck.

I created my very first large print edition for my book *The Author Estate Handbook*. This also happened to be the first book I ever published through IngramSpark, so I purchased an author copy.

The copy arrived in the mail, and I was satisfied with the quality, book cover, pages, and so on. As far as author copies go, it was a fine specimen.

However, to my surprise, I thumbed to a random page and noticed that something was wrong with the header. The chapter title was truncated. Instead of saying "ABCDEFG," it said "ABCDE..."

Seeing that was a punch to the gut. I stopped everything I was doing and immediately inventoried which of my books have chapter titles in the headers. Fortunately, the only books in my catalogue that have chapters in the title are the *Indie Author Confidential* series.

It turns out that if your chapter title is greater than 35 characters, then Vellum will truncate it. You would think that Vellum would prevent this from happening by warning the user. It does not.

This is a critical quality error, and one that could easily be missed under the right circumstances (like mine). Most authors don't order proofs if they trust their designer and have been doing this for a long time (like me). The only reason I ordered this proof was because it was my first voyage at IngramSpark. If I hadn't done that, I wouldn't have noticed this for a very, very long time.

Of course, I take responsibility. But this would be an easy thing to address programmatically in an app. Just sayin'.

I fixed this problem once and for all. I identified three books in this series that had the truncated header problem. I contracted a developer to write a Microsoft Word macro. This macro identifies chapter headings, counts the number of characters in the chapter title, and inserts a comment with a warning for any chapters that exceed 35 characters. Problem solved. I made the change to all of the books, reuploaded them, and took a big sigh of relief.

If you haven't checked your proofs in a while, maybe you ought to do it more frequently. I have decided to check the proofs for Book 1s in series and every fifth nonfiction book. I still think it is overkill to check proofs for every title (and expensive), but I don't want to be surprised like this again if I can avoid it.

THE MORE THINGS CHANGE, THE MORE THEY STAY THE SAME

The more things change, the more they stay the same. I was talking with an author recently about the progress of technology in the writing world. We were talking about writing on your phone.

This author (who was a few decades older than me) talked about how writing on your phone was actually a thing before it was a thing. She explained that she used to have a PDA and how she could write text on them via an app. She could then upload that text to a computer and convert it to a text file or a Microsoft Word file. This would have been perfect back then because most people who were writing any kind of manuscripts were probably using Microsoft Word or WordPerfect anyway.

I like to think that if I were an author in the 90s or early 2000's, I would have discovered this hack.

But it just goes to show you that the more things change, the more they stay the same. There is always a will and a way for those who want to improve their word counts.

ESSENTIAL COMPUTER SKILLS FOR WRITERS

I read an article about essential computer skills for writers. It said that writers needed to have a professional-looking email address, not share an email with a spouse, and they needed to observe email etiquette. They also needed to learn Microsoft Word.

I agree with those suggestions, but they're woefully inadequate. This was true in 1997.

Today (at the time of this writing) is 2022 and the world has changed.

Here are the skills that writers in today's age need, and it's more than just email skills and Microsoft Word. These skills are not just required; they get you in the door. In other words, you can't expect to have a successful career unless you master them at some level. These skills are merely the cost of competing—we won't go into advanced concepts like pay-per-click advertising or copyright.

Microsoft Excel. You also knew I was going to say this.

Email productivity. Sure, you need to know email basics, but you also need tools to help you destroy your inbox with ruthless efficiency. Email controls our lives whether we admit it or not, and we have to deal with it. If you can't manage your emails swiftly, you'll potentially miss out on opportunities, and you may miss issues that are happening across your portfolio.

Email marketing. Knowing how to build a list, segment that list, write good copy, and create engaging autoresponders will be more important than ever.

Basic data analysis. The future belongs to the writers who will become data masters, but knowing how to analyze things like your sales and market trends are becoming increasingly important. Authors are not generally numbers people, so this will be a disadvantage to many.

Teleconferencing skills. If you can't run or participate in a video call at this point, you're in trouble.

Audio/visual production and editing. Knowing how to edit audio and video is a critical skill in a world that religiously consumes multimedia content like videos and podcasts.

Media interviews. I don't care how much of an introvert you are; knowing how to give a good interview or media appearance is important.

Hiring work. No one can do everything. You will need to hire people to help you with one-off tasks. You would be surprised at how many people struggle with this. The key is to articulate succinctly and efficiently exactly what you need so that you eliminate any back-and-forth. Your goal should be for any freelancer you hire to complete the work on the first try or second try with minimal revisions. This is easier said than done and requires experience.

Book formatting. Even if you use software like Vellum or Atticus, you still need a basic understanding of ebook and print layout.

Cybersecurity. You need to know how to avoid malware,

random attacks, and other acts by bad actors. Otherwise, you could expose your writing business to hackers.

Website creation and maintenance. Most people use WordPress. Whichever content management system you use, you must master it. You must also understand how to navigate the underbelly of website hosting in case you become a victim of an attack.

Are those the only skills writers today need? Heavens no, but it's a good start.

EFFICIENT CAPITAL

What does a more efficient writing business look like? I don't mean writing better or faster. I'm purely talking business here.

Most people would look at the money coming in and going out. Expenses are certainly one way to think about this problem; they have a wonderful way of hiding inefficiencies.

I define efficiency as being able to operate such that you obtain a profit faster than your competitors.

If you review your expenses, the key question you should ask is "how can this expense pay for itself?" To me, that should be the North Star of creating an efficient writing business. Every dollar that comes in should work much less than the average author's.

Let's go through the different categories of expenses and figure out how they could pay for themselves.

Website domain and hosting. These cost an average of $200 per year. Do you sell books directly on your website? If so, that can easily defray some of the hosting costs each year. Direct sales grow over time. What if you also allocated your Amazon Associates commissions and other affiliate link income to your website? What if you could rig it so that your website domain and hosting are technically free each year?

Costs of book production. Until recently, I didn't think there was a way to defray these costs outside of having a Patreon or similar service. However, Kickstarter has changed the math considerably. More and more authors are using Kickstarter to fund their novels. After Brandon Sanderson's amazing success, that number is only going to change. This quarter, I backed a novel by Kevin J. Anderson that earned over $5,000. I've only corresponded with Kevin once or twice, but I can guarandamntee you that it didn't cost him $5,000 to produce the ebook and paperback versions of the novel. I'd be shocked if that cost more than $1,000. The Kickstarter campaign basically allowed Kevin to produce his novel for free, at a profit.

Imagine running a successful Kickstarter campaign a few times per year. It could effectively zero-out your business's expenses, even after taxes...

Advertising. Can you write good ad copy and learn pay-per-click advertising so that your ads generate a profit each month? Could you tweak your ads so that you decrease wasted ad spend as much as possible? That's the pathway to efficiency here.

Annual business costs. Things like PO boxes, Secretary of State filings, and other legal fees can't be defrayed, but if you do them correctly, they don't cost very much anyway. I pay $225 per year for my mailbox, $150 per year for a registered agent service, and $85 every other year for my Secretary of State filing. That's $460 per year just to operate my business. Not bad, especially if I can make almost every other area of my writing business efficient. I can't think of many businesses that can operate for less than $500 a year. That is a blessing for authors that not enough of us appreciate.

Next, some data analysis. If I created a spreadsheet with my expenses in Column A, the amount of money recouped in Column B, and the amount offset in Column C, I'm curious what the total number would be. If I can drive that number down to the lowest possible (without being ridiculous about it), that number is my competitive advantage.

Think about it: Author A spends $10,000 in expenses per year. Author B allocates their expenses to income and spends $10,000 as well, but through allocation, they're *technically* only spending $4500. They have more money in their bank account at the end of the day and can use that to pursue additional advantages, whereas Author A's money will be far more inefficient. And, most importantly, everything Author B earns over $4500 is pure profit, so they arrive at a profit much faster (and more efficiently).

Making your business more efficient is a beautiful thing.

PITFALLS WITH INDIE AUTHOR PRICING

Recently, I was working with a fellow writer on developing a resource that people could use to price their books better in international currencies.

I see this is one of the great problems that we face as writers.

How should you price your book? There are many factors to consider that make this a Rubik's cube of a problem:

- country
- format
- genre
- length
- economic considerations like the cost of printing a paperback or producing an audiobook)
- reputation of the author
- retailer
- venues such as libraries
- how traditional publishers are pricing their books
- and more

My opinion (and I seem to be alone in thinking this) is that authors need to be told what to price their books. They don't want to or have time to weigh all these factors, and they certainly don't want to have to keep all this straight. I've talked to people who believe a book should be priced differently at different retailers; I don't know if that's right or wrong, but most people I know don't have systems in place to track or monitor a strategy like this. It takes a lot of skill and effort.

Again, that's why I think people just want a number. It's not useful or productive to give them a big range. People just want to know what to put in the box.

The best thing someone can do for the community is embark on an intensive research project in at least the major currencies of the world (USD, GBP, EUR in its major variations, CAD, AUD, and a few others). This research would encompass how books are priced, reader habits and considerations, and additional competitive analysis to figure out how traditionally published authors are pricing versus self-published authors. This research should become the basis of a recommendation.

That recommendation should be in the form of a database with one-to-one mappings of currencies. Ideally, an author could go to this database, select their home currency and other attributes such as genre or format, and then get an instant list of recommendations for price points in all major currencies. $4.99 USD would equal £3.99 GBP, €4.99, and so on. The author could save that spreadsheet to their computer to reference when publishing a book. Or, they could use it as a starting point and tweak it from there.

But this would require a lot of work. I almost embarked on this project myself, but I determined that it wasn't worth it right now.

LOOKING FORWARD

ANALYZING THE 2022 FUTURE TODAY INSTITUTE REPORT

The Future Today Institute released its 2022 Trends Report. If you're not familiar with FTI, you should be, as their reports are must-reads. I usually stop what I'm doing to read the reports the moment they come out. This year is 668 pages of future trends that will shape our society. Wow—no mere mortal can read all of this, but I like to scan the digest to see if there are any trends that will potentially impact my writing business.

Here are my takeaways.

Synthetic media will be used to generate popular likenesses to deliver a range of personalized products and services at scale.

Synthetic media is any software that uses AI to generate content. Right now, you see it in apps that generate art based on a description you enter (especially on Twitter with people generating art based on Taylor Swift song lyrics, for example).

The team at OpenAI released a demo of a program called DALL-e, which takes this to the next level.

In DALL-e, you type in a sentence that describes the image you need, like "a chair that looks like an avocado" or a "tiny radish walking a dog." DALL-e then generates a panel of images that are inspired by what you wrote. And wow, the images are surprisingly good. Look it up.

This will be the future of stock images. Imagine browsing Shutterstock and you can't find the image you need. Click a button, tell Shutterstock what you want, and it will generate some options. Click the one you want, pay for a license, and boom. You will literally be the only person in the world to have that image. Why does Shutterstock need content creators, then? (I'm not advocating for this, just making an observation).

More specifically, DALL-e can even generate clothing renders. I saw one example where the user asked for a mannequin wearing a checkered flannel shirt. It generated several options in several poses. I could change the clothes on the mannequin with a click of a button.

The next-next level is being able to generate faces that go on that model, and customizing those faces... and then you'll literally be able to type in a description of your main character, get a character render, and then be able to use that on your cover royalty-free. This will be great for authors like me who struggle to find models of color. I'd be very nervous if I was a vector artist or stock photography model, though.

Face generation technology does exist and it's quite good, but I haven't seen anyone bring the two pieces of tech together yet (synthetic art + synthetic faces, bodies, and poses). When that happens, the game will change.

But more importantly, this will fundamentally change how cover designers work. It will enable them to create better covers that match both theirs and the author's visions. The downside is that the designers who specialize in compositing will find their skillset less in demand as these types of apps proliferate. I'd also be nervous if I was a compositor.

More practically, imagine writing a blog post and needing an image. Open a WordPress plugin, tell it what you need, and boom, you've got a beautiful, high-quality image for your blog that will keep readers engaged.

Companies are looking to upskill their workforce in machine learning and the basics of AI.

If companies are looking to do this, then we should be too. What skills should every author know twenty years from now? Figure that out and start learning today.

A few skills that I think are critical to have at least basic proficiency in would be data literacy (being able to look at data and make accurate decisions based on what the data says), basic programming understanding (Python, Java, and so on), and cybersecurity best practices. Those are a great start.

Some skills that are key right now will remain key in the future: copywriting, storytelling, knowing how to run your finances, and so on.

If you don't upskill, you're going to get left behind.

Until about 2007, the skills an author needed were pretty basic—they needed Microsoft Word proficiency, storytelling prowess, contract negotiation skills, and basic marketing skills. Then, the advent of self-publishing came along and authors had to add Internet savviness, book formatting, cover design, and more to their skillsets. The advent of AI and machine learning becoming mainstream and woven into the fabric of everyday lives will require them to become even more adept.

If you don't like it, be ready to get left behind.

There are plenty of sites that can teach you basic skills quickly. Coursera, LinkedIn Learning, Skillshare, and Udemy are a few. Unlike in the past, the information is out there.

To paraphrase Wayne Gretzky, you just have to figure out where the puck is headed, educate yourself, and then start small. I'm not advocating for people to become programmers or AI scientists—but you do have to understand how to speak the language.

Machine learning is transitioning, as new platforms allow businesses to leverage the power of AI to build applications without the need to know specific code.

As more developers become comfortable with AI, they'll start offering more AI services to the author community. At some point, I expect writing apps to be interlaced with AI capabilities, and that's where folks will have to be careful.

What those services will be, I don't know, but a critical skill in the future will be to understand how your data is going to be used.

If someone wants to scan your manuscript to give you insights, your data will almost certainly be used for other purposes. In an age of AI, you'll have to weigh whether it is worth it and what the benefits potentially are. There will be a lot of small startups and companies trying to offer new technology, but not all of them will succeed. You should be very selective who you give your data to because it's akin to giving them money. I forget who said that giving your data to an AI company is like investing in them, and you get paid with the benefits of the service rather than money. I think that's a wise way to think about new AI tools instead of "Wow, this is free! How cool!"

People will create multiple digital versions of themselves, each tailored for specific purposes. This will lead to fragmentation—and a widening gap between who a person is in the physical world, and who they project in various online platforms.

If you thought reaching readers was hard now...

This will completely disrupt advertising. Instead of advertising to people, you'll be marketing to their avatars, which will make it much harder to determine buying habits and behaviors.

The flip side is that people could create avatars that are easier to market to. I could create an avatar that is all about urban fantasy, for example. Maybe I WANT that avatar to be advertised to with UF books and new authors.

But there will inevitably be people who become harder to reach in a fragmented world. Some of those people are people who we're currently advertising to. Like I said, I think PPC advertising's days are numbered in its current form. I have no idea what will replace it, but if you're one of those authors who derives much of your income from advertising, I'd start diversifying now. Some good ideas: direct sales, Kickstarter, investing in your email list, going wide, getting into audio, etc. There are lots of choices.

. . .

Ransomware will become the new "smash and grab" of cybercrime.

I've been saying this since early 2020, and that was before attacks started spiking. It's a wise idea to educate yourself on cybercrime and how to protect yourself and your business.

China will push for the broader use of its digital currency, the e-CNY, within and outside of the country.

This idea will spread all over the world, with many countries instituting their own digital currencies. Every transaction will be tracked. The ramifications of this are scary: if you think cancel culture is bad now, wait until the government starts monitoring your transactions and blocks you from purchasing certain things from certain people for any reason. Such a scenario will make the current moment of heated cancel culture feel like the good old days.

If you're a writer writing erotica, for example, and a state government doesn't want its citizens to purchase erotica, they could freeze you out. Or, if you're writing work that is political or challenging to the status quo in any way, you could be targeted.

To get around this, I predict that people will use alternative forms of currency like crypto to purchase disfavored items.

Blockchain-based applications are being used to track the origins of content online, and permanently store original assets, improving the ability of consumers and businesses to authenticate infor-

mation. This is a powerful tool for combatting censorship and misinformation.

In the future, no one will know what is real and what is false, and no one will really care as until they need to care. That's scary. There will be no such thing as a shared historical experience. Up until now, everyone grew up consuming the same media and was exposed to the same cultural items. That won't be true of children born from now. Everything is going to be fractured, with individuals and populations having their own fragmented experiences.

From a consumption standpoint, there were so many books I wish I would have known about when I was younger. I would have devoured them. Readers will live in a future where every book recommendation is optimized. Which books get recommended and which ones don't?

Those are a few of the takeaways that I'm watching closely. I look forward to reading next year's report.

LOOKING BACK

This volume represents the first volume where I can look two years into the past. I started the *Indie Author Confidential* series in Q2 2020, so I thought it would be fun to start a new recurring segment that looks at the previous years at the same point in time to see what I was discussing and how it panned out.

What was I discussing this time one year ago? Two years ago? *Five* years ago?

One Year Ago - Q2 2021

Become a World-Class Content Creator

The 5-5-50,000 Challenge. I tried a crazy challenge where I tried to write 5,000 words per day for 10 days to achieve a 50,000-word novel. I failed tremendously. I still think I would fail today if I tried it, though my voice recorder hack would help me get closer to a 5,000-word quota. I'd like to try this sometime in the future, but not any time soon.

Complaining About ISBNs. This time last year, I said I would not buy ISBNs. Funny how things change quickly! To be fair, the only reason I ultimately purchased them was because my accountant told me to make some big purchases by end of year to minimize my tax liability.

Livestreaming Experiments. This time a year ago, I hit my stride with my "Power Hour" livestreams. It started on a whim and I didn't think anyone would be interested. They turned out to be a huge hit, and I've been doing them every month ever since.

The Looming Cover Designer Shortage. For the first time in this series, I predicted the cover impending cover designer shortage. It hasn't happened yet, but as I wrote in later volumes, the prices of cover designers skyrocketed again *after* I wrote about it. We're in for a rude awakening at some point in the very near future.

Become a Technology and Data-Driven Writer

The Importance of Being Nimble. I wrote about slipping in my driveway on a patch of black ice and how that got me thinking about the critical need to learn how to write in alternative methods. For instance, if you break your wrist, you aren't doing any typing for a while. Knowing how to dictate can keep you productive while you're healing. My experiments with dictation, transcription, and writing on my phone continue to help me insulate myself against being unable to write. As of now, I can write anywhere, any time, and in any position. That's one of my strategic advantages.

Deepfakes. The Tom Cruise deep fake came out around this time, and I wrote about how scary it was. There hasn't been much deep fake activity since, at least none that have caught my eye.

Two Years Ago - Q2 2020

Become a World-Class Content Creator

Writing with the Audiobook in Mind. Writing a novel is hard enough; it's easy to forget about tricks that help you write for audio. I was onto something. Earlier this year (2022), I spoke with a company who is developing a tool to help writers with this issue. The software scans a manuscript and alerts authors to potential troublespots for narrators. I really hope the company succeeds. I was definitely ahead of the curve on this one.

Become a Technology and Data-Driven Writer

Ransom Attacks. If you need any proof that I was one of the first people in the indie author community talking about ransom attacks, mark Q2 2020 down and see if anyone said anything about it earlier than that. Here's what I wrote: "Ransom attacks are on the rise. I talk about this exposure at length in my course *Writing in Hard Times*. I believe it is an emerging threat for writers, but I don't talk about it publicly for fear of bad guys hearing it.

"A ransomware attack is when a cybercriminal gets access to your computer and then shuts it down and makes you pay money to get access back.

"Many people think ransomware attacks only happen at large organizations. I've read industry statistics that somewhere around 60-70% of ransomware attacks are actually on small businesses.

"Writers are small businesses. In fact, we're what the industry calls "micro small businesses."

"It's just a matter of time before ransomware creators realize that self-published writers are worthy targets, so start preparing now."

Anyway, now it's 2022 and ransom attacks are still on the rise. Start protecting yourself now because it's going to become a serious problem for authors.

My immediate recommendations:

- Educate yourself on cybersecurity.
- Install antivirus software on your computer.
- Keep your website and any website plugins up-to-date.
- Use a password manager to protect your accounts.
- Use two-factor authentication wherever and whenever possible.
- Back up your work in multiple places so you can recover your backups.
- Use a backup service like Backblaze to create secure, time-stamped backups.
- Use an encryption service like BoxCryptor to protect any files that you store in the cloud.
- Consider cyber liability insurance.

I'm very careful not to share these tips publicly because I don't want to draw too much attention to this issue. If you're reading this, you're lucky because outside of my *Writing in Hard Times* course, I have never shared my recommendations publicly.

Be careful out there!

Become the Writer of the Future/Looking Forward

Four Areas Where AI Can Help Writers. I wrote that there were four areas that authors could benefit greatly from AI:

1. Developmental editing
2. Writing assistance
3. Marketing assistance
4. Writing to market

Have there been any developments? Not quite. There is promise with writing assistance apps—Sudowrite is gaining popularity and I believe it will be successful. Apps like it will be integrated into writing apps in the near future. However, we're still too early for the others. There aren't any (viable) developmental editing tools yet; there are marketing assistance tools but none that are wildly successful for *authors* yet; and there aren't yet any AI tools I know if for authors wanting to write to market. Like I said, it's still early.

Brandon Sanderson Kickstarter. No, not the multi-million dollar one in 2022 that many writers are bitching about (for no real reason other than jealousy). I'm talking about the one Sanderson did in 2020 to create a leather-bound limited edition of one of his novels. I cheered him on then and I'm cheering him on now.

The Fall of Indies. We are currently living in the greatest time in history to be an author. All good things eventually come to an end. What will the transformation of self-publishing into the next era look like? Here's what I wrote:

"I don't know. Global economic recession or depression is my first thought.

"A close second is a trend away from books toward more interactive experiences—gaming, movies, or even virtual reality in the long-term. Authors who don't pivot will be left behind.

"Also, another event that might initiate this is Amazon taking some sort of action that hurts all authors, such as reducing its sales commissions, or restricting the 70% commission to KDP Select authors only, or introducing some sort of new sales commission scheme that drives authors to make less money overall. This happens all the time.

"Another might be a traditional publisher 'comeback.' Maybe the pandemic forces traditional publishers figure out that they need to start innovating and spend a lot of money on technology and marketing value-adds for its authors, enticing more people to seek traditional publishing (and sign the same old terrible contracts). Perhaps innovation technology gives them a clear market advantage over indies, maybe through artificial intelligence. They'll undergo a brand refresh as well.

"It's also not hard to imagine a political event that precipitates a societal distaste for self-publishing, such as a self-published writer who commits a mass murder and leaves behind a trail of books that espouse hatred and very obvious motives. I pray to God that never happens, as it would turn governments and public sentiment against indie writers.

"But honestly, I don't know what an extinction event for

indies would look like, or how bad it would be. It's worth asking the question, as when it happens, it will seem like it came out of nowhere, but will have been glaringly obvious in retrospect."

The fall of indies hasn't happened yet and doesn't appear to be on the horizon, and that's a beautiful thing. However, the concerns I pointed out are still valid. I find myself thinking *a lot* about a traditional publisher comeback. I also find myself thinking a lot about censorship and cancel culture. Earlier in this section, I wrote about governments introducing their own digital currencies so they can track everything you do. In addition to tracking you, they can censor what you buy.

We also seem to be nosediving toward fascism in many countries in the world. In fascism, the language of *everything* is the state. Everything one does must be in service of it. My biggest fear at the time of this writing is that, in my lifetime, the death of the author world as we know it will be due to fascism and governments gatekeeping who can publish and who can't. Traditional publishers could become the state's instrument to do so, and retailers won't do anything to stop it.

A fascist state has no use for an author speaking out against the system. It also has no use for people with active imaginations. The act of writing and the life of intellectualism must be reconditioned in the service of the state in order to survive. That is terrifying, but I don't see how it won't happen, especially in the United States.

I sure hope I'm wrong, but every election cycle, I can't shake the feeling that this may be how the current golden era ends. It won't happen tomorrow, but when it does, it will play out in ways that no one can predict.

How Long Will Smartphones Last? I wrote that smartphones' days are numbered. Hasn't happened yet, thank goodness! I happen to like smartphones a lot and I fail to see the metaverse overtaking them at this time. It will probably happen, though.

That was a fun walk down memory lane. I look forward to seeing how this segment will grow along with the series.

COPYLEFT TROLLS

I read a concerning article from Cory Doctorow about copyleft trolls. The article (which is quite long and detailed but worth reading) details the early days of Creative Commons and a loophole in the standard that attorneys are now exploiting to bleed potential copyright infringers of money. It's far too technical and nuanced to explain in detail here, but before 2008, there is a loophole in Creative Commons licensing where, if you didn't attribute a text correctly, you violated the license, and therefore were subject to a copyright infringement action. The Creative Commons foundation identified this and closed the loophole in 2008, but it still exists for creators and licensees who used the standard before 2008.

As a content creator who regularly relied on Creative Commons early in my career, the article made me nervous. I've written before about trademark trolls and how they could one day bring their evil services to the copyright world. I believe this is how they will do it.

Here's how they operate: they go to media sites that have Creative Commons licenses and use software to scan their databases. They look specifically for works licensed under the old

Creative Commons standard. Then, they scan the internet for any content creators that have attributed the works in question. They then look to see if the attribution is correct. Doctorow points out that many people (even today) still do not attribute Creative Commons works correctly. This was much more so 20 years ago. It's very easy to accidentally do it wrong.

If the attorneys catch even a single typo in the attribution license, they then threaten the content creator with copyright infringement if they don't pay a significant fee. The creator has no choice but to pay. The worst part about all of this is that it is done primarily via software. It is doubtful that there are any attorneys personally reviewing the infringements.

This is precisely what the Creative Commons foundation sought to avoid when they closed this loophole. Upon reading the article, I asked myself (as I always do), "What's my exposure here?"

I don't use Creative Commons anymore, mainly because I prefer to use licensed stock media. It's less risk. Creative Commons has been great for me over the years, but my biggest problem with it has been that some media I have used under a Creative Commons license no longer exists. I don't know if it's because the creator changed their mind or because the media they uploaded wasn't really theirs. I'll never know for sure. That's what scares me. I've always been careful to document any media I use for fear of exactly this type of scenario happening. I keep a spreadsheet that tracks the media I license, where I got it from, a link to the media, and information on the creator.

Doctorow's article helped me identify how I could make the spreadsheet stronger. It also helped me come up with an idea to restructure the spreadsheet so that all the column inputs could be strung together into a formula that gives me the correct Creative Commons attribution every time.

Creative Commons attribution isn't complicated, but it's not intuitive. My exposure is to make sure that whenever I use Creative Commons work that I attribute it correctly. That was my takeaway. I was pretty satisfied with my spreadsheet and very glad that I put it together. I was also glad that I read Doctorow's article because this is an issue that many writers may have to deal with at some point. Many writers can't afford to purchase stock images early in their careers. They use Creative Commons images on their blogs, websites, and even their books. Yet, I don't see very many people talking about this problem.

COLLECTING ADVANTAGES

I've been thinking about advantages lately. In studying the works of successful authors, I've noticed that many of them have advantages that helped them become successful. This is not just true of writers; it's true of successful people in general. There are usually one or two skills that they have or have perfected over the years that contribute to their success.

(I won't talk about survivorship bias here, but that is real. We're just talking philosophically here.)

When I listen to a podcast interview with a successful author, I no longer listen for advice. Much of the advice given anymore is the same.

But when I listen for advantages instead, I take a lot more from the conversation.

For example, I believe that a person's work history can tell you a lot about the skills they have. There's a certain skillset you need to have to be a doctor or military personnel, for example. That's fascinating.

Does that mean that I want to go to medical school or join the navy? No, but it's worth asking the question to figure out what the answer could be. I bet there are lessons you could take away if you studied that profession.

That's just one example of an advantage.

What are my advantages? In other words, what are the skills I have that, when I become successful, people will say are my strengths?

My Work Ethic. I am disciplined and I consistently produce books day in and day out. I also consistently make progress every day toward my writing, rain or shine.

My Sustainability. I have been able to sustain my productivity for the last 10 years with no slowdown in output. In fact, I have gotten faster at producing books over the last 10 years. Burnout isn't in my vocabulary because I'm having fun. I know many authors who could not sustain the pace and volume that I have without burning out.

Prolificality. I am extremely prolific. I am not the most prolific author in the world by any means. I know authors who write circles around me. I consider myself to be a medium-slow author. I'm not too fast, and I'm not too slow, but I'm consistent, which is why I am prolific.

Writing a Book in One Draft. I focus on getting my text down correctly the first time. I don't get hung up on drafting. Therefore, in addition to being consistent, I produce my novels faster than the average author. That is a strategic advantage because it increases the number of books I publish each year.

Alternative Writing Methods. It's no secret that I write on my phone and use dictation to bolster my word counts. (I dictated this very chapter at the sink doing my dishes.) Learning how to write on my phone increased my word counts by 40 percent. Dictation has doubled my word counts, and even tripled it in some cases. And because I write cleanly, I focus on getting my words right the first time. Learning dictation and writing on my phone also has the benefit of helping me write anywhere, anytime, and in any position. It also allows me to continue writing even in the event of an injury or potential disability. That helps me maintain my consistency, which helps me maintain my prolific status.

Advanced Editing. I have an editor who works quickly and turns around my manuscripts faster than the industry average. That's an advantage. I also use editing macros in Microsoft Word to help me catch common errors that my editor would have caught. This results in cleaner manuscripts, which will reduce my editing costs and improve the quality of my work. I also have developed a framework of thinking about my editing in terms of data and analytics; this has helped me to identify true weaknesses in my writing and shore them up accordingly.

Format Parity. By the end of this year, I will be in the position to publish the ebook, paperback, hardcover, and large print editions of my books on day one. The more formats you publish and the earlier you publish them, the more long-term earning potential you have.

Audiobooks. I'm still not at the point in my career where I can afford to produce audiobook versions of all of my books. However, I have enough titles in audio that it is a lucrative investment for me. As I become more successful, I look forward to the day when I will be able to release the audiobook edition very quickly after my other formats. Some authors have developed a workflow where they will produce the audiobook and launch it on day one, but I don't agree with that philosophy because you can spend a lot of time waiting for your audiobooks. As soon as a book is ready, I would much rather publish it. You can always let your readers know about the audiobook later, and that serves as good marketing because you're continuing to make people aware that your book exists. But sure, there is definitely a time and place for launching your audiobooks on day one.

Narrating My Own Audiobooks. In the future, when I am in a better position to do so, I would love to be able to narrate many of my audiobooks. If I did that, then I probably *could* release the audiobook on day one. Narrating your own audiobook is a place where even angels fear to tread, so this is something that makes me stand out. I narrated the audio version of *150 Self-Publishing Questions Answered*, so I know the process of producing an audiobook and I know how to do it quickly and correctly. Hell, I passed Audible's and Findaway Voices' QA standards on my first try!

Being "Wide." I am not a fan of Kindle Unlimited. I have used it over the years, and I've made money with it for the years, but I don't believe it is a sustainable strategy if you want to have a long-term career. While I have dabbled with Kindle Unlimited in KDP Select over the years, at the time of this writing, 100 percent of my titles are available wide. Readers can buy any of my books anywhere and in whatever format they desire. I wish my Apple, Google, and Kobo sales were a little higher, but they have been increasing over the years. What matters is that readers can find my books on those platforms. This way, if I have a breakout success, readers will have over 80 books in my portfolio to choose from. In a decade, that number will be much higher.

Podcasting and Video. I have been a podcaster and YouTuber since 2014. That has helped my writing and my marketing tremendously. I'm well-recognized in the indie author space, I'm always in demand for interviews, and I like to think that I deliver a good interview when I show up. Because I constantly teach writing concepts, I can express them simply and in a way that sounds good in audio and video formats. If I become far more successful than I am now, this will be to my benefit because it will help me sell more books and connect with more readers. Most importantly, perhaps, the advice I'm giving will help more people.

Law School. I went to law school and have education on contracts, copyright, and other legal topics. This is an advantage, even though I will never be a practicing lawyer (or qualified to be one). But I know how to think like a lawyer, and that's valuable.

Work History. Insurance turned out to be a good career for me and my writing. I have specialized in general liability, which means that I understand the dangers that businesses face every day. I also know how to avoid some of these dangers. My particular line of work has also helped me develop additional skills such as data analysis, advanced Microsoft Excel skills, public speaking, and more.

Automatic Sales Insights. In 2020, I discussed my process of automating the aggregation of my sales reports. At the click of a button, I can run all of my sales reports through a workflow that adds up all of the sales for all of my titles into a single report that I can use to mine for insights. For example, I can tell you to the penny how much money I made from my book sales in Germany across all retailers in all formats in the second quarter of 2015. That's powerful, and I use this data to drive my marketing decisions.

Consistent Cover Branding. In 2017, I embarked on a journey to rebrand my titles under a unified pen name design. Most of my Michael La Ronn covers have my name in big letters in the same font. This way, if you look at one of my titles, you know it's one of my titles. Ten years from now, when I have a significantly larger fiction portfolio, this will magnify my brand. It's still amazing how few authors do this.

Fan-mail. Anyone who has filled out my contact form knows that I respond to emails quickly. I receive a lot of fan-mail, and I make it a priority to respond to my fans. Even if people are asking simple questions that I've received a thousand times, I still take the time to respond.

Why do I do it? First, because I care. The people reaching out are usually struggling with some aspect of writing, and I have always tried to never lose sight of the struggles I had when I was an aspiring writer. I understand the emotions, the mindset, and the struggles. If I can help somebody in a small way, I see this as paying it forward.

Second, more practically, it keeps me in touch with what people are struggling with. It also helps me determine if the advice I'm giving is actually helpful or if I need to re-tweak it. I can use those personal one-on-one interactions to help my audience at large.

Third, it's good marketing. A reader reaching out asking me about one of my fantasy series and receiving a prompt response has the potential to become a fan for life.

Fourth, almost no one else in the writing space does it, especially when they get over a certain level. I don't want to become one of those writers. I like to think that, even if I reach a point where I receive a thousand pieces of fan-mail a day, that I would be able to find a system to answer all of those people's questions personally, whether it be from me or an assistant.

Fan-mail always deserves a personal response. If someone spends their hard-earned money on your book, and your book moved them to the point of typing a beautiful email, then that person deserves a response. I write about this in my book *The Reader's Bill of Rights*—check it out if you're interested.

I hope this chapter didn't come across as too vain. That's not my intent. I just want to reflect on some of my strengths. I encourage you to do the same. I also encourage you to look at the strengths of other successful indie authors. You may be able to learn from them; you may also realize a strength in them that you have in yourself but are not realizing yet. That's the most beautiful type of self-discovery because it connects you with who you are meant to be.

I believe advantages are worth studying for that reason alone.

WHY YOU ARE YOUR OWN WORST ENEMY

I recently watched a YouTube video called "Nietzsche - You Are Your Own Worst Enemy" on the Freedom in Thought YouTube channel (published August 12, 2021). This eight-minute video perfectly explained why you are the biggest obstacle to your success.

Your biggest enemy is you. Not marketing. Not learning the craft of writing. Not learning business. But you.

I highly recommend that you look at the video and watch it for yourself, but I will attempt to summarize the main idea. The YouTube channel is a philosophy channel that summarizes the ideas of the world's greatest philosophers.

The video is a dialogue between an acrobat and a circus master. The acrobat wants to become a famous acrobat but doesn't feel that he can because society doesn't value artists and his family will think less of him for pursuing this profession.

The master takes him to task and explains that:

- fears arise from your thoughts.
- thoughts arise from your desires.

Therefore, it could be said that your desires lead to your thoughts, which lead to your fears.

The master explains that the young acrobat wants society to value artists and he wants to get paid. But his fears and thoughts are holding him back.

However, you can't change your desires. Instead, they fall away on their own through understanding. Therefore, if you seek to understand a problem on a new level, you can change your thinking, which will change your fears, possibly eliminate them.

To assuage the acrobat's fears about society not valuing artists, the master explains that people will value anything that is a necessity. If the things you create are a necessity, then people will pay for them. He also explains that people respect you when you live according to their values. If you live according to your own values, then there will always be people in the world who don't respect you, but you will attract the right people into your life. If you don't do that, you will become resentful and regret the choices you have made in your life.

Wow. Such a powerful message in just an eight-minute video.

I wish I could do the video proper justice, but my main take-away was the premise of the video: your fears arise from your thoughts, which arise from your desires. Change your desires through understanding of yourself and your world and you will change your life. That's a philosophy to live by.

FEEDING THE INSATIABLE WRITING BEAST

I am on a journey to publish 100 books by the end of 2023. I began this journey in 2012, and I'm looking forward to putting my number of published books in the triple digits soon.

It takes a lot of time, energy, and effort to accomplish a feat like this. It is the result of many early mornings, late nights, time alone at my desk, and discipline, dedication, and commitment.

What happens after I achieve 100 books?

I'll want 200 books, and after that, 400. And after that, if I'm lucky—1000 books.

I have realized that I must be careful in this pursuit. It is an insatiable beast that must always be fed. No matter what I do, I will always want to increase the number. If I'm not careful, this could be akin to playing with fire.

I have known several authors who wrote at a breakneck pace only to burn out, negating any progress they made. Burnout scares me, but I have never thought that it was an issue for me. The best vaccines against burnout are to have fun, take care of yourself, and stay connected with why you are writing in the first place. You should know enough about me to know that I don't have any problems in any of those areas.

But still, I have become more aware of the writing beast in the lead-up to accomplishing my goal of 100 books. I also need to be reading, marketing, and doing things that will help me run a viable and profitable writing business. If I focus too much on productivity, I risk throwing all of the other elements of my writing business out of kilter.

But let me tell you something: there is nothing like feeding the beast. I love preparing a novel for publication, hitting that publish button, and watching the counter go up.

My theory is that there is a big marketing difference in saying that you have published 100 books versus anything in the two digits. People are always impressed when you have published one book. They are *really* impressed when you have published in the double digits. Their heads explode once you get over 50. Publishing over 100 books is simply unfathomable for most people; publishing 1000 books is otherworldly, and, dare I say it, a little suspicious to most people.

My point is that I don't think there will be that much of a difference in people's reaction moving forward once I have passed 100 books. Whether the number is 100, 200, or 999, the reaction will be the same type of bewilderment.

I would love to surpass the 1000 book mark, but I highly doubt that will happen. Therefore, I will have to be comfortable with three digits for a long time, which I most definitely will be.

What should my priorities be after publishing 100 books?

First, I don't intend to slow down. I do, however, plan to introduce more things into my daily routine to ground me, like reading more. I still read many times more books each year than the average person, but I could be reading more. And I will.

Ultimately, I don't want to fall prey to the writing beast. In my book *The Indie Author Bestiary*, I write about burnout and the many other beasts of the writing world. I'm very much aware of the impact they can have in your life.

In the meantime, I'm going to race for 100 and then reevaluate once I have achieved that milestone.

Q2 2022 STRATEGY PROGRESS

I'm now halfway through 2022. It has been a good year so far. Here is the progress I've made toward my goals.

BECOME A WORLD-CLASS CONTENT CREATOR

To achieve my goal of becoming a world-class content creator, I will focus on the following tactical priorities:

•Demonstrate a commitment to learning the craft of storytelling and teaching

•Demonstrate a commitment to outstanding quality AND quantity

Examples of day-to-day activities that will help me carry out my tactical priorities include:

•Keep learning through online courses and workshops taught by professional writers who are further down the path I want to write

•Reading

•Developing mentorships

•Finding new ways to increase my daily word counts

•Mastering different writing methods

•Documenting my process of becoming a successful writer in the *Indie Author Confidential* series

•Cleaning up my platform to ensure a consistent quality reader experience

What did I do to become a world-class content creator during Q2 2022?

- I have taken approximately 20 workshops from Dean Wesley Smith and Kristine Kathryn Rusch on writing craft.
- I have read (and studied the craft in) 20 books so far this year.
- I am still on track to publish 100 books by end of 2023.
- I exploded my dictation word counts by purchasing a voice recorder and implementing some hacks to help me dictate and transcribe more cleanly.
- I improved my fiction editing benchmark to 1 edit per 300 words, which represents a 3x improvement over my writing in 2018, which was 1 edit per 110 words.
- I rebranded *The Good Necromancer* and *The Chicago Rat Shifter* series under Michael La Ronn, concentrating my urban fantasy footprint. I also renamed my *Magic Trackers* series to *The Dream Mage* to improve its standing in the portfolio.
- I licensed the ebook version of *The Author Estate Handbook* and *The Author Heir Handbook* to The Alliance of Independent Authors. Later this year, it will be available as a free download to ALLi members as part of their membership. The ebook is

licensed as a special edition and it doesn't impede on my rights in the least. This will make the books available to a global audience and expand my reach.

BECOME A TECHNOLOGY AND DATA-DRIVEN WRITER

To achieve my goal of becoming a technology and data-driven writer, I will focus on the following tactical priorities:

- Use technology to make the business more efficient
- Use data to get insights

Examples of day-to-day activities that will help me carry out my tactical priorities include:

- Developing a tax plan
- Developing an estate plan assisted with technology
- Learning how to design my own covers
- Hiring a personal assistant for small tasks where it makes sense
- Developing a metadata database for my work
- Improving my readers' experience on my website
- Implementing direct sales for my fiction

What did I do to become a more technology and data-driven writer during Q2 2022?

1. I implemented my tax strategy and it worked very well.
2. I continued to take steps with my estate planning.
3. I took the first steps in learning how to design my own book covers.
4. I made some minor improvements to my website, making it a little easier for readers to find works they will enjoy.

5. I successfully implemented direct sales for my fiction.
6. I began doing "deep quality checks" for a handful of titles in my portfolio to double-check that they were uploaded correctly. A deep check includes reviewing the work on all the retailer dashboards, something I don't do during my normal QA process.
7. Signed up for Kindle Trends to get insights into the urban fantasy genre.

2022 is still off to a great start. Next quarter, I will continue doing more of the same: focusing on growing my portfolio to 100 titles and focusing on maximizing the value of my portfolio through new formats and quality assessments.

As I said at the end of 2021, 2022 is the final year for me to get my fundamentals right. I'm excited about that, and I'm looking forward to what the next quarter brings.

CONTENT CREATED WHILE WRITING THIS BOOK

This section recaps the books I've published and media I've created during the quarter. To keep the book evergreen, I will not include links to podcasts or magazine articles because sometimes links break over time, especially with podcasts if the hosts stop podcasting. You can easily search for them to see if they're still active at the time you're reading this book. If they are, enjoy! If not, please accept my apologies.

Books

The Dream Mage (formerly Magic Trackers)

New name, same great characters and story!

Aisha Robinson is a dream mage. She can read your dreams and even jump into your mind and control what you dream about. She's built a business helping people unravel their dreams so they can solve their problems. Join her and her cousins as they keep people safe from dream-eating demons.

Buy at www.michaellaronn.com/dreammage.

. . .

The Good Necromancer Series

Follow the adventures of Lester Broussard, necromancer extraordinaire who uses his powers for good. Talking to the dead and controlling them are Lester's specialties, and he does them to keep the city of St. Louis safe from evil demons and other things that go bump in the night.

Buy at www.michaellaronn.com/thegoodnecromancer.

The Chicago Rat Shifter Series

Meet Cyrus Grant, rat shifter. After a bad breakup, getting turned into a rat is the last thing he needs. Now he must survive the brutal world of rats under the city of Chicago. Sometimes, big heroes come in small packages.

Buy at www.michaellaronn.com/ratshifter.

Podcast/Video Appearances

"How to Balance Writing with a Busy Lifestyle" on The Self-Publishing Show

In this interview, Michael talks about building a writing business while raising a family, working a full-time job, and attending law school classes in the evenings.

"Estate Planning for Authors with Michael La Ronn" on The Indy Author Podcast

Michael talks about estate planning essentials and not-so-obvious pitfalls that are waiting for authors' heirs.

VOLUME 10

INDIE AUTHOR CONFIDENTIAL

Secrets No One Will Tell You About Being a Writer

VOL. 10

M.L. RONN

INTRODUCTION

2022 continues, and it has been one of the more eventful years in my writing life.

The "time of great forgetting" is in full swing. Summer is the time when writers forget to write. After all, it's nice outside.

Fortunately, the "time of great forgetting" forgot about me. I still maintained record levels of productivity even though the number of books I published this quarter was small. Next quarter will more than make up for it due to the timing of a few projects hitting late in the quarter and my annual Beast Mode challenge, which starts mid-August. This is still shaping up to be a solid year for writing output.

Yet, I dealt with problems. My wife is still battling long COVID and suffered worsening symptoms this quarter. I also had kidney stone surgery at the beginning of the quarter that slowed me down a little due to some complications.

Despite the setbacks, I still made some signature achievements this quarter.

My Core Strategic Priorities

As a refresher, my mission is to create content that entertains and/or educates my audience, preferably both, and to remain nimble in an ever-changing industry. I do this by focusing on three strategic priorities:

- Become a world-class content creator
- Become a technology and data-driven writer
- Become the writer of the future (looking forward)

What's in This Volume

In the World-Class Content Creator section, I discuss experiments with voice recorder dictation that laid the groundwork for doubling my word counts moving forward. I also discuss writing craft lessons learned from bestsellers, collaborating on a book with a friend, and adventures with AI audiobooks.

In the Technology and Data-Driven Writer section, I discuss falling currency exchange rates, running profitable Facebook Ads, and thoughts on new tools that have helped me be more productive.

In the Looking Forward section, I share how my wife's battle with long COVID has impacted my writing as well as thoughts on cancel culture and how to remain balanced in my everyday writing life. I also talk about where I was this time a year, five years, and ten years ago, with a special anniversary taking place this year. It's fun to look back at my career from time to time.

Enjoy this volume.

—*M.L. Ronn*
August 20, 2022
Des Moines, Iowa

BECOME A WORLD-CLASS
CONTENT CREATOR

LESSONS IN DIALOGUE

I read a book with a dialogue scene that stuck with me. I decided to study it to see how the author kept me captivated.

I won't share the name of the book because that's not important. What matters is the analysis itself.

This was a 700-word section of a scene between the main character and an ex-girlfriend who happens to be his boss. The main character was just injured in a scary attack, and his boss is visiting him in the hospital, chastising him for being reckless. The scene is a medium-paced (not fast but not slow) conversation between two characters. The scene is mostly witty dialogue.

Here are my takeaways.

1. The author established the setting within the first 200 words. There were three major focus points in the setting. That's an admirable thing to shoot for— amazing setting and world-building early so the reader stays engaged.
2. The author established the secondary character with just three pieces of description, yet she's a

relatively important character in the novel. I've always operated under the theory of *the more important the character, the more details they get throughout the book*. This turns that on its head. It just goes to show you that anything's possible as long as you execute.

3. There is some overwriting in the chapter. There are a few lines that really aren't needed and don't add to the experience. In fact, I don't even remember HEARING these lines when I listened to the audiobook, and I didn't even hear them the second time when I listened to the chapter. It was only when I studied the chapter visually that I noticed them, and even then, my eyes glossed over them. I paid careful attention to the phrases so I can avoid them in my own writing.

4. Approximately 25 percent of the dialogue lines do something other than "said." In other words, the author did something a little different to vary up the conversation every fourth line (on average, not in practice).

5. There were three lines of AMAZING writing in the section I studied (I could argue that there were more, but there were three lines that grabbed me). What if I aimed to write one to three arresting/interesting/very vivid images in every chapter? This isn't necessarily something to aim for; it's just food for thought.

This analysis only took me about 30 minutes. I don't like to spend a lot of time doing this. Studying the craft can become a big time suck with diminishing returns.

I'm a big believer in reviewing a section, carving it up like a turkey extremely quickly, writing down *actionable* takeaways that I can apply in my *next writing session*, then completely forgetting about it. I always keep my takeaways at a very high level and I never write down phrases or words the author uses. The goal when studying should never be to copy, plagiarize, or commit copyright infringement. The goal should be just to see the techniques other pros are using so you too can use those same techniques with your own style and your own words.

I'm grateful to this novel for helping me see yet another way to write dialogue between two characters.

LESSONS IN COMICS

From time to time, I like to change my reading habits. For the last year and a half, I have been alternating between fiction and nonfiction. Specifically, urban fantasy and nonfiction. This strategy has been working, so I don't plan to fix it.

But every once in a while, I like to read something out of left field. I don't remember how or why I stumbled upon comics, but I made a split-second whim decision to read IDW's *Teenage Mutant Ninja Turtles* comics. This series is a fresh retelling of the *Teenage Mutant Ninja Turtles* story that began in 2011 and, at the time of this writing in 2022, is still going strong.

I have never confessed it publicly, but I have always been a big TMNT fan. I grew up with the 1987 series, and I played the Super Nintendo games *Turtles in Time* and *Teenage Mutant Ninja Turtles: Tournament Fighters* games to death during my childhood. And, of course, I watched the live-action 90s films many times. I have many fond memories of my childhood time with the Turtles.

I also enjoyed the 2003 animated series, which I thought was a lot darker and more mature compared to the 1987 series.

I know my Turtles terminology and characters (in their various iterations) down cold.

I wasn't sure what to expect when I started reading the IDW series. Many people raved about it. At first, I wasn't so sure. I have always thought that the Turtles' origin story has always been a bit hokey. There's just no good way to get from real turtles to mutant turtles without a few mental gymnastics and suspension of disbelief. The IDW comic definitely is the best origin story for the series.

There is so much that the series does right, and I binge-read the entire thing because it was the most fun I had reading this year. Without getting into the characters or story too much, there is so much I took away from this comic series that inspired me to write better fiction.

Teams

The *Teenage Mutant Ninja Turtles* is one of the most iconic teams in entertainment. When most people think of teams, they think of teams with humans, like the *A-Team*, *Star Trek*, *Grey's Anatomy*, and many others. Most people don't put the *Teenage Mutant Ninja Turtles* in the same sentence as a team, but teamwork and brotherhood is the central theme of the series.

The Turtles are four brothers who must stick together no matter what. Leonardo is the leader of the group and the most disciplined, who serves as an elder brother. Raphael is a hothead and a defender, practicing vigilante justice in his free time. Donatello is the brains of the operations. Michelangelo is the immature youngest brother who just wants to have a good time no matter what he does. Combine these four brothers with

Master Splinter, a quiet but profound father who serves as their mentor and martial arts sensei, and you have one of the most legendary teams ever made.

The IDW comic amplifies the team aspect of the franchise. It does things with teams that I have never seen before.

The Turtles and Master Splinter are the core team, but other good guys float in and out depending on what is going on in the story. There is April O'Neil, the human who discovers the Turtles and befriends them. There's also Casey Jones, April's love interest, and a fellow vigilante along with Raphael. And there are many more. The "good guy" team is quite large and varied. Generally, each issue arc of the comic (about four issues) focuses on two to three good guys at a time. The others take the backstage.

There is also the Mutanimals, led by Old Hob, who is a mutant cat who was exposed to Mutagen at the same time as the Turtles. Old Hob starts off as a villain, but alternates between good and evil depending on what his goals are at the moment. He has a team of other mutants around him.

But there's a bad guy team too. There is Shredder, who needs no introduction. Shredder has a second-in-command, who is his granddaughter Karai. There's Baxter Stockman, an evil scientist who works for whoever is most expedient at the time. There are Bebop and Rocksteady, two mutant goons who do Shredder's dirty work. There's Hun, a former gang boss off the street who also does Shredder's dirty work (and is Casey Jones's father). And then, of course, there is the entire Foot Clan of ninjas that work for Shredder. Shredder works with Kitsune, a god who helps him see visions of the future and cast spells.

And then there are the really bad guys, led by Krang, an evil alien from Dimension X who is trying to restore his dying race of aliens to former glory. Krang has minions that serve him too.

So, really, this comic is a battle between four different teams. One good, one sometimes good, one bad, and one really bad. It's a masterful lesson on how to interlock teams and their different storylines together.

This comic taught me that when executing a team, it is best to think about two components:

- Who's on stage
- Who's in the spotlight

Who's on stage is who is in the scene. For example, the four Turtles might be doing a night run on the rooftops.

Who's in the spotlight is who is driving the scene. For example, the Turtles might be arguing about Donatello's plans to destroy the Technodrome, so Donnie is in the spotlight and he gets the most lines and the most face time.

In any four-issue arc, two to three good guys will be in the spotlight as well as two to three bad guys. Then, that arc ends. The next arc picks up where the previous one left off, but this time through the lens of another character.

Micro Series

Another great feature of this comic is the micro series. In the first few volumes, there is an issue devoted to one of the team members from each team.

Leonardo's issue is about him focusing on his training and inadvertently catching Shredder's attention, something that will haunt him later.

Raphael's is about vigilante justice.

Donatello's is about Donnie sneaking away to a scientist conference and meeting a man who becomes his rival and friend.

Michelangelo's is about Mikey sneaking off to a costume party, discovering a heist in action, and apprehending the bad guys.

And so on. The micro series are wonderful character studies. In many cases, what happens in the micro series has a direct impact on the plot later in the bigger arc, and the reader is so much more invested as a result.

I was also blown away by how this was executed. One lesson I have learned in my fiction lately is just how problematic origin stories can be. In comics, origin stories are expected; they are one of the main comic book tropes. But in fiction, origin stories can't be executed in the same way. If book one of a series is an origin story, readers will go into the sequels with expectations that the sequels will be similar to the origin story. But structurally, that is not possible.

In any origin story, there is the hero before the transformation, the events leading up to the transformation, the transformation itself, and then the hero learning how to adjust to their powers.

In a sequel, the character already has their powers and is somewhat comfortable with them. Books two and onward will be more similar to each other than to book one. If you take a few books to hit your stride as an author, you aren't giving your series the best possible chance. This is why origin stories can be problematic with fiction. It's also why many best-selling indie authors start their series with their characters already comfortable with their powers, and these authors reserve origin stories as prequels and/or list magnets. I never truly understood this until recently.

There's also something to be said about having a repeatable

structure in every book. It makes the reader comfortable. They always know what to expect whether they are buying book one or book nineteen. There is power in that.

Anyway, back to the micro series. I would like to try to do something similar with my next fiction series using the lessons I learned from reading the micro series. It might take the form of a short story collection that collects the characters' origin stories. Or, I might find a way to weave a micro series into the main narrative. I'm not sure yet, but it's got me thinking.

Annuals

If you have ever read a comic series, then you are no doubt familiar with annuals. In an annual, which is usually the last issue in a collected volume, the art style, storyteller, and the overall aesthetic are different. The story, while often continuing the narrative in some way (but not always), is told by a different team of artists and writers. Annuals give great opportunities to new voices to showcase their skills.

To apply this to my fiction, I don't plan on inviting anyone to write in my worlds, though that is certainly one way to do it. Instead, it would be fun to take an annual approach to the main narrative in some way. For example, maybe I do certain things in every novel at a predictable point that changes up the narrative while still continuing the story. Or, this could be a short story collection or series of novellas. Again, at the risk of repeating myself, I'm not sure how this will manifest itself in my fiction just yet, but it left an impression on me. I normally don't like annuals that much because in previous comics I have read, they never grabbed me. IDW's *Teenage Mutant Ninja Turtles* annuals are one of the few that I have enjoyed in all the comics I have read, and I do like comics.

I am looking forward to how these inspirations will one day show up in my fiction. I learned a lot from this comic series, and I am sure that it will be one that I read again in the future.

LESSONS FROM STUDYING AN INTERPRETER

I had to attend an insurance training for my job. The training was at a hotel business conference center, and it was a nice way to get out of the house for a few days.

I have attended these types of training many times, but this time was the first time one of the participants was hard of hearing and needed the assistance of an American Sign Language (ASL) interpreter.

The interpreter sat in a chair in the front of the room. For eight hours, she translated every single thing that was said in the room, even questions from other participants.

I cannot stress enough how difficult a skillset this is. It's one thing to listen to someone, pause, and interpret what they say. It's another thing entirely to interpret what they're saying in real-time. I still can't truly wrap my head around how one could do this. I suppose your brain has to be wired a certain way.

Studying the interpreter was a great people-watching session. For starters, she wore all black. I've seen interpreters do this so that the participants have an easier time focusing on their face and hands. I have seen other interpreters who didn't wear black, though, so this doesn't appear to be a requirement for the profession.

She kept one eye on the instructor at all times, alternating between facing him and the participant who needed her assistance.

She was extremely expressive in how she moved her hands and face, almost as if she were talking to a child.

Some words just can't be translated into sign language in any meaningful way. These terms include "commercial general liability", "asbestos", "nano materials", and many more torturous insurance terms that were uttered repeatedly throughout the training. I felt bad for her until I realized that she would just mouth the term to the participant rather than sign it.

During a break, the interpreter admitted to everyone that she had never read an insurance policy let alone attended an industry seminar. A few people's heads exploded.

During breaks, she spoke almost exclusively to the participant she was working with. She continued to sign and have conversations with him even when she wasn't actively interpreting. I could tell they shared a special connection even though they had never met each other.

Throughout the training, the other participants were just as captivated and intrigued by the interpreter as I was. I would frequently catch the other participants glancing over at the interpreter right after the instructor said a difficult word, just to see how she would interpret it. During breaks, there were many sidebar conversations about how great the first interpreter was.

On the second day, the wonderful interpreter was replaced by another whose skills were just as adept, but she did not have the same connection with the participant. In fact, I rarely saw her speak to him during breaks. She did not socialize or mingle with the other participants, and when it was time to go home, she was the first one out of the room.

In conclusion, I was glad for this people-watching experience. It taught me a lot about the interpreting profession and how I might write an interpreter into a story one day. It also illuminated more facets of that ever-morphing and infinite diamond that is human nature.

LESSONS FROM THREE ASSHOLES
IN AN AIRPORT

While traveling home from a writing conference, I got stranded at O'Hare Airport in Chicago. O'Hare is one of my least favorite airports, but I won't get into that. I found myself staring at a delayed flight with an extra three hours to kill.

I had planned on being home in the early afternoon, but now I wasn't going to be home until after dinner. As a result, I was going to be at a serious deficit in my daily word count.

I needed to get words in. I was working on *Year of the Rat* (The Chicago Rat Shifter Book 3) and I was close to finishing it, so I didn't want to waste any time.

I'd brought my voice recorder with me, but I forgot my lapel microphone, so I had to hold the recorder directly to my mouth. This wasn't ideal, but lately, I have been disciplined when it comes to my daily word count. I don't care how I get the words as long as I get them and they are as close to first-draft final as possible.

The concourse I was stuck in had a hallway that served as a loading area and supply transport for the United and Delta airport lounges. The hallway was long, quiet, and had almost no foot traffic. I found a secluded corner and went to work with my dictation.

Several chapters later, three African American men passed by. They made remarks about me that I won't repeat. They didn't say them to me directly, but they made sure that I heard them. They laughed at me and then kept going. The experience left me feeling insulted and upset.

Now, I will be the very first to admit that I put myself in that situation. After all, I was sitting in a dark hallway, speaking into a voice recorder like a crazy person. I suppose I deserved to be laughed at, or at least stared at with a little curiosity. But what they *said* was what bothered me. It was uncalled for.

I took a walk, listened to some music, and forgot the encounter until it was time to write this chapter.

The experience got me thinking about those guys and what kind of people would make a comment like that. They represent a type of person I haven't written about in fiction before.

There are some in the black community who believe that black people must behave a certain way, particularly males: you've got to be hard, have street cred and swagger, and fall into the typical black stereotypes. If you don't fit that mold even a little, you're worthy of contempt because you're not black or manly enough.

I feel sorry for these people because they've usually suffered some sort of trauma in their lives and are subconsciously offloading it to others. In other words, they're manifesting their hurt by trying to hurt other people.

As I walked through the airport reflecting on my emotions after the encounter, I decided to turn that negativity into something positive. Writing this chapter was one way to neutralize that negative energy.

Growing up, I was bullied by a fair share of black men like

this. These bullies treated me badly, but it was only because they were jealous.

My encounter with those three men took me back to my middle school and high school days when I endured treatment like that daily. I was frequently called an "Oreo" (black on the outside, white on the inside). I got into a lot of fights.

My childhood experience is one reason why I prefer to spend most of my time alone, and why I am extremely selective about who I surround myself with. I have no patience for negative people.

Most of those people who bullied me in my childhood have done nothing with their lives; in the end, I became successful in spite of them.

What's the difference now between me yesterday and me today?

First, I've gotten a lot older and had time to reflect on my life. I'm not bitter about things like I used to be when I was young. When I was younger, an experience like the one in the airport would have made me upset and moody for weeks. Today, it bothered me for a few minutes and then I quickly forgot about it because my novel was much more important than the opinions of some random strangers that I will never see again.

Second, I'm a writer. The three men in the airport represent a character that I've never written about in my fiction yet. At some point, I'll write a character based on these guys because I think there's strong material there.

Black folks complain about racism in the United States, and while it's true that there is racism in this country, no one treats us as badly as we do ourselves. Not by a long shot. That's worth exploring in a novel someday.

A CHALLENGING FANTASY
SERIES IDEA

I came up with an idea for a new series this quarter. It will be my most challenging series yet, but I'm excited about it.

However, it's going to require a lot of research. It's also a very tricky concept from a marketing perspective—maybe one of the trickiest I've ever come up with.

The initial concept is a mythological urban fantasy story, with a flavor of superheroes. This just so happens to be a pretty hot genre right now. I didn't plan it that way. The idea just happened.

I've seen people fight to the death on whether superhero fiction can be considered urban fantasy, or vice versa. I generally think that superhero fiction and urban fantasy are mutually exclusive, but there is a lot of overlap. The trick, if I were going to do it, is to adhere very, very carefully to all the main tropes in every overlapping genre that the concept touches:

- Fantasy: there is a conflict between good and evil and the good guys win, there is a team of good guys, there is magic, and there is a magic system.

- Urban fantasy: takes place in a real city, there is magic and it is hidden, and there are supernatural creatures.
- Mythology: the characters from the mythology feature prominently in the story, the heroes are linked in some way to those characters (or are gods themselves), and the mythology serves as the tapestry and impetus for the story.
- Historical: any historical sections need to be accurate and believable. They don't need to be 100 percent historian-approved, but I do need to do my best.
- Superhero: has to play by the rules of UF, but also have origin stories, a strong team, supervillains with a strong team around them and a good rogues gallery, no crazy multiverses (this isn't typically done in UF). There should be no science, aliens, or space travel (those don't play well with the fantasy genres listed earlier).
- And so on.

Holy crap. This is a huge challenge for someone who writes into the dark. And I haven't even gotten started on what the book cover or book description should look like.

If I do this series, I'm going to follow some important steps based on key lessons I've learned over the past few years since making urban fantasy my main genre. These will hopefully set me up for success:

1. I'm going to write the entire series, or at least the first three to five books, before talking about the actual concept. I may honestly do five books, which is a little crazy, but this concept is so challenging

that if it doesn't work, I would prefer to have it fully formed and stand on its own as a complete set so I can move on if I want to.

2. Regardless of what the market says, I'll still finish the idea. I don't abandon ideas once I commit to them. You never know how reader tastes will change.

3. I'm going to structure the series so that it can go on for a very long time, at least for 20 books. I keep saying I'm going to do that, and I did it with *The Good Necromancer* finally. This time, I'm going to do it better.

4. I've really got to do my research on some of the historical and mythological elements in the story. This will definitely be the most challenging research I will have ever done, and the stakes are pretty high if I screw up. Fact-checkers will be doubly important with this series. The concept is 50 percent material that I know well and 50 percent material that I don't.

5. I am going to design the covers backward. That worked like magic with *The Good Necromancer* series. So, if I write five books, I'll start by designing Book 5 first, then work backward. Once done, I will pick the strongest one and make *that* the Book 1 cover.

6. I may not put a stock model on these covers. You can find as many white people as you want to put on book covers; black people, not so easy. I'm honestly tired of fighting this battle. Illustration is an option, but it may be a bad choice 1) because it's expensive 2) because of the genre-targeting I mentioned above and 3) because just because you illustrate it doesn't

mean you'll nail it. Illustrating a series with 20+ book potential is a ridiculously expensive mistake if I get it wrong. According to K-Lytics (a data and analytics company that specializes in self-published data on Amazon), over 90 percent of urban fantasy titles have people on the cover. Over 60 percent of those are females. Around 30 percent are males. Only 10 percent of books in the genre have symbols on them. This story has a male character, which already puts it in the minority. If I go with symbols on the cover, I am already potentially operating with two gigantic strikes against me unless I found a way to NAIL the concept without a person, which I think can be done, but carefully. Symbol-driven covers are usually the province of epic and high fantasy (and thrillers and mystery too), but I think I could get away with it by 1) being smart about the background, using it simultaneously to convey urban fantasy AND mythology and 2) strong and bold typography. Symbol-driven covers have downsides, but they have the advantage of being cheaper and easier to sustain long term. It's much easier to hire someone to illustrate a symbol than it is to illustrate a person. Also, it's much easier to do these types of covers yourself if a designer builds you a strong template. Again, these are little talked-about reasons to consider symbol covers. I'm still early in my thinking, so this could change.

7. I'm going to run a Kickstarter campaign to test the idea. If the Kickstarter fails, the series will probably fail. I will, of course, have all the novels done, edited, and packaged before running the Kickstarter.

8. This story is going to have a strong team. There will be a central main character, but I'm going to use a bigger team instead of the two to three characters that I usually do. The villain will also have a team. I do this in my novels already, but I'm going to be a bit more intentional about it.

9. There will also be some romance, though it won't be substantial.

10. I am going to avoid the thing I screwed up with my last two series without realizing it until it was too late. Books 1 of *The Good Necromancer* and *The Chicago Rat Shifter* are origin stories. That resulted in Book 1 being different structurally from the sequels in the series. For example, with *The Good Necromancer*, I follow a very specific structure with Books 2 and onward that doesn't exist in Book 1. My theory is that there is probably some cognitive dissonance there. That said, the series has a very good read through and I wouldn't change a thing about it. I think it would have been better if I had executed Book 1 differently, though.

Anyway, that's a lot of information about a concept that's early in my head and still evolving every day. But I'm excited about it, and regardless of how it shakes out, I will have a lot of fun writing it. I look forward to cataloging my experience writing it in future volumes of this series.

AUDIO: THE GREAT CONCEALER

I was listening to a fiction audiobook that I enjoyed immensely. In fact, I enjoyed it so much that I listened to it twice.

The novel taught me a lot about characterization and dialogue. As with all novels I read that I enjoy, I study them afterward to determine how the author kept me spellbound.

When I loaded the e-book edition and reread the chapters I loved, I noticed something strange. The pages didn't *look* like what I was used to.

When I read the works of a mega-bestsellers, I am used to seeing shorter paragraphs and sentences for faster-paced scenes, and the opposite for longer-paced scenes. Most scenes fall somewhere in the middle.

This novel didn't follow that rule at all. The fast-paced scenes were big and blocky, and the slow-paced scenes were even bigger and blockier. This broke some of the rules that I know mega-bestsellers adhere to.

The author that wrote this book was *not* a mega-bestseller (though they are extremely successful in their own right, and, in my opinion, one of the best practitioners in their genre).

I thought about this disconnect a lot, and I came to the

following conclusion: audio is a very good concealer. It masks issues that would otherwise turn off e-book and print readers.

Here's why:

Audiobook listeners usually consume audio while they are multitasking. I myself listen to audiobooks while doing the dishes, driving, and mowing the lawn.

When people are listening to audiobooks, they simply don't use the time-scrubbing feature most of the time. Audiobook apps allow you to skip ahead and jump back in intervals, such as 30 seconds. If you're driving to work and listening to an audiobook, you aren't going to use those buttons. If you're doing the dishes, you aren't going to touch the screen with wet hands unless you really need to. In other words, you have no choice but to listen to whatever happens.

Many audiobook listeners consume audio at higher speeds, such as 1.5x or 2.x, so they don't hear issues with craft as readily.

Narrators will often intrinsically correct pacing issues through their narration. They will narrate fast-paced scenes faster and with more animation, for example.

Some people listen to books almost exclusively in audio. They may never see the e-book or paperback editions.

When you consider these facts, you can get away with a lot of bad habits, such as improper pacing and overwriting.

Remember, the listener isn't going to skip past it and isn't going to think too much about whether the book is overwritten unless the author goes over the top.

Ironically, this novel was extremely long. I would argue that it was twice as long as other books in the genre and filled with approximately 15 to 25 percent filler descriptions. I'm not knocking the book because I still enjoyed it, but I can't deny what I saw.

My point is that you can get a lot of mileage out of an audiobook. If you're still improving your craft, audio will hide many of your flaws. As long as you write a story that is *good enough*, readers will buy the audiobook, and they will enjoy it.

If you pad your story with filler, maybe spend more time and money promoting the audiobook version—readers won't know the difference. I don't plan to use this tip for evil; I'm just telling it like it is.

WRITING MORE SHORT STORIES

I love writing short stories. There was a time in my writing career when I wrote them exclusively. I once told a friend that I couldn't imagine writing a novel because they were so intricate and complex.

Now, at this stage in my career, I almost exclusively write novels.

Once I published my first novel, I stopped writing short stories. When you step onto the novel train, it demands all of your time, energy, and attention. Suddenly, the only thing you care about is writing more novels. More novels mean more stories to get lost in, more readers, and more money. It's an intoxicating drug.

Yet, novels take much longer to write than short stories, and they come with higher risks.

I've been saying for a while that I want to write more short stories, but I haven't put my words where my mouth is. This year, I committed to taking small steps to change this over the medium term.

First, I started reading more short stories this year.

Second, I wrote two short stories in my *Good Necromancer*

series. Both stories were approximately 5,000 words, and I followed the Lester Dent plot formula. I had a great time writing the stories. I licensed one story to an upcoming urban fantasy anthology; I have been shopping the other story around to fantasy magazines. That was a meaningful step.

Third, I responded to a push from a mentor. The mentor asked me what my strategy was for short stories, and I gave him a squishy response--something about wanting to grow my short story portfolio over time. He asked how many unpublished short stories I had. The answer was about 12. He challenged me to submit one of those unpublished stories to a magazine market within the week. His advice was that magazine submissions take a long time, so it's best to ease into the submission process so that you start getting answers (acceptances or rejections) in a steady stream. But it takes a long time to build up to that steady stream.

I listened and submitted three short stories to different markets this quarter. It's not much, but it's a start.

My thought is that if I can write and submit one short story per month, that will eventually get me to the goal state that my mentor recommended. I'm not there yet, and it's going to take me a while to build short stories into my workflow, but I'm excited about it.

The hardest problem I have right now with short stories is getting back into the short story mindset. Since I have developed a novel mentality, it has been difficult for me to transition back to simpler short story structures. I like the short stories I wrote this year, but I still think they have a novel mentality. It's going to take me a while to disabuse myself of that.

I look forward to talking about more short story endeavors in the future.

MASTER DICTATION MACRO

In the previous volume of this series, I discussed my adventures with a voice recorder dictation—an advanced but superpowered way of writing stories with insanely high daily word counts.

I'll recap my process here:

1. I use a Sony UX 570 voice recorder that I purchased on Amazon for approximately $70. Voice recorders are engineered to capture the human voice, and they do a much better job of it than smartphones.

2. I purchased a harmonica neck holder and put the voice recorder inside the holder. I put the holder around my neck and dictate while walking around and multitasking. This ensures that the voice recorder is approximately two inches away from my mouth at all times. No matter what I'm doing or how I am moving, this ensures more accurate dictation and transcription.

3. When I'm in public, I use a lapel mic hooked up to my voice recorder so people don't think I'm *completely* crazy.

4. I also have learned to enunciate more and speak more exaggeratedly when I am dictating. This also ensures more accurate transcription.

5. I upload my audio to Dragon and use its transcription feature. Transcription takes approximately 10 to 20 percent of the time it takes to dictate.

6. I put my transcribed audio into Microsoft Word.

And that, my friends, has been an unbelievable boon to my word counts. However, this method comes with problems:

1. You still have to speak in "Dragonese," meaning you have to speak with dictation commands. (Another option is to hire a transcriptionist, but ain't nobody got the money for that.)

2. The cleanup is absolutely, positively horrendous. Anyone who has dictated stupendous word counts and then had the unfortunate displeasure of editing those words can tell you that this is extremely painful.

I have spoken with several authors who use voice recorder dictation. For them, the speed at which they can fly through their stories outweighs the disadvantages of the cleanup (which they admit is painful).

But...you should know me well enough by now to know that dictating crazy word counts and spending hours cleaning them up is not my cup of tea. At all.

I tried to solve this problem using... wait for it... technology and automation!

I have spoken at great length about Microsoft Word macros in previous volumes, so I won't explain them here other than to say that they are the best way to solve this problem that I can think of.

I came up with a two-part idea. The first part was to create dictation commands that I used while speaking that would allow me to edit and format my text in real-time as I was dictating. The second part of the idea was to create a Microsoft Word macro that identifies those dictation commands in the transcribed text and takes certain formatting actions based on the commands. The macro then deletes the commands afterward so it looks like they were never there. The macro would then make edits in the document as tracked changes. I could then review and accept all of the changes with the click of a button.

This macro is *the* signature accomplishment in my writing business this year.

Here is a recap of the commands and the macro.

COMMAND #1: Delete the current sentence. When you're dictating, it's not uncommon for your mouth to move faster than your brain. You might say a sentence, but realize that you said something incorrectly. Or, you may have used a word you didn't mean to use. Whenever this happens, I say the command "Pikachu period." The macro will then delete every sentence that contains that phrase. This is wonderful editing in real-time. When I make a mistake, I can simply say the phrase quickly and then say what I meant to say. You would not believe how much time this saves.

(You're probably wondering...why "Pikachu"? Because it's an easy word to say and there are no words in the English language that sound quite like it. If you teach it to Dragon, it will recognize it correctly most of the time. Plus, it's fun to say.)

COMMAND #2: Delete the previous sentence and/or paragraph. Sometimes, you may finish a sentence and realize that it needs to be deleted. Without special commands or a macro, you have to remember that the sentence needs to be deleted. This will require you to go back and reread what you wrote, which takes a lot of time. That won't do. Instead, I use the commands "delete previous sentence" and "delete previous paragraph" while I am dictating. The macro will then do just that. When combined with the Pikachu command, what remains on the page are only the sentences I meant to say. The macro deletes everything else.

COMMAND #3: Interruptions. When I dictate, I am often doing things around my house. For example, as I was dictating this very chapter, I was walking around my office. My daughter came downstairs and told me that she wanted a snack. If I were not using special commands or a macro, I would have had to pause or stop the recorder to answer her question. That's not terribly efficient.

Instead, I use the command "Bulbasaur." When I heard my daughter coming downstairs, I said the command, then kept the tape rolling. I went upstairs with the harmonica holder around my neck, fixed my daughter a snack, served her, and made sure she had everything she needed. I did all of this with the recorder still on. Then, as I walked downstairs, I said the command "Bulbasaur" again and continued this chapter where I left off. When I loaded the text into Microsoft Word, the macro identified both instances of the command "Bulbasaur." Then, it deleted the commands and everything in between—including everything I said to my daughter.

This command is a godsend when you are multitasking and can't readily push a button on your voice recorder.

This command has served me well in several scenarios, particularly when I am running errands.

- Once, I was at a drive-thru and dictating a story while I waited for the hostess to take my order. When she approached my car, I simply said, "Bulbasaur," rolled down the window, gave her my order, and paid. As soon as I rolled my window up, I said, "Bulbasaur" again and continued my story. I did the same thing when it was time to grab my food.
- When I'm washing the dishes, if my wife or daughter need something while I am dictating, my hands are usually wet. I don't want to ruin the recorder with dirty dishwater. I simply use the "Bulbasaur" command.

COMMAND #4: Lists. When I am dictating nonfiction, such as the *Indie Author Confidential* series, I frequently use ordered and unordered lists. Lists are part and parcel of nonfiction writing. When I'm ready to start a list, I simply start a new line and use the command "list item" for an ordered list and "number list item" for an unordered list. I use these commands for every line in the list. The macro will then format each line accordingly and capitalize the first letter in each line.

COMMAND #5: Insert comment. Sometimes when you're dictating, you need to remind yourself of something. Maybe your third paragraph should be the opening paragraph, or you need to remind yourself to research something. The scenarios are endless.

You know that I am committed to writing clean text correctly the first time. As a result, I don't use comments as a way to write sloppily. I use them only when I truly need them. When needed, I use the command "insert comment colon."

When I run the macro, this will create a comment and paste everything to the right of the colon into a comment box.

COMMAND #6: Style commands. I use this for bold, italic, and underlining. This command works similarly to an HTML tag. I use the command before the word or phrase I want to format.

After I've spoken that word or phrase, I say the command again. For example, I would say, "You should italic really italic try the ice cream."

The macro will then format everything between the commands (and delete the commands).

COMMAND #7: Find and replace array. In previous volumes, I talked about a Microsoft Word macro developed by Paul Beverley called FREdit. FREdit is a scripted find and replace macro that allows you to change words quickly. I got the idea to build FREdit into my dictation macro so that it automatically corrects things such as proper nouns or Dragon mishearings. For example, if I dictate the words *The Good Necromancer,* Dragon will represent the words as all lowercase. But this is a proper noun. The macro will find and replace the text accordingly. This is helpful when I mention my books or series titles. Dragon can also do this, but it's a little clunky. It's easier to update an array inside macro code (for me, at least).

As another example, I have a character in my *The Good Necromancer* series named CeCe. No matter how clearly I pronounce her name and no matter how much I train Dragon to recognize her name, it almost always transcribes her name wrong. I simply add the different variations of CeCe's name into the macro so that it will find and replace those incorrect variations for when Dragon gets it wrong. This is extremely powerful, and it is a godsend for recurring proper nouns in your story.

COMMAND #8: Sentence case and formatting for proper nouns. This was the most difficult command to solve. Proper nouns are my biggest bugbear with Dragon. It's unreasonable to expect Dragon to recognize every proper noun in the English language, but I suspect that authors spend a lot of time cleaning up proper nouns such as *Teenage Mutant Ninja Turtles, The Good Necromancer*, and so on. It's just not fun to clean up all those proper nouns.

I worked with my developer to create a sub-macro that has two parts:

1. turn proper nouns into sentence case (while keeping articles in lowercase)
2. bold, italicize, and underline those proper nouns if needed

Some proper nouns don't need to be italicized, but I wanted to build this flexibility into the macro. It wasn't easy, but we were able to figure it out. The result is that I can designate and format proper nouns in real-time as I speak.

Putting It All Together

My dictation macro makes all of my changes with the click of a button:

- I can delete incorrect sentences or paragraphs in real-time.

- I can manage interruptions with the peace of mind that they will be deleted without any effort on my part.
- I can format lists, create comments, and format the text in any way you can imagine—on the fly.
- I solved the proper noun problem.

To say this has been a game changer is an understatement. It has allowed me to dictate faster, more cleanly, and more accurately. And I spend almost no time cleaning up my transcribed text because it is accurate the first time.

Dragon still makes mistakes, though. Most of those are easily cleaned up with Microsoft's Word's Editor, Grammarly, and PerfectIt. I catch the rest as I review the text (which I already have to do anyway—no dictation session is perfect).

I am proud of this accomplishment and it has already paid dividends in helping me explode my daily word counts.

ACHIEVING NEW LEVELS OF PRODUCTIVITY

I've been thinking a lot about the impact that adopting voice recorder transcription is going to have on my productivity. In short, it is going to have a seismic impact. Honestly, I haven't truly comprehended just how seismic it is going to be.

As I was writing this book, I had a dictation session where I walked around my basement for an hour, dictating chapters from this book. I dictated 3,000 words. This is the number I dictated after applying my dictation macro. As a reminder, these words were all clean and required only minimal editing. It took less than ten minutes to edit the text and mark it as final.

That means I can dictate 3,000 words an hour on average. When I first discovered this, I thought it wasn't that much. Then I did the math and it blew me away.

To put the 3,000 words per hour in perspective, if it takes one hour to dictate 3,000 words and 10 minutes to clean up those 3,000 words, that's 70 minutes to create CLEAN, first-draft-final text.

If you do the math on an entire day's productivity, it gets really interesting.

Say you start dictating at 7 a.m. On the hour every hour, you take a 15-minute break, followed by a 15-minute clean-up session. Assuming a full workday(ish), you would dictate a total of 6 hours, which would net you 18,000 words in one day. All clean.

In a 5-day week, that would net you 90,000 words If your novels are 50,000 words, 1.8 novels.

In a month, that would net you 360,000 words, or 7.2 novels.

In a year, that would net you 4.3 million words, or 86.4 novels. I'm willing to bet you that there is a rarefied, upper echelon of writers out there doing even better than this. I write between 500,000 and 700,000 per year and am considered extremely prolific.

Now, the math looks nice, but in practice, your actual results would be far below that 4.3 million because you have a 4.3 million other things to do in your writing life, like marketing, taxes, and business.

But what if you could write even just a third of that (1.4 million words) per year? That's insane.

That's what this voice recorder and transcription have allowed me to do—get to the next levels of productivity. Or, put another way, they have helped me "level up."

Such a revelation reminds me of the importance of a few things:

1. The true question is how my editing results are. Am I accruing more errors from my editor, or is the level of editing required roughly the same? I'll know after I've produced a few books exclusively with this method.

2. I need even more refined ways of being productive. To the extent I can optimize my dictation macro, I should do so. Everything is going to depend on how

quickly and cleanly I can speak the words, lightly edit them, and move on. If my goal is to be a first-draft-final writer, then I need to scale my operations accordingly.

3. I need to start doing my own covers, yesterday. You saw the math. There is no way even the most affluent author can afford to pay for professional book covers for so many books.

As I become faster and more productive, I am starting to see the upper echelons of author productivity. These are echelons I have never seen before.

The pulp writers wrote millions of words per year... on a typewriter. Today's authors have the benefit of technology, and they are still mostly typing. Those who are using dictation and transcription are probably not doing it the way I am doing it, which means they are doing it sloppily. Or, they're spending a fortune on human transcriptionists.

Few authors can type 3,000 words an hour for 6 hours. That's just asking for carpal tunnel syndrome. Speaking that much is easier; the only friction is your imagination. I've found that my imagination does a pretty good job of keeping up with my pace.

Therefore, I think the fastest authors writing today are using voice recorders to achieve their speed, and they're probably writing somewhere between five and six million words (sloppy). I don't think annual word counts over 6 million are possible unless you're a cyborg, but I could be wrong.

What would it mean to suddenly write several million words per year, when I am only writing around half a million at the time of this writing? That's profound.

When discussing my voice recorder adventures on my YouTube channel, I encountered another author who mastered this method and gave me some advice after expressing some hesitation with achieving such high word counts. He said, "You're right to question the power, but it's worth it."

That's a great way to think about it. Onward I go, and harness the power, I will.

AI AUDIOBOOKS: THE WATERSHED MOMENT

In 2021, Google Play opened a beta program to turn e-books into audiobooks using its AI voice technology. The goal was to take a book and have it narrated by a life-like AI.

I wasn't in the first beta, so I can't speak to how well it went, or what the quality was. Some initial comments I remember were that people thought the voices were a little too stilted. I wasn't terribly impressed with the voices myself, but the story was an interesting signal to track.

Fast-forward to today, and Google has expanded the beta. With the click of a button, Google converts your e-book to audio. If the AI narrator mispronounced a word, just click a button and teach it how to pronounce it. You can also edit the audio by editing your text; the narration will update automatically.

Google has expanded the number of voices available and also has made significant advancements in the quality of the AI narration. The advancements are significant enough that, while people were laughing at the first round of samples, they're not laughing now.

Google states that it is focused on helping authors create

audiobooks for books that probably never would have made it into audio. The company states that the best candidates (at the time of this writing) are nonfiction and other work that doesn't require much emotion in the narration. Fiction is NOT recommended.

First, let's discuss the quality of the voices because it is the least important factor in this conversation. If you know anything about AI, then you should know that it advances quickly. Successful services almost always start as laughingstocks. Then, suddenly, they're not. Remember when people laughed at Apple Maps for nearly sending people off cliffs? You don't hear stories like that anymore. Apple learned.

Now that Google opened the beta to all authors, they are now effectively training their AI models with a copious amount of data. They will have hundreds of millions of words to analyze. And with authors able to make corrections to the text, Google will be able to train its AI models much faster than previous iterations. (By the way, if you use this service, you're helping Google train their models. That's why you're getting this for free initially.)

The quality of these voices is going to make unbelievable strides now that anyone can use the tech. If quality is the only thing you are focused on, then you have missed the point, and you are in danger of missing the boat on this technology.

Quality is a red herring. What ultimately matters is convenience for the end user. In this case, the end users are authors and readers. Authors need low-cost ways to enter the audio market. The costs and barriers to entry are quite high. Readers want more books available in audio. Some readers only listen to audio. Additionally, some nonfiction readers don't really care WHO is narrating a book so long as it is engaging and gives them the information they need. For these readers, the narrator is irrelevant. If an AI reads it, so be it, as long as it doesn't sound completely mechanical.

And longer term, readers will want to be able to personalize their audiobook experience. If you want to hear a black man narrate a book, you'll be able to change the narrator with the click of a button. If you want to hear someone narrate with an Australian accent because that's what makes you comfortable, you'll be able to. That's extremely attractive.

As I said, many of the loudest voices against this technology are going to make fun of the quality. Don't fall for that. In just a few short years, those people are going to eat their words.

Next, let's talk about Google. People are skeptical of Google, and that feeling is justified. They're certainly not angels when it comes to our data. But when it comes to being the first mover of this technology, it's going to be Google, Apple, or Amazon/Audible. Take your pick. Frankly, I'm relieved Audible wasn't the first mover. This is exactly the kind of competition we need in the audiobook space.

This announcement is going to force Audible's hand. I'm positive they've been working on something similar—I'd put money on it. Now they have to do something in response to this, and that's something we should be celebrating. Healthy competition is a win for readers and a win for authors.

That brings me to the elephant in the room: narrators. It's undeniable that narrators are the biggest losers in this week's announcement.

Narrators are right to be concerned about what a technology like this will do to their livelihoods. I'm not cheering for the destruction of their profession, and I certainly don't want the narrators I've worked with to be out of a job as a result of this technology. But there's also not much any of us can do about it. Trying to stop this technology is like standing on the beach, trying to beat up the ocean. Anyone who thinks they can stop its advancement is delusional. I don't believe that this tech is going to eliminate narrators completely. There will always be readers who want a human narrator, just like there will always be readers who prefer paperbacks.

Trying to pretend reader tastes aren't changing and/or trying to stop it from happening is not productive. Narrators will have to find ways to shift their skillset to compensate for the impending changes. I don't like that any more than the next person, but I think the sooner people accept that change is coming, the faster they'll be able to find a solution that helps them move forward.

That brings me to something I've seen some people say about Google auto-narration (and AI narration in general) that is headshakingly stupid and misinformed. The statement goes something like this: "We can't let Google/Amazon/whoever flood the market with a tsunami of crap!"

Remember my comments on quality. Also, I don't consider myself a self-publishing historian because I haven't been doing this nearly as long as others, but...the words "tsunami of crap/flood of garbage/etc." should have special meaning for indies.

I recall a time not too long ago when people made that very argument against self-published books. Ten years ago, I remember people saying to my face that self-publishing was garbage—why would I even think about it? They begged me to sign with a publisher to save my career. (These people, by the way, had never published a book.)

I remember the Kindle gold rush. I was working on my first book when it happened. I remember the bitter debates people had about the "value" of traditional publishers. If you think the debate between traditional and self-publishing now is bad, you have no idea how vociferous it was ten years ago.

Anyway, my point is that I remember too vividly the battles

that people like me and other seasoned authors in this space had to fight to blaze this path. I haven't heard the words "tsunami of crap" in a long time, and now it's coming back again, this time from authors and narrators who have no understanding of recent history or technology.

If you're an indie author uttering these words, shame on you. You wouldn't be publishing if it weren't for that "tsunami of crap." If all those people who hated self-published authors had their way 10 to 15 years ago with the advent of the Kindle (which by the way, wasn't warmly received by many in the industry at first either), then you'd be signed with a publisher and miserable...if you got published at all. Or worse, you'd be lamenting the fact that you paid a vanity publisher and have stacks of books in your garage that no one will buy.

If you're a narrator uttering those words, I understand the pain. Still, many narrators today wouldn't be where they are if it weren't for that self-publishing "tsunami of crap" back in the day. Because that's just it—the "tsunami of crap" wasn't actually crap. Sure, some of it was. But while critics were busy pointing out the crap, many, many GREAT authors, narrators, and free-lancers were able to make a living. Many of these people who would not be where they are today if it weren't for the advent of self-publishing.

What critics failed to understand in the early days of self-publishing was that it was actually a tsunami of opportunity. Those who recognized it early have amazing success to show for it. Those who did not eventually came around to the status quo. Or, they're no longer around.

So, I hope detractors of this new AI technology dispense with the "tsunami of crap" line of reasoning because it's not a good look. It's hypocritical at best and disingenuous at worst. Any time people start romanticizing the way they do business, that's never a good sign. Your alarm bells should go off and you should immediately question everything you hear. You should also be skeptical of anyone in the indie space trying to "stop a tsunami of crap." Again, it shows no understanding of recent history.

As this technology heats up and the voices start getting loud, the most important thing you can do is make decisions based on logic, not emotion. The plain fact about AI narration is that it's here, and now it's here in a big way. You can choose to embrace it or reject it.

Unfortunately, the universe doesn't care what you decide. Even if Google fails at this endeavor, the bell has been rung at this point...

My recommendation is to do your own research, validate it with your own experience, and ignore the loudest voices—both opponents AND proponents. As with all things, the truth is usually in the middle.

Now, let's talk about Google again. I spent some time playing around with the technology. The quality of the voices is much, much better than I expected. I would reserve any judgment on the voice quality until you've heard real results. They're shockingly good. I converted one of my books, *Indie Author Confidential Vol. 1* into AI audio, and the results were very good.

It's clear Google has been working on this for a while, and the product development is on-point. The problem with Google is that they don't always commit to its products. But if they stay committed to this one, it's a game changer.

The product has still has some rough edges. There are still moments where you definitely know you're listening to a bot. But, honestly, in the audiobooks I produced, I would say that the recordings were 90 to 95 percent perfect. I only had to make minor corrections here and there. No one is going to be fooled that this is *not* an AI, but that's not the point. The point is that the AI is pleasant to listen to. It'll only get better.

If Google can figure out ways to make the editing just a little faster, and if they keep improving the quality of the voices, we're probably 5 to 7 years away from viable fiction AI narration, maybe sooner. And then everything will change.

I didn't think Google would be the one to make the first move, and I believe this is the watershed moment that people have been waiting for. It's hard not to see Audible and/or Spotify making a move into AI narration after this.

Also, I should also point out that I reviewed Google Play's auto-narration terms of service, and I didn't see anything unusual at first glance. No rights grabs, no funny business, or no unclear language. Yet.

Google also gives you the ability to sell the audio on your own website as long as the audiobook is for sale on Google Play. That's pretty generous. I think readers will initially be skeptical, but they'll be pretty quick to embrace this technology, especially if authors price their audiobook editions correctly.

I believe in the technology so much that I produced AI audio editions of the entire *Indie Author Confidential* series. Moving forward, AI audio will be a launch format for new entries in the series.

I don't know for sure, but AI audio now feels like self-publishing did in 2011 and 2012. That's an exciting feeling. It's going to be a little messy at first, but if history is any indication, the first movers will reap the biggest advantages.

I think we're in for a crazy ride in the audio space.

PORTFOLIO MANAGEMENT
ACHIEVEMENTS

I have talked at length about portfolio management and how important it is in my long-term strategy of being a world-class content creator, technology and data-driven writer, and writer of the future. When you have as much intellectual property as I do, you have to develop a way to manage your work quickly, effectively, and with the same agility as an author who only has a few books. This sounds somewhat counterintuitive, but I have proven that it can be done.

My master publishing file is how I am accomplishing this agility. My master publishing file is an Excel spreadsheet that contains all the metadata for my books. You name it, it's there: title, subtitle, series title, ISBNs, links to retailers, and so on. It sounds simple—and it is—but it's amazing how many people don't have all of this information in one place at their fingertips. They often have to go hunting for it. I don't.

I made some improvements to my master publishing file this quarter that will be beneficial for me in the long run.

First, I performed "deep checks" for a subset of my books this quarter. A deep check involves reviewing all sales pages at all retailers as well as how the book is set up on retailer dashboards, looking for anything wrong. A deep check takes approximately 30 minutes per book, and it is a failsafe to ensure that nothing is terribly wrong. I make sure the right version of the book is published, that the right version is for sale, that it has the most up-to-date book description, and so on.

Next, I updated the file to include links for my books on Barnes & Noble. I have neglected Barnes & Noble for a long time, and they are still not a major part of my distribution strategy. However, when I schedule promotions, many of the venues want a Barnes & Noble link. This prompted me to add Barnes & Noble links for all of my books to the master publishing file. This took approximately two hours, but I don't have to worry about hunting for those links anymore.

Next, I reduced the number of hyperlinks in my e-books. At the beginning of my career, I was a little too undisciplined with how I handled hyperlinks. I did foolish things with links in my books.

- I linked to book sales pages on other retailers. Not only is this a no-no, but it also doesn't age well.
- I linked to podcast episodes. This is unwise because if the podcast host stops paying for their show, it becomes unlisted. Therefore, your links become obsolete overnight (and you won't even know).
- I included affiliate links to products on Amazon. This is foolish because products go off sale all the time on Amazon, especially when there is a new version of that product. Therefore, my affiliate links were sending people to invalid product pages and/or obsolete products.

In reviewing my link strategy, some things didn't make sense anymore, like including a million links on my author biography page. I streamlined that.

I also reduced the number of links on my copyright page. I used to link to my cover designers' websites, but I stopped doing that because I realized that if my cover designer goes out of business or stops accepting work, the website could become invalid. Instead, I just mention their names. It's far more evergreen.

I updated the interiors for all of my books and reduced the number of links by anywhere from 80 to 90 percent. This made a big difference in the evergreen potential and professionalism of my books.

As I mentioned in a previous volume in this series, I created a master link log that contains all the links in all of my books with an Excel macro that checks whether the links are valid. Every time I publish a new book, I used Calibre to export all the links in the book into an Excel file that I combine with my master link log with minimal effort. Then, on January 1 of each year, I have a calendar reminder set to run my master link log macro. In just a few minutes, I know if there are any broken links in my books. If I run the master link log at 8 a.m., I can have changes identified and published at all retailers by 8:30 a.m. For *all* of my books. That's what I'm talking about when I talk about agility and being nimble. I can catch and fix broken links quickly and fix them quickly.

I also discovered a problem with my e-book files. In Vellum, I was not using store-specific exports. Vellum allows you to export a different EPUB file optimized for each of the major retailers (Amazon, Apple, Google, Kobo, and so on). When I first started using Vellum, I disabled this feature because I only wanted to worry about one EPUB file. I discovered that this was a mistake. For starters, it was causing the "look inside" samples on Amazon to be improperly formatted. When readers would preview the book, the background would be blue. (When they purchased the book, everything looked fine, but the sample suggested that I didn't know how to format my books. Oddly enough, this didn't happen for all of my books, but it happened for enough of them that it was a problem.) I believe this could have cost me some sales. Fortunately, readers never said anything about it, but it bothered me to have this type of quality error.

At the same time I reduced the number of links in my books, I also regenerated my books to include store-specific exports from Vellum. I then re-uploaded these new versions of all of my books, followed up a few days later to make sure the correct versions were published and available, and I updated my master publishing file accordingly.

This was a colossal amount of work, but it now ensures that my books are compliant with all book retailers and (hopefully) look good on a broader range of devices now.

I also took the opportunity to improve my pricing on Google Play. Google Play's interface used to be pretty bad. In fact, I would argue that it was one of the worst publishing interfaces in the industry. They've come a long way.

When I first published my books on Google Play, setting a price was a hassle. It was counterintuitive and overly difficult. When Google Play updated the Google Play dashboard, it made setting book prices much easier (in addition to moving to an agency pricing model, which was a welcome improvement).

When I began using the new dashboard, I segmented my pricing so that the major currencies were priced appropriately: US dollars, British pounds, euros, Australian dollars, and Canadian dollars. However, my earlier books did not have this level of pricing segmentation. I had set the US dollar price and then let the system convert the price to other currencies automatically. That is never a good idea when you can help it.

I still am not a fan of Google Play's pricing segmentation. I feel that it is too many mouse clicks and you shouldn't have to choose which currencies you want to set pricing. They should make it easier to set currencies more quickly like their competitors. But, it is what it is. I set aside an afternoon to go through my older books and segment the prices accordingly. This will make my entire portfolio more attractive to Google Play readers all over the world.

Amazon also introduced further pricing segmentation for Poland and Sweden. I set aside another afternoon to update my book prices in these currencies to make them more attractive to readers in those markets.

Payhip also introduced a feature where you can segment your product into different formats. Previously, if I wanted to sell the e-book and audiobook on my website, I had to create two different products with two different links. Now, I can create one product that has an e-book version, an audiobook version, and a combined version. I went through my portfolio and updated the products that could benefit from this more sophisticated format segmentation.

And last but not least, Google Play introduced a new AI audiobook tool that I discussed in a previous chapter. I developed the entire *Indie Author Confidential* series into audio within a couple of weeks. That broadened my reach for this series and made it available to more readers. Plus, I could also sell the AI audiobook versions on my website.

Those are my portfolio management achievements this quarter.

SPEAKING ENGAGEMENT SUCCESS

I attended my first in-person speaking engagement since 2018.

My, how the world has changed. It was great to be among writers again in-person. I attended Inkers Con in Dallas, Texas, and the annual Writer's Digest Conference in New York City in Midtown. Both events were great.

Now that I am back on the conference circuit again, I have taken some actions to make it easier to prepare for speaking events.

First, I now think twice about any speaking engagement that is not directly tied to one of my books. If I wrote a book about it, I can speak about it, and that cuts my preparation time in half. Otherwise, I will need to start from scratch, which will require a higher fee. This has allowed me to build a bank of presentations that I can recycle in the future. This is more efficient, and it saves me money while also providing good credibility to the organizer. Organizers like to see presentations ahead of time; it shows them that you are prepared and gives them a taste of what to expect for their event.

Second, I developed a new presentation template. I purchased a premium PowerPoint template from a design website. The slides are professionally designed, easy to customize, and visually stunning without being over the top. This will be my new template for the next few years. This way, everything will be branded and consistent.

Third, I adopted a sales technique I observed one speaker do. It was so smooth and effortless that I wondered why I had never thought of it.

The technique was as follows:

- At the end of the presentation, the speaker concluded the slide deck with a question slide that contained a QR code.
- The QR code took participants to a sales page on the speaker's website that contained an image of the speaker waving from a recognizable landmark at the hotel the conference was in, which was a great personal touch. It also included a link to the PowerPoint presentation, a few other bonuses, and a button to schedule a consultation with a discount.

I thought this was brilliant. I implemented this same strategy and it worked extremely well. The only thing I will change is the administration of the QR code. I found that many participants loved the fact that I offered a QR code, but it wasn't the easiest thing to manage on a smartphone internet browser when you only have a few minutes. What I should have done was created a printout on premium card stock with images of myself, my book, the link, and the QR code. This way, participants could scan the code in their own time and engage with the content without worrying about having to run off to the next speech at the conference. Including the link on the card would have also been helpful for people accessing the sales page on their desktop computers. In other words, everyone wins.

I also had some setbacks. Both times I traveled, my return flight was either delayed or canceled. I had to spend the night in Dallas because the last flight to my city for the day was canceled. Then, when I got to O'Hare Airport in Chicago, my flight was delayed. I spent eight hours at O'Hare Airport.

My trip home from New York City wasn't much better. I was also stranded at O'Hare airport for four hours (when I was only supposed to be there for one).

The current economic climate has wreaked havoc on airlines (actually, the airlines did this to themselves, but I digress). The result is that traveling is significantly more difficult than it used to be. I don't see this ending anytime soon. As someone who enjoys speaking but has a full-time job, this is problematic for me because I have to take off work to attend a speaking event. Therefore, I have decided to be more deliberate in the speaking engagements I take on.

For every event I attend, there is an opportunity cost. I have to spend time preparing for the event, traveling to and from, being at the event, and catching up when I return. This cost for me is worth it, but the unpleasantries of traveling right now and the fact that I live in a city that is hard to get in and out of makes me have to think twice about in-person invitations for the foreseeable future. That's not a bad thing. Ultimately, I feel it was good to have these bad airport experiences because they made me realize the importance of discipline.

Anyway, it feels good to be back at in-person events.

THE IDEA WELL

I thought it would be fun (and helpful for me) to start a new recurring segment in this series. I'm calling it the Idea Well, and it will contain inspirations and influences that made it into the books I wrote for that quarter. This will be a useful way for me to reflect on where my ideas came from, and it could be a fun Easter egg for fans of my work.

Year of the Rat (The Chicago Rat Shifter, Book 3)

This is the third and final book in my urban fantasy series about a protagonist who can shift into a rat. He is turned into a rat against his will, and since Chicago is one of the rattiest cities in the world, he's in good company.

Chicago features prominently in this series. I've always believed that the setting is a character in urban fantasy. I sprinkled little Chicago references throughout the series, but the most prominent are the epigraphs that I start each book with. The epigraphs are taken from the *Spoon River Anthology* by Edgar Lee Masters. Masters' poetry captures the spirit of life in Illinois in the late nineteenth century. Masters also spent time in Chicago as a practicing lawyer, and he was inducted into the Chicago Literary Hall of Fame in 2014. His poetry is free verse that expresses the epitaphs of different people who live in the fictional town of Spoon River. I read his poetry in college and was always taken by it. He has such a way of capturing the human spirit. Because his work is now in the public domain, I was free to use it in my novels.

The epigraphs (which are epitaphs) mirror the villains. They could be narrated by the villain themselves and encompass the villain's theme. Book 1 is about being drawn toward someone who doesn't love you; Book 2 is about stunted growth and living with death (the villain is a necromancer); Book 3 is about the cruelty of life. Again, the themes match not only the story but also the villain's aesthetic. Ironically, this was purely a coincidence that I didn't realize until I wrote this chapter.

In *Year of the Rat*, the villain is a hardscrabble demon collector who stores his collection of evil beings in the bodies of willing servants. He's stuck in the 1970s, is high on weed for most of the novel, and has an affinity for mink coats. He's the kind of guy who goes bump in the night, and not the kind at all you want to mess with. Some of his scenes were terrifying to write.

His name is JoJo Skaggs. He was inspired by a great song called "JoJo" by Boz Scaggs. The first line of the song is "Look out behind you, JoJo's got his gun."

In JoJo's first scene, he pulls a gun on his bartender, who is snooping around the back office of JoJo's nightclub. He jams the gun in the bartender's back, who can't turn around or he'll get shot. That's an homage to that infamous song lyric.

JoJo has a down-on-her-luck girlfriend named Simone, whose name is taken from a song called "Simone" on Boz Scaggs's *Middle Man* album, the same album that contains the song "JoJo." I always like to find ways to pay tribute to great musicians in my work. *Year of the Rat* continues this tradition.

I also discovered another interesting piece of Chicago history while writing the book. In the late 1800s and early 1900s, there were underground freight tunnels in downtown Chicago that were used to transport trash and merchandise between the buildings downtown. These tunnels had little trains that ran through them daily. It's a fascinating piece of history and testament to what an amazing architectural wonder the city of Chicago is. (Frankly, it is a miracle the city even exists, but that's another topic.)

Those tunnels are the fodder of fiction. The inner writer in me couldn't help but weave this piece of history into *The Chicago Rat Shifter*. In the novel, my hero, Cyrus, encounters a clan of gnomes who are protectors of the earth that dwell underneath the city.

There are many more inspirations that made their way into *Year of the Rat*, but those are the most prominent.

BECOME A TECHNOLOGY
AND DATA-DRIVEN WRITER

LESSONS IN COVER DESIGN THIS QUARTER

I took some meaningful steps this quarter to position myself to learn the art of cover design. I'm still behind where I want to be, but I am making progress.

The current inflation crisis is a constant reminder for me that I need to get moving on this. I anticipate that cover designers will raise their rates again soon. Why wouldn't they? Inflation is crazy right now.

In the previous section, I talked at length about my adventures with voice recording, dictation, and transcription. I have paved the groundwork to start accruing words in a significantly faster manner than I ever have in my writing. If I'm going to do that, I *must* start designing my own covers. I simply don't have a choice, especially if I write more than 20 books per year, and especially if inflation continues (which it will).

Next, I had an illustrated cover done for *Year of the Rat*, and while I liked the cover, it's another reminder that I need to find a more sustainable way to handle my cover design.

Finally, I obtained a mentor who is quite adept at cover design. I can now ask him any question I want about design, and he has graciously agreed to help me build a branded cover template. He also agreed to look at any covers I create. Having him in my back pocket will be critical as I begin learning.

Again, this is a short chapter, but it is my way of holding myself accountable for the steps I've taken. It is also my way of showing that I am beginning to walk the walk and put my money where my mouth is.

BUILDING AN EASIER MASTER PUBLISHING FILE

Google Play announced enhancements to its publishing dashboard this year. The enhancements are mostly visual and are aimed at making it easier to use their platform.

Google made it easier for authors to use its batch upload feature. Google Play, PublishDrive, and StreetLib are the only retailers I know of that allow for bulk uploading and changes. For example, if you want to upload ten books at the same time, or make changes to those ten books at the same time, these retailers provide an Excel spreadsheet template that you can use to facilitate the changes more economically. Unfortunately, each retailer has three different spreadsheets, but you get the picture.

(On a slightly related note, publishers make bulk changes using the ONIX standard; I've talked about it at length in previous volumes of this series. It's possible for indies, but too technical for most people).

Google has offered bulk uploading changes for a long time; they just make it easier now.

Google now provides a spreadsheet that you can download that contains the metadata for all of your books. I think you had to request this in the past. When I say they provide everything, I mean they provide *everything*. If you want a shortcut to building a master publishing file, then just use Google's template. They've done all the hard work for you. Hell, if I hadn't built a master publishing file, then I would definitely have used Google's. It's a great start, and you can add other columns as needed. This would have saved me a lot of time in 2021.

I'm just passing this tip along.

AUDIOBOOK PROOFING WITH AI SOFTWARE

I produced audiobook versions of *The Author Estate Handbook* and *The Author Heir Handbook*. I hired a professional narrator to do the job.

We followed the typical audiobook production process, which is as follows:

1. I provided a list of proper noun pronunciations for any words that might not be immediately obvious.
2. The narrator provided a sample for me to review and comment on.
3. The narrator then recorded the entire book and sent me all the audio files upon completion.
4. I listened to the audio and provided feedback.

However, I did something different this time that was a follow-up on a chapter that I wrote in a previous volume in the series. The idea was to use a proofreader for the audiobook.

Over the past few years, I have encountered individuals who listen to audiobooks, compare the audio with the text, and provide a summary of any differences, mispronunciations, or formatting errors, such as missing sentences. I thought this was a great idea, and I promised to hire an audio proofreader the next time I produced an audiobook.

Fortunately, they aren't hard to find. I found one on Fiverr. I sent the proofer the audio files with detailed instructions on what I wanted her to look for; one week later, she sent me a report with everything wrong with the audio. This freed me up to simply listen to the audio for major issues without having to do the tedious work of comparing the audio to the text. I sent that report to the narrator, who made corrections, and I performed the final listen-through of the book to make sure that the changes were made correctly.

I am not a big fan of "waving away" my responsibilities. Just because I'm not doing the work doesn't mean that I ignore my proofer's work product. I checked the proofreader's work to make sure she did a good job, and she did.

Another tool that I used in this process to ensure higher quality was Pozotron. Pozotron is also a service that I covered in a previous volume of this series; it is an automated audiobook proofreading software that uses artificial intelligence to catch errors. It scans your audio, compares it to the text, and flags any discrepancies. It works quite well.

For *The Author Heir Handbook*, I trained the audiobook proofer to use Pozotron. I granted her access to the project, and she went through and reviewed the discrepancies as well as performed a customary listen and proofread of the audio. The result was outstanding. The narrator and I both felt that we had eliminated almost all errors with the first draft of his narration.

Moving forward, when I produce audiobooks, I will let the proofing software and the human proofer do the tedious work, then I will follow up as the last line of quality defense. This process, while adding two extra steps, increases the quality of the audiobook production.

FIXING A MISTAKE IN A LIVE AUDIOBOOK

After I published the audiobook version of *The Author Estate Handbook,* I caught an error that the narrator and I both missed. (I did not use Pozotron for this book. If I had, it would have most definitely caught this problem.)

The error was relatively simple. There were a few paragraphs that didn't belong in one of the chapters. It would have made the listener tilt their head for a few seconds, but it was a relatively minor offense.

I did not want to inconvenience my narrator, so I figured out if I could fix the problem myself.

It helps tremendously that I produced my own audiobook four *150 Self-Publishing Questions Answered,* so I know the technical parts of audio production. I also know the problems that narrators run into when submitting audio for quality check.

The fix was as easy as loading the MP3 of the chapter in question, cutting out the unnecessary paragraphs, making sure that the "tail" of the audio met audiobook retailer standards, and re-exporting the file with the proper specifications. I have a free audio editing software called Audacity that has a plug-in called ACX Check. ACX Check scans your audio to determine whether it is compliant with Audible's technical specifications. If it's not, it will tell you why. Fortunately, the file passed ACX Check.

I re-uploaded the audio to Audible and Findaway Voices. Within a week, the new changes were published and live. I sent an email to the narrator afterward with a summary of what I changed and asked him to make the change when he had an opportunity.

Why would I email my narrator to tell him this? When I licensed my estate planning books to ALLi, I told them that I would review the books in three years to determine whether anything was obsolete, and I committed to keeping the books up-to-date. This means that I must also keep the audiobooks up-to-date. And to do that, it means that the narrator and I must stay in sync. When I engage him in 2025, I am going to have to give him a list of edits and timestamps. If those are off by even just a few seconds, it will cause massive confusion.

Thank goodness I was organized and technical enough to solve this problem. It saved me some time and money, and my narrator was grateful that he did not have to stop what he was doing to help me out.

BULK FILE RENAMING

In the previous section, I discussed Google Play's new AI audiobook feature and how it is a watershed moment in the audiobook world.

Google allows you to download the audiobook files so that you can sell them in other places, such as your website. However, when they give you the files, the metadata on the files is blank. The only thing Google does for you is number your chapters. That's not helpful for anybody!

If you want to manage your audiobook properly, you need to know which file represents which chapter; you also need to have complete metadata so that when you upload your file somewhere (or someone downloads your files onto their device), they know what they're listening to. This was a major oversight on Google's part.

Fortunately, there are apps to help with this problem.

Here's what most people would do: they would manually change the file names and the metadata by themselves (if they did it at all). This is time-consuming and laborious.

Here's how to handle this problem using technology, data,

and automation. It requires several steps, but it will produce good results.

First, the important thing is to remember that problems like this are data problems, not effort problems. When you think about your metadata and audio files as *data*, you will think about this differently.

Ultimately, your audiobook files are a giant block of data.

I found a Windows application that allows you to create a comma-separated value (CSV) file with the old file names in one column and your desired file names in the second column. That begs the question of how you can get your chapter names into Excel. The answer is no, you don't type them in.

Calibre has a feature that allows you to export the table of contents as a CSV file. You can then take the data from that file and paste it into your Excel template in just a few seconds.

Once you set up the Excel file properly, the Windows application will change all of your file names in seconds.

That solves the file name problem. But we still have to solve the metadata problem.

If you have ever looked at the metadata of an MP3, it is stored in what is called an ID3 tag. An ID3 tag contains all the information anyone would ever want to know about a file: track title, artist, album, album artist, track number, cover, and more. ID3 tag editors are easy to find, and they are often free. Many can edit your ID3 tags in bulk.

I found a cheap ID3 tag editor that allowed me to import the audiobook files (with fresh new file names) and edit the tags for all the files at the same time. The metadata looks something like this:

- Album: *Indie Author Confidential: Vol. 10*
- Artist: M.L. Ronn
- Album artist: M.L. Ronn

- Year: 2022

I was able to update all the files with this metadata in just a few seconds. I was also able to create another Excel template that imported the file names as track titles. Lastly, the editor allowed me to apply track numbers so that all the files would be loaded sequentially when the reader opens them in the app of their choice.

When I was done, I had audiobook files with clean file names and metadata. The overall process took approximately five minutes, which is much faster than someone doing this manually. I repeated this process for every AI audiobook in the *Indie Author Confidential* series, and I will continue to use this process for every AI audiobook that I create until Google develops a fix for this problem.

This is yet another example of how understanding data allows you to do things in minutes that would take other people hours. This is why understanding data is a critical advantage for every author in today's digital world.

CLIPBOARD MANAGER

I don't remember how I heard about clipboard managers. Maybe I saw a video for one on YouTube; maybe someone told me about them—it's fuzzy now, but boy, am I so glad that I stumbled upon them.

A clipboard manager is an application that stores everything that you copy to the clipboard. It functions similarly to a word processor storing every instance of undo and redo. The only difference is that you can recall everything you have ever copied to the clipboard.

Why would you want an application like this, you ask?

Let me count the ways that clipboard managers can be extremely useful:

- when you have to paste the same data over and over again. I scheduled an ad stacking campaign earlier this year and found myself having to input the same links, ISBNs, and other items that required so much time and effort to hunt down.

- when you paste something, copy something else to your clipboard, and need to recall the original pasted item quickly without searching for it.
- when you copy something and would have otherwise lost it if you couldn't recall it.

With a quick keyboard shortcut, I can pull up everything I have ever copied to my clipboard. I can even save favorite copied items. It is amazing. I can't tell you how much time it has saved me and my everyday operations. The app I bought was surprisingly affordable too.

Anyway, I strongly recommend clipboard managers. I don't know how I ever lived without one.

AUTOMATING REVIEWS

I recently had a service done at my house. A few hours after the service person left my home, I received a text message with a request for a review and a link. The link took me to a screen that gave me the choice of leaving a review on Google, Facebook, the Better Business Bureau, the company's website, and a few other places. I left a review on the platform of my choice. It was very easy and I only had to sign into my account for that platform. The entire process took two minutes.

This is the sort of thing I dream about as an author. How grand would it be to send an email to a reader with a link to leave a review on their retailer of choice? It would make gathering reviews a breeze!

I found a way to *kind of* do this with Genius Links. You can build a Genius Link Choice Page that contains logos and links to all the retailers you want people to leave reviews to, and you can use special links that take readers directly to the review page for a given book. However, it does have some downsides and it doesn't function nearly as smoothly as what I just described above.

The best application for this would be for direct sales—if

someone buys one of my books, an autoresponder could send the reader to the review page for that book.

The only difference between homeowners and readers is that homeowners have had the service performed and it will be fresh on their minds; readers may not read a book right away, so a request for a review would be annoying. This is where I think retailers could step in to solve this problem, but they don't seem to be terribly interested in it.

That said, this was a great customer experience, and I hope indie authors can get something like it someday because it would be a game changer.

LESSONS IN FACEBOOK ADS

While at Inkers Con in Dallas, I attended a session on Facebook Ads. I sat next to an extremely successful romance author who gave me some pointers after the talk. The chat, which lasted five minutes, left me feeling enthusiastic about finally getting around to Facebook Ads. I made a promise to myself at the conference that I would make my very first Facebook Ad before I got on the plane to go home.

Well, I would have broken that promise to myself because I ended up being preoccupied with conference activities on the last night. Suddenly, I found myself sitting on the plane with no Facebook Ads to my name. Imagine my surprise when the pilot came on the intercom and announced that the flight was canceled due to a maintenance issue with the airplane.

Everyone had to get off the plane, and I couldn't find another flight home until the next morning. I had to stay at a hotel.

Sitting in the hotel room, I realized that this had to be a sign from the universe. It kept me from breaking that promise to myself. I spent the rest of the night learning about Facebook Ads, and I made not one, but two ads before I went to bed.

Upon arriving home, I discovered that the ads were complete disasters, but they did give me some valuable data that I was able to use to improve my next ad. One week later, my ads were profitable! That month became the best sales month ever in the history of my writing business. My sales increased and have not dropped to pre-Facebook Ad levels since.

It's funny how the universe works sometimes. I could have bitched and moaned about being stuck in Dallas for an extra night. I could've taken my wrath out on American Airlines, an airline that I will never fly on again, even if it's a cold day in hell. But instead, I kept my eyes on the publishing business, and it was one of the best successes I enjoyed this year.

Am I perfect at Facebook Ads? No. I've run a lot of ads that haven't done well since. But a lot of them have, and that's something to be grateful for.

ANOTHER WAY TO RUN AMAZON ADS

I've been running Amazon Ads since 2017. In the beginning, I had middling success with them. It wasn't enough to keep them going.

I decided to invest in a premium course in 2018. That taught me the ins and outs of the platform. I quickly recovered the money I made on the course in a very short time, and my Amazon Ads have not produced a loss for me since 2019.

The school of thought of the course I purchased a few years ago was to never trust the Amazon dashboard. Amazon is slow to report data, and the data they report is not always complete. Therefore, you don't really know how effective your ads are.

Lately, I've been coming across people who are vehemently disagreeing with that school of thought. They argue that no, the Amazon dashboard is *very* accurate. It is slow, but only by about 14 days. If your dashboard says that you're taking a loss, then you're taking a loss. This school of thought is adamant that the other school of thought is full of scammers. After all, it's awfully convenient for an ad guru to say that the ad dashboards don't work so that you can't hold them accountable for poor results. If your results are good, they may not actually be because of the instructors' advice because—well, you can't trust the data. This school takes a different tactical approach to ads, bidding high on a small subset of target products instead of a shotgun approach that the first school advocates for.

I believe both schools have some merits. The first school is valuable because it has gotten many people comfortable with the ad platform. The second approach is valuable because it teaches people to think with their heads, not their hearts.

I tried both methods, and I can't definitively say that one is better than the other. I think they both have their time and place.

What I can say is that the answer is probably somewhere in the middle. We should probably give Amazon's data more credibility than the first school does, but we shouldn't rule out the fact that a decent amount of book sales could be coming from sources other than the ads.

It goes to show you that there isn't just one way to do anything in this business.

REEVALUATING CURRENCY
EXCHANGE RATES

The euro is heavy on my mind. Recent reports have shown the value of the currency being 1:1 with the US dollar.

This means that collectively, a book sale in a euro country is worth less than it was two years ago if you're an American like me. I historically benefited when Europeans bought my books because of strong currency exchange rates.

I'm going to meander for the next few paragraphs, but there is a point at the end.

I've talked many times about how I created Excel macros that slice and dice my sales reports into a nice database that I can run reports from.

One component of these Excel macros is currency conversions. Every retailer except Amazon does currency conversions for you, and you don't even have to think about it when you look at their sales reports.

Amazon is a pain in this regard because its detailed sales reports don't tell you what you actually got paid in your home currency when you sell books in foreign stores. For example, if I sell a €4.99 book in Germany, the report will tell me that I made approximately €3.45, not what I made in dollars. To get the dollar amount, I need to look at a separate monthly payment report that includes a German exchange rate factor. Then I must multiply the commission by that factor to get the actual amount I got paid. And even then, because of rounding, it'll never be 100. But it will be close.

Also, Amazon's bank uses different exchange rates than any other bank I've tracked, so you can't do this math with publicly available exchange rates. If you do, your numbers will be way, way off.

Amazon could solve this problem once and forever by simply including the exchange rates on the detailed royalty report and then do the math for you. But alas...I have to do it with an Excel macro instead.

If you don't account for exchange rates on Amazon, then you will never have accurate sales figures. There is one very prominent sales tracker on the market that, last I tested, did NOT do this math. It doesn't even convert the currencies. It's headshakingly bad. But I digress.

Anyway, my Amazon sales report macro does this math by estimating the past 6-year average of the Amazon bank's exchange rate between 2014 and 2020 for every month I got paid during that period, and then it applies that factor to my foreign royalty amount to get an accurate conversion and estimate of what I made in any given month. Because exchange rates fluctuate over time, you're better to use an average. In my tests, my currency conversions got me to within 90 to 95 percent of what I actually made, and my numbers were just as accurate if not more than Book Report, a prominent sales tracker on the market right now.

Anyway, maybe you don't care about that. Maybe you never thought about it. But I do because I want my database of sales to always be accurate and up-to-date. I know to the penny of what I made for every book in every country in every format, and I can get those numbers in just a few minutes. Very, very powerful, and unlike some people who use sales trackers with browser extensions, my data is private.

With the falling euro exchange rates, I think it's time for me to go in and redo the math on my euro factors. They're current through 2020. For Germany, the Netherlands, Italy, and Spain, the average exchange rate was about 1.12. This means that a €4.99 book at a 70 percent royalty would net me about $3.86 (3.45 x 1.12). In France, the historical exchange rate has been a little better at 1.68, which would net a $5.79 royalty.

With current exchange rates, if it's true that the euro and dollar are close to 1:1, then that means that the same sale would now be $3.45 (everywhere but France), which is objectively worse in all euro countries. But again, I need to review Amazon's exchange rates to see just how bad it is.

Honestly, I probably need to do this exercise for all my currencies again by adding the last 24 months into my current average. It would strengthen my factors from 60 months to 84 months and therefore lead to better and more accurate conversions when I slice and dice my reports into my database.

I think the wrong thing to do right now is to raise my euro prices. I'll probably wait until the war in Ukraine ends, assuming it ends soon. Otherwise, if you raise your prices and the exchange rates rally, you'll shoot yourself in the foot. Plus, people raising their prices is what leads to more inflation. That's ultimately bad for readers.

This is the kind of stuff I sit around and think about when I have spare time and am procrastinating on a novel...

SELLING ENTIRE BIBLIOGRAPHIES OF MY WORK

I was looking for some music to listen to, and I stumbled upon Bandcamp. I have been a Bandcamp listener since 2010, and I know I can always find good music there. Bandcamp has a feature that allows you to purchase an artist's entire discography for a discounted price. I have done this in the past for artists whose work I love. For a good price (or a price that I choose), I can support an artist and get lots of great music to add to my library.

This got me thinking about how to accomplish something similar on my direct sales platform.

There's no denying that being able to offer your entire bibliography to your truest fans is a beautiful thing. It is even more beautiful if you give them additional bonuses that they can't find elsewhere.

It's a great idea, but there are some logistic issues. Let's talk through them.

When you upload the books to your direct sales platform, you would have to do it as a ZIP file unless the platform uses technology to make this easier.

Assuming that you would have to do this manually, you

would have to maintain a master file that contains the most up-to-date versions of all of your books. If you update one of your books, you will also have to update this master file and re-upload it to your direct sales platform. This requires extreme organization, and it would be time-consuming.

Next, let's say that a reader does buy your entire bibliography. If they buy it on January 1, by December, you will have added more books to that bibliography. Does the reader get the new books? Probably not. But how will they know that the new books exist? How could they update their bibliography if they wanted to? In other words, if someone purchased all of your books once, and then want to do it again, how easy would it be for them to do that?

Those are the major issues I see with this sales technique. Technically, you could hire a developer to create a PowerShell or AppleScript that could grab the requisite files from all your book folders and compile them into a master file. Anytime you want to recompile the directory, just run the script. This is doable.

Another way around this problem could be to sell bundles of your work from certain periods. For example, you could structure your bibliography much like a poet structures multiple collected works. You could do a bibliography from 2010 to 2015, 2016 to 2020, and so on. This way, readers always know where they are in the bibliography. You just have to release a new bibliography every few years. Is it still clunky? Yes, but with the right finesse, it could be accomplished.

This is yet another technology that I hope makes its way to the author world one day. It would allow authors with decent platforms to make meaningful money and serve their fans.

LOOKING FORWARD

A PERSONAL TRIAL

Through 2022, I endured a personal trial unlike anything I have experienced in my life. It took me away from writing for a time, and it was life-changing for me and my wife.

In January 2022, my family contracted COVID-19. My daughter caught the virus first. I believe she brought it home with her from school because there was an outbreak in her classroom.

My daughter was sick for a few days and then recovered. Then, I got sick for a few days and recovered.

My wife, however, did not fare so well. Her bout with COVID was minor at best. She was only sick for a few days. Then, she got better for a couple of days, to the point where we thought everything was back to normal. The next day, she woke up with extreme dizziness.

She also had strange visual disturbances that she described as "like being on a boat." Her symptoms persisted no matter what she did. When she rested, she was dizzy; when she was active, she was dizzy. Nothing seemed to alleviate it.

Days went by, then weeks. Both of us were starting to get

concerned. A quick Google search of long COVID symptoms was enough to send both of us into despair. I watched YouTube videos and newspaper articles about long COVID patients. So many of the patients spotlighted in articles couldn't work, and required around-the-clock care. Their prognosis hasn't improved.

Before this happened, my wife was a very high-functioning person. She is very much like me, able to do many things at the same time. She was pursuing a Master's degree, and she had all the responsibilities of a wife, mother, and daughter. To say that this disrupted her life is an understatement.

My wife went to every doctor you can think of: primary care, internal medicine, cardiologist, neurologist, ENT, pulmonologist, physical therapist (two types), chiropractor, and psychiatrist, and that's just scratching the surface. She wanted answers on why she was feeling this way, but most of the doctors just shrugged off her symptoms as anxiety. They were unwilling and unable to help.

Yet, my wife didn't stop. She wouldn't take no for an answer.

A long COVID clinic confirmed our suspicions—she indeed had long COVID. Before this, when I thought of long COVID, I thought of persistent flu-like symptoms. However, it is not that.

My wife's COVID only lasted a few days. All traces of it are gone from her system. However, we learned that by sheer bad luck, the infection spread to her ear, destroying the nerves there and causing minor hearing loss and a condition called labyrinthitis. Labyrinthitis is the inflammation of the inner ear. It lasts for a few days or weeks, but the long-term effects are devastating; they include severe dizziness that doesn't go away matter what you do, anxiety attacks, heart palpitations, visual disturbances, hearing loss, and many other symptoms. The disease presents similar to chronic fatigue syndrome (CFS) and pain disorders such as fibromyalgia.

The most important thing with labyrinthitis is to catch it early. Unfortunately for my wife, because of doctor incompetence, we did not catch the labyrinthitis as early as we could have. The result was a complete upheaval in my family's life.

My wife would suffer panic attacks for no reason. It turns out that when the nerves in your inner ear are destroyed, the brain perceives dizziness as life-threatening. Its response is to panic. If you have ever witnessed a *true* anxiety attack or experienced one yourself, then you know just how devastating they are to both the person experiencing it and the people around them. My wife had several anxiety attacks every day. When she got them, she wasn't herself. It was as if she transformed into another person. The experience is very much like watching someone have a seizure. The attacks left her disoriented and with no energy. They were very scary and emotionally draining for me.

Eventually, YouTube videos led us in the direction of discovering labyrinthitis. My wife suspected that she had it, and she had to raise the topic with her doctors. Not once did any doctor say, "We think you have labyrinthitis or a vestibular issue." She had to bring it up. If that's not an indictment on the United States healthcare system, I don't know what is.

After weeks of advocating for a labyrinthitis diagnosis, my wife eventually found a doctor who requested that she do a VGN test.

In reading about VGN tests, I thought they were relatively benign, like a CT scan or an MRI. No—this test was hell. They attach many sensors to your head to track your nerve function. Then, they induce vertigo to see how your body reacts. My wife says that it was the most hellish experience she has ever endured in her life. It left her shaken, disoriented, and unable to function for a week.

Fortunately, the VGN test confirmed the labyrinthitis diagnosis. Finally having a diagnosis was a huge sigh of relief for us. After dozens of tests, we ruled out that she didn't have cancer, she wasn't going to have a heart attack, she didn't have a brain tumor, and that despite the gravity of the symptoms, she wasn't in any mortal danger. The doctors told her that it would take anywhere from 9 to 18 months for her to make a full recovery, and even then, the doctors weren't entirely sure about her prognosis because this bout of labyrinthitis was brought on by COVID-19. There's a lot that the medical community still doesn't know about COVID-19.

My wife's symptoms got so bad that she had to take short-term disability at work. The prospects of my wife not making a full recovery and never working again weighed heavily on me as it was possible that I would have to be the sole provider in my household. I'm fortunate enough to have a good job, but this sort of change in a household would be difficult for any family to absorb. To say I was worried about our finances and financial future is putting it lightly.

My wife and I both have made very smart financial decisions in life. We paid off our student debt early. In fact, we have no debt. We are very careful with our finances and we have been diligent about saving for retirement. The fact that we made all those smart decisions, did what we were supposed to do, and we *still* could have been wiped out by this incident is another indictment of the political and economic atmosphere here in the United States.

You would think that, in the middle of a pandemic, citizens would be able to get healthcare that is not tied to an employer. You would also think that, with incidents of long COVID being so common, it would be easier for people to get short-term disability, medical care, and benefits such as therapy and mental health counseling that they need in a time like this.

At the time of this writing, there are no benefits available to me and my wife as a result of this crisis. We had to navigate it alone. We have healthcare through my wife's job; if she loses her job or has to quit, we won't have healthcare and we'll have to buy gap insurance until I can enroll my family with my employer's health insurance plan. Private insurance is extremely expensive.

All those medical bills we have to pay for—that's our responsibility. Any permanent and long-lasting medical conditions that my wife will inevitably have as a result of this crisis are her responsibility.

What are world governments doing to address this problem? My wife was one of the lucky ones. There will be more people who, before catching COVID, were healthy, high-functioning, ambitious, industrious, and independent people. When they suddenly can no longer take care of themselves or find themselves facing bankruptcy or some other godforsaken reality, our governments will do nothing. If they do anything at all, it will be to punish those who were not lucky or rich enough to survive a personal health crisis.

As horrible as the pandemic has been so far with the lives we've lost, the worst is yet to come with long COVID.

One of my wife's long COVID doctors told her that COVID is really a mental disease. Its physical effects do not last very long. The mental effects are the most devastating. To paraphrase what he said, "We are finding that for many of our patients, COVID has rewired their brains to make them feel as if they are constantly under attack and still fighting the disease even though it has left their body. It is similar to post-traumatic stress disorder. Therefore, the recommendations we have been making to patients have been not only to treat the physical symptoms as they appear, but also to retrain their brains to function in this new neural condition that COVID has caused."

We already have a mental health crisis here in the United States with drugs, opioid addiction, mass shootings, and veteran suicides, to name just a few symptoms. If COVID is literally and figuratively putting people out of their minds, I can't imagine what this world will be like in another decade after COVID has had the opportunity to infect, reinfect, and devastate a significant amount of the world population with long COVID and its associated symptoms and conditions.

My wife and I have a long road ahead of us, but the day I wrote this chapter, we got promising test results that indicated that she is most definitely on the right path to recovery. Every day is a new struggle, but things are getting better.

This experience has completely changed my wife's life. She had to lean very hard into her faith. It has made her a stronger person, but she will not be the same person she was before January 14, 2022, when she got her positive COVID diagnosis.

I share all of this because the *Indie Author Confidential* series is my way of articulating lessons that I've learned on my path to becoming a successful author. Boy, did I learn many lessons from this experience.

I learned something that I always feared: life can strike at any time. I've been careful in my writing life to prepare for this as much as possible. This is why I created a course in 2020 called *Writing in Hard Times*. In that course, I outline my strategies for dealing with life's struggles as they arise. You can't prepare for everything, but you can damn well try. Looking back, that was a smart move, and it confirmed that I was definitely thinking about my career (and life) in the right manner.

I also learned the power of optimism. During a time like this, it is easy to fall into despair. During the first few months of this crisis, I had no idea what was going to happen to my wife.

Yet, I stayed optimistic. Even when it was hard, I found a silver lining in every day, in every diagnosis, and in every interaction with a doctor. I don't know if it ultimately made a difference, but I know that it helped *me* keep a clear perspective. That helped me support her.

I learned the power of momentum. I stepped away from my writing for a few weeks to help my wife through this difficult time. Not once did I have any regrets. Not once did I wallow over the fact that I couldn't get any words. I dealt with the problem, set a date to return, and I returned.

I kept working even when it was easier not to do so. Even though I took time off from writing, I still continued making progress in my writing business every day. I published several books. I traveled to writing conferences and appeared as a guest on podcasts. I kept making YouTube videos. I produced two audiobooks, fixed typos in my books, and did other things that I had a better mental capacity for. As a result, most people didn't even know I was away. I continued writing my nightly blog, even though I had nothing to say on many of those days.

Everything in life is a season. Just as summer cannot be endless, neither can a personal crisis. I knew that my future self would appreciate it if I kept even just a modicum of momentum during this crisis. That's what I did. This year, I am still on track to have one of my best word count years ever.

I also learned the true sweetness of that age-old quote, "Be kind to everyone you meet for they are fighting a great battle." I always liked that quote; I like it a lot more now.

This chapter is just to show you that everyone in life goes through hard times. You may be going through a hard time in your life right now. It won't last forever.

I'm sure that, in the grand scheme of the universe, there was some reason that my wife and I were chosen to go through this.

We may never know, but at least we made it. What got us through was faith, optimism, and prior preparation.

If you are not going through a hard time right now, one is sure to come. That's why I recommend taking steps now to prepare and plan. For writers, this means learning new ways to write, thinking about the future, and streamlining your existing production processes. I have detailed much of my experience in these areas in the *Indie Author Confidential* series.

AUTOMATED WEBSITES

I stumbled across a service that offers website creation for authors. That in and of itself is not unique, but the way this company approached creating those websites was.

I have said several times throughout this series that maintaining an author website becomes more challenging as you become prolific. It's a relatively easy affair to update your site when you only have one or two books. When you have 80 books, and you realize that you need to update something, you have to do it 80 times...

For example, I recently had a bug in my website that was causing some of the links on my book pages to be invalid, but I didn't know which pages were affected. I had to go through every book page and test every link. That was a pain.

Other little problems come up from time to time that add up in the long run. That's why I have said that the next website I build will utilize automation for gathering the metadata for my books. I don't know what that automation will look like, but this website service that I am going to discuss offers an intriguing solution.

The idea is this: instead of building a website page for each of your books, the service gives you templates to choose from and then scrapes the data off your Amazon sales page. Any time you update the sales page, your website will also be updated overnight. The service also crawls retailer websites regularly, so when you publish a new book, it will automatically create a page on your site.

This is ingenious. I thought the best way to handle this would be through building a database using my master publishing file as the basis, but this is much more economical if you think about it. Your sales pages are always up-to-date. If such a service were to take off, it would virtually eliminate the issue of website maintenance for your book pages. You would only have to monitor your pages from time to time (which you could do adequately with WordPress plug-ins). Under this model, an author who has hundreds of books would spend almost as much time maintaining their site as an author with only one or two books. Of course, there will always be issues endemic to large portfolios, but this is the type of solution we should be encouraging in the community.

There were a few things I didn't like about the service in question—namely that it is still early and the functionality is limited. The service also didn't take into consideration authors like me; it is mostly targeting new authors at this time. That's why I am not mentioning the name. However, I believe their business model is a sound one, and if they offer customizable and dynamic templates, infinite scaling, and relatively few bugs, I believe this is the future of author websites.

I'm so glad I found a service like this because it challenged me to think about the future of my own author website.

THE RISE OF CANCEL CULTURE

At a conference, a best-selling author used a certain outdated term to refer to black people. The author was praising another member of the panel who was black.

The author who made the remarks could be considered elderly and is a product of a different era.

I'm not going to mention names in this post because the names aren't important.

Many in the community quickly labeled this person as a racist and demanded a boycott of their books. The controversy spread like wildfire. As usual, people split into two camps: those who were against this author because this person was a purported racist, and those who supported this author (who were labeled by the other side as purported racists too). A prominent author organization disavowed the author, despite having given this person its most prestigious award the year before. The award was revoked.

As a black person, I understand the concern around the use of the term in question and why some people were offended by it. I wouldn't have been, though I would have certainly tilted my head at this author if she referred to me using the term. I would have pulled her aside afterward and said something to her. I have seen nothing online previously to suggest that this author hates black people.

I don't believe that the majority of people in this country are racist. Ignorance is a far more widespread problem, but ignorance is not the same as racism. Trust me, I would know.

I grew up in St. Louis, Missouri, which is one of the most segregated cities in the United States, even today. My great-grandparents were sharecroppers and picked cotton in the Deep South. They told me stories of what real racism was like. My great-grandfather fled Mississippi because if he hadn't, he would have been on the shortlist to be lynched.

My grandparents grew up before the civil rights movement, and they fought a type of racism that doesn't exist today, particularly in the workplace.

During my elementary years, I was the victim of overt racism at least twice (that I know of). These experiences weren't someone making an offhand remark about me; they were life-altering.

I went to college in a small town in Iowa, where many people never had an interaction with a black person. There were definitely ignorant people, but I wouldn't call (most) of the people I went to school with racist. I say that because my freshman year, I lived a few doors down from a self-described white supremacist. He broadcasted it publicly and he was proud of it. I had several conversations with him. I learned a lot from those encounters. Because of that, I know racists when I see them. Most people are not racists.

My point is that many of these people pointing fingers and crying "racist" have probably never met a real one. If they did, they would choose their words more carefully.

You can't talk to a racist. They can't be reasoned with. You *can*, however, have a reasonable conversation with an ignorant person and change their perspective. When two rational people have a conversation, both walk away having learned something. That's the point of discourse. It makes us better.

All these allegations of racism against people who may or may not be racist is ultimately hurting everyone. Calling someone a racist is an easy way to shut that person down. When people hear the term, they lose the ability to think critically. If someone is racist, how could you support them? No one wants to be affiliated with one, and rightfully so.

I have no love for racists, but I object to people using allegations of racism to advance a political ideology or personal agenda. To call someone a racist should be, as it has always been, a very grave allegation reserved for the worst that society has to offer—not cheaply thrown around on social media as a way to make a statement to people you don't know (and who don't care about you) on what your values are.

It appears that this author is going to suffer considerably from this fallout, and I don't believe it was justified. No one in the community should be able to make unfounded allegations and destroy someone's career so easily.

I think about authors who have been canceled due to their words or actions. Maybe the backlash against some was justified, but if even one innocent person loses their livelihood because of something that could have been a teachable moment, that is a human tragedy. That doesn't give people license to keep saying bad things, but we have to have some compassion and grace and pray that people can learn from their mistakes. We should extend the same compassion and grace that we would want extended to us.

Everyone should be allowed to publish the books they want on their own terms. Every reader has a right to purchase the books that they are interested in. If you don't like someone's politics or someone's views on a certain matter, then don't buy that book and don't support that author. If you don't like the politics of a conference or a publishing house, then don't support that conference or publishing house.

People seem to forget that the writing profession is a business of opinions. Everybody has opinions. Some of those opinions will probably offend you. *Your* opinions will probably offend somebody else.

Whether it's a remark at a conference or written opinions in a book, having to deal with things we disagree with (sometimes viscerally) is the cost of living in a free society. When someone says something ignorant, they *should* be corrected. But when we start trying to censor others, we start down a slippery slope that, at some point, will be so slippery that we can't turn back.

When all we focus on is identity politics, we risk losing our own identities as authors.

R.A.M.P-ING UP MY CAREER

I have been focused on improving my discipline as a writer. I'm already pretty disciplined, but I believe I can improve.

One area I am trying to improve is balancing my daily activities. I love to write, so that's where I spend the majority of my time. I'm happiest when I am in the land of a new story.

However, I am so focused on word production that sometimes other areas of my business drop off for a time. This results in an ever-growing mountain of emails, tax receipts that need to be organized, and other obligations that I need to attend to that I put off for a few days when I am in the heat of finishing a book.

I need to take a more balanced approach to my writing life.

My strategy as a writer is as follows:

1. Become a world-class content creator
2. Become a technology and data-driven writer
3. Become the writer of the future.

What are the tactics that I need to be taking every single day to support that strategy?

I came up with an acronym that explains the four key activities I should be doing every day. The acronym is R.A.M.P.

R is for reading.

A is for analyzing data and opportunities.

M is for marketing.

P is for production of books, specifically, new words every day.

The question I have been asking myself every day for the last few months has been, "What does the picture of good look like today?" That is a great question because it keeps me focused on what I am doing every day to further my career. However, the question often leads me down rabbit holes.

I have changed the question. Instead, I ask, "What am I doing to R.A.M.P. up my career today?"

In other words:

- What did I read today?
- How did I use data in some capacity to glean an insight into the business?
- How did I market today?
- How many words did I write?

I have a daily blog where I talk about my activities for the day. I have built a great community of people who have been interested in my day-to-day adventures. I adopted the R.A.M.P. acronym as a way to structure the blog posts so that they're easy to scan.

My R.A.M.P. posts hit the highlights of everything I did that day. They have been a hit with my community.

Each letter of the acronym allows for a jumping-off point for my posts:

- I might be reading a book where the author used a technique that captivated me. I will talk about that technique generally on the blog (and in this series).
- If I uncover an interesting insight with my advertising, sales, or dictation, I discuss those on the blog too.
- I talk about things I'm doing to market my work.
- And--most popularly--I share my word count for the day and how my writing sessions went.

Developing the R.A.M.P. acronym and sticking to it has been helpful for me in keeping my priorities straight.

ENCOUNTER WITH A SAVVY
AUTHOR ESTATE

This quarter, I had a run-in with a savvy author estate. Given that I wrote two books on estate planning this year, I have been paying careful attention to author estates.

I happened to be on a speaking panel on Zoom, and afterward, one of the audience members reached out to thank me for the advice I gave on the panel. This person was the personal representative for a very wealthy author estate that you would recognize. After a nice email exchange, the representative asked for my address to send me a care package. I was blown away by what I received, not only because it was very generous, but because it was a master class in author branding and marketing.

Here is what it contained:

- several handsome paperback copies of the author's books
- bookmarks
- audiobooks of the works on a USB drive that was branded to the cover of one of the author's books
- a brochure with more of the author's works and appropriate links

- a handwritten note

Wow. It was impressive. It set the kind of standard that I want to achieve myself one day. It would be easy to send a reader a paperback copy of my work, a bookmark, a copy of the audiobook, and a brochure, along with a handwritten note. That is stunningly easy. It's so easy that I kicked myself that I had never thought of it.

My encounter with this estate is proof that it is indeed possible to make long-term plans for your work and have people continue your legacy long after you're gone. It inspired me to double down on my estate planning efforts. If I'm lucky, I will leave an estate that can operate on such a high professional level.

THIS TIME LAST YEAR

I thought it would be fun to continue a segment every Q3 that looks back at previous volumes to see how I have advanced and how the industry has changed.

What was happening a year ago in Q3 2021? Some of the things that were important for me:

- Things were starting to return to normal after a crazy 2020. My family began going out to restaurants for the first time since 2020.
- It was a little easier to plan for the future. The hysteria of the pandemic was starting to wear off.
- Honestly, as I think back to Q3 2021, it was...kind of boring. Looking back on it, that's a wonderful thing.

Content Creation

.   .   .

This time last year, I wrapped up many responsibilities that were draining me every day: law school, podcasting, and teaching insurance classes. I didn't realize the gains at the time, but ceasing these activities allowed me to be more disciplined.

Technology and Data

This time last year, I was experimenting with AI tools. Most were dead-ends.

Become the Writer of the Future

Ironically, I commented on Google Play's auto-narration tool. I said this: "That said, I downloaded a few public domain titles and listened to them. The narration wasn't good, but it wasn't bad either. It clearly sounded like an AI was reading the book, but it sounded a hell of a lot better than current voice-to-text software on phones and computers. The voice still reads too fast and doesn't handle sentence breaks or proper nouns well. Still, it's promising.

"With any new technology, people are quick to judge or write it off without understanding the rate at which technology advances. I'd give Google's effort a C-. In five years, however, if they continue the program and continue improving the technology, it'll be a B+ or an A-, enough for customers to start paying attention. Then, overnight, the technology will be mainstream and everyone will be using it."

Wow.

A few chapters later, I wrote about how authors are tired of

AI. They just don't seem to be interested in the new tools that are popping up. I wrote, "I suggest that it is up to you to figure out your artificial intelligence strategy. At this point, no one is going to do it for you, and I don't see anyone dedicating themselves to creating advanced tools to help authors as a whole. If they do, they'll do it without too much input from the authors who need it most—those who will be left behind."

Now, here we are in 2022. What a year.

THIS TIME FIVE YEARS AGO

I was thinking about how far I've come compared to five years ago. I'll continue my trip into (not so) old memories.

In 2017, I wrote a 9-book space opera series called *Galaxy Mavericks*. In July 2017, I was just wrapping up the publication of the series. I had a blast writing it. I wrote the entire series before launching it. Almost all of the major lessons I learned in 2017 came from *Galaxy Mavericks*.

Galaxy Mavericks was the series that taught me the importance of branded covers. In 2016, I started a campaign to clean up my covers and make them more consistent. I followed a similar style for all my books moving forward, with my author name prominently at the top of my covers. When you have 9 books that have a consistent look, it looks GREAT on a bookshelf. With this series as the visual anchor, all the books in my portfolio started to gel visually.

Galaxy Mavericks also taught me the importance of research, and that I wasn't doing my research correctly. I got the space details in that story horribly wrong, but readers still loved the story. I would carry the research mistakes I made from this book to my future series.

Galaxy Mavericks also contains the fastest novel I've ever written to date. *Zero Magnitude* (Book 3) clocked in at six days. I still haven't written a faster novel since.

Galaxy Mavericks also taught me how to write books out of sequence. I wrote Book 2 first, then 1,3,4,5,6,7,8, and 9. It also taught me a tremendous amount about writing into the dark. To write a 9-book series without an outline is a gigantic feat.

2017 was a good year, but for some reason, it's not as prominent in my memory as 2018. We'll talk about that next year!

THIS TIME TEN YEARS AGO

Since we're on the topic of traveling back in time, I might as well look at the last decade...

July 2022 is exactly 10 years to the month that I had my near-death experience. This time 10 years ago, I was leaving the hospital.

In July 2012, I fell ill with food poisoning after eating a nice dinner at a restaurant. My wife rushed me to the hospital... where I didn't leave for a month. I had food poisoning but then picked up an infection in the hospital, and doctors almost didn't catch it. The only reason I survived was because of sheer luck. My wife's old roommate was in medical school at the time, and when she heard about my symptoms, she told me what to tell the doctors...and then they discovered what was really wrong.

In fact, an article came out in the *USA Today* newspaper about the type of infection I caught and how it was killing people across the country, mainly because of bureaucracy, lack of sanitation, and inaction on the part of hospitals. The article is titled "Far More Could Be Done to Stop the Deadly C. Diff Bacteria."

It is dated August 16, 2012, which is right around the time I got out of the hospital. It honestly might have been that exact week; I can't remember. I used to have a paper copy of the newspaper, but it's probably long gone now. I kept it to remind me of what my life was like at the lowest point.

While I was in the hospital, I asked myself what I was doing with my life. I worked a crappy job as a claims adjuster (and got yelled at every day, all day, in English and Spanish), I had a ridiculous amount of student loan debt (loans were half my paycheck), a car payment that took up another third of my check, I lived in a tiny studio apartment, and I had only written some short stories and poems that no one would look at. I had some novel ideas, but agents wouldn't even give me the time of day.

I swore on that hospital bed that I would become a writer and I didn't care what I had to do to make it happen.

This time, ten years ago, I got out of the hospital, recovered fully, and shortly afterward, I discovered self-publishing. I'm pretty sure it was "The Creative Penn" first, followed shortly by The Alliance of Independent Authors (which was founded in 2012). I learned what was possible, and I couldn't wait to try it for myself. A few months later, I came up with the concept for my first novel: *How to Be Bad* (now *Magic Souls*), and I spent the entirety of 2013 learning about self-publishing, learning how to write my first book, and working with my first editor (Gary Smailes at BubbleCow, an amazing guy). I spent $40 on a pre-made cover from Goonwrite.com. I bought Scrivener for $35.

On January 6, 2014, *How to Be Bad/Magic Souls* was finally published. Three people bought it: me (because I wanted to generate a sales rank for the book), my writing buddy at the time, and my mom. I made $5.79 in January 2014 and somewhere around $50 total for the book during that first year.

Yikes. I made just about every tactical error you can think

of, but I kept listening to podcasts, reading blogs and books, buying paid courses (if I could afford them), and asked people in the community for advice. Somehow, I survived that first year without doing anything too stupid.

Fast-forward a decade later and it's crazy how far I've come. Joanna Penn was the person who got me into self-publishing; this year, I'll be on her show for the third time. ALLi gave me a lot of confidence and helped me find good information; I'm the Outreach Manager at ALLi now and have done countless podcasts & speaking events on their behalf. I even wrote a book for them.

I work a much better job now (thank god), I have written more books than I ever dreamed of, I'm constantly amazed by my book sales, and I'm especially amazed by how many people recognize me at speaking events. I've been published in "Writer's Digest," spoken at countless events, and have a pretty recognizable name in the indie space. Sure, I'm not a full-time author yet, but I definitely am on a path to getting there.

All of this took ten years. Ten years. Put another way, I'll be 35 this year. This took nearly a third of my life. And I've still got a long way to go.

If you're wondering whether the writing life is for you, keep at it. Keep writing. Keep reading. Keep learning. With every book you publish, aim to make at least one fewer mistake. Stay optimistic no matter how crappy things get. Get a mentor. Keep learning business, copyright, covers, book descriptions, etc. Dreams do come true!

I'm now two-thirds of the way through 2022. It has been a good year so far. Here is the progress I've made toward my goals.

BECOME A WORLD-CLASS CONTENT CREATOR

To achieve my goal of becoming a world-class content creator, I will focus on the following tactical priorities:

- Demonstrate a commitment to learning the craft of storytelling and teaching
- Demonstrate a commitment to outstanding quality AND quantity

Examples of day-to-day activities that will help me carry out my tactical priorities include:

- Keep learning through online courses and workshops taught by professional writers who are further down the path I want to write
- Reading
- Developing mentorships
- Finding new ways to increase my daily word counts
- Mastering different writing methods
- Documenting my process of becoming a successful writer in the *Indie Author Confidential* series
- Cleaning up my platform to ensure a consistent quality reader experience

What did I do to become a world-class content creator during Q3 2022?

1. I secured a mentor who is a very successful indie author.
2. I have read (and studied the craft in) 30 books so far this year.
3. I am still on track to publish 100 books by end of 2023.
4. I exploded my dictation word counts with a voice recorder and Microsoft Word macros.

BECOME A TECHNOLOGY AND DATA-DRIVEN WRITER

To achieve my goal of becoming a technology and data-driven writer, I will focus on the following tactical priorities:

- Use technology to make the business more efficient
- Use data to get insights

Examples of day-to-day activities that will help me carry out my tactical priorities include:

- Developing a tax plan
- Developing an estate plan assisted with technology
- Learning how to design my own covers
- Hiring a personal assistant for small tasks where it makes sense
- Developing a metadata database for my work
- Improving my readers' experience on my website
- Implementing direct sales for my fiction

What did I do to become a more technology and data-driven writer during Q2 2022?

1. I learned how to run profitable Facebook Ads and had one of my best sales months ever.
2. I developed a killer Microsoft Word macro for cleaner and faster dictation and transcription.

As with this quarter, I will continue doing more of the same: focusing on growing my portfolio to 100 titles and focusing on maximizing the value of my portfolio through new formats and quality assessments. I will also ramp up my lessons in cover design in the final quarter of the year.

As I said at the end of 2021, 2022 is the final year for me to get my fundamentals right. I'm excited about that, and I'm looking forward to what the end of the year brings.

CONTENT CREATED WHILE WRITING THIS BOOK

This section recaps the books I've published and media I've created during the quarter. To keep the book evergreen, I will not include links to podcasts or magazine articles because sometimes links break over time, especially with podcasts if the hosts stop podcasting. You can easily search for them to see if they're still active at the time you're reading this book. If they are, enjoy! If not, please accept my apologies.

Books

Year of the Rat (*The Chicago Rat Shifter*, Book 3). The third and final novel in Michael's wildest urban fantasy yet. Cyrus Grant searches for a way to cure his sister from the grips of a demon possession. The cure? A ruthless demon collector who peddles in lies and shadows.

Buy at: https://www.michaellaronn.com/yearoftherat

Grab the complete trilogy at: https://www.michaellaronn.com/ratshiftertrilogy/ratshiftertrilogy

Learn more about *The Chicago Rat Shifter* series: https://www.michaellaronn.com/ratshifter

Podcast/Video Appearances

"Estate Planning for Authors" on The Creative Penn

Michael and Joanna Penn talk about all things estate planning for authors, and how you can organize your affairs and leave a legacy for your family.

"How Get the Most Out of In-Person Speaking Events" on The Indy Author Podcast

Michael and Matty Dalrymple talk about their experience at the 2022 Writer's Digest Annual Conference, along with tips about how to maximize your experience at in-person speaking events.

VOLUME 11

INDIE AUTHOR CONFIDENTIAL

Secrets No One Will Tell You About Being a Writer

VOL. 11

M.L. RONN

INTRODUCTION

Here we are at the end of another year. Honestly, I'm glad to see the end of 2022. My introduction will be thin this quarter.

My Core Strategic Priorities

As a refresher, my mission is to create content that entertains and/or educates my audience, preferably both, and to remain nimble in an ever-changing industry. I do this by focusing on three strategic priorities:

- Become a world-class content creator
- Become a technology and data-driven writer
- Become the writer of the future (looking forward)

What's in This Volume

In the World-Class Content Creator section, I discuss my return to short fiction and how it will help me build my platform.

In the Technology and Data-Driven Writer section, I

discuss lessons in cover design, upgrading my audiovisual setup for my YouTube channel and interviews, and a powerful new transcription tool that could change the way I dictate.

In the Looking Forward section, I share thoughts about economic downturns, a once-in-a-lifetime trip to Saudi Arabia, and my thoughts on mastering the fundamentals.

Enjoy this volume.

—M.L. Ronn
December 23, 2022
Des Moines, Iowa

BECOME A WORLD-CLASS CONTENT CREATOR

USING STOCK PHOTOS AT SPEAKING ENGAGEMENTS

I am always cautious about the graphics I use.

Early in my career, I frequently used images from the public domain or the Creative Commons. I (mistakenly) thought that because these images were allowed to be used for free and commercial use, I would be covered.

I was wrong.

As I learned more about copyright and protecting the creative works of others, I realized that relying on Creative Commons and public domain work was unwise.

First, you have no way of knowing whether an artist has created that work or if they have stolen it. If an image is removed from a Creative Commons search engine due to theft or a copyright infringement allegation, you don't know about it unless you happen to look up that image one day and discover that it's gone...or you get sued.

Therefore, I no longer use Creative Commons images or anything public domain in my books or marketing. It's just bad business.

I have switched to using paid stock media instead. It is not cheap, and you can't always find what you're looking for, but you don't have to worry about copyright infringement or theft (for the most part). This is because stock media sites do a good job of policing their content. Many also offer a liability guarantee so that if you are accused of copyright infringement when using an image from their site, they will step in and defend you. Also, if you can produce a license from a stock media site, you're probably not going to be sued anyway.

I did a speaking event that required visual aids. Normally, I do not like to put images in my presentations. It makes everything easier because the organizer doesn't have to worry about where the images came from. For this particular event, I decided to do something different. Once I built the presentation, I purchased all the necessary licenses. Then, I downloaded each license (which has my name, the date purchased, a small thumbnail of the image, the image asset ID number, and a stamp of authenticity). I then built a table in a Microsoft Word document that listed the slide number, a description of the image, and a link to the image on the stock media site where I purchased it. Every slide had a corresponding entry on the table. When I sent my slide deck to the organizer, I included the Word document with the table and a link to a Google Drive folder that contained copies of all the licenses I purchased. I made it very easy for the organizer to do their due diligence on my due diligence.

The organizer was impressed with my documentation and fast-tracked my presentation for approval. I have a hunch that the company's attorneys also looked at this document because the organizer said their legal department appreciated my attention to detail.

This was an incredibly successful exercise that I will duplicate whenever I want to use visuals in my presentations. I still won't use visuals unless I have to, but it's good to have a process in place that will protect the organizer and me if I do.

WRITING ONE MILLION WORDS PER YEAR

Now that I have improved my writing process workflow and can consistently achieve between 3,000 and 5,000 words daily, it's time to take my planning to the next level.

I have always wanted to achieve pulp-level productivity. I have always been intrigued by how the old pulp writers wrote millions of words per year nonstop.

I have written many times in this series about how I admire prolific personalities. I gravitate toward them because they possess a skill that I also have and want to perfect. When I study the lives of prolific personalities, I feel as if I have unlocked something within myself.

Therefore, I am ready to try something different. I have consistently written between 500,000 and 600,000 words for the last eight years. Depending on the books I wrote, this equated to somewhere between 8 and 12 books per year. The average is eight. I have been happy with that number, and while it has given me an amazing portfolio, I know I can do better.

The next level for me is one million words per year. This equates to 2,750 words per day, 21,000 words per week, and 84,000 words per month.

This is a tough, tough word count goal to achieve, but it only represents the minimum level of what the old pulp writers could do. Imagine a career with a writer writing several million words each year without missing. When I think about that, I think about all the new worlds, characters, and lessons I could meet. It's an endless journey on which there is no destination. I find that fascinating.

So, I will try to write one million words in 2023.

It's not as easy as simply sitting down to write and hoping for the best. It requires a surprising amount of planning and foresight. For example, you have to be able to tell one story right after the other. Most authors I know like to have a "recharge" after they finish a book. They view finishing a book as a monumental challenge worthy of celebration and rest. There is no doing such a thing when you want to write at pulp speed. Because of the math, you literally cannot take a break.

To write one story after the other, you always have to know what to write next. What do you write? How do you determine what to write next? When you start writing *really* fast, you realize just how deep your creative well needs to be to sustain such a fast, consistent pace. This is not for the faint of heart.

My biggest challenge in writing one million words has been twofold.

First, I have had to systematize what I write next. I now must know what I will write at least *two* books in advance. This way, I always know what's next when I finish a book. Also, my daily word quota minimum is 2,750 words per day. This means that if I finish a book and I am at 2,000 words for the day, I must find 750 additional words, which means I need to start another project right away, often immediately after I type "The End." That takes guts and a complete elimination of fear to pull off.

The second challenge is dealing with bottlenecks. For example, once I have finished a book, I have to review it one more time to ensure everything is good to go. You know me well enough by now to know that I write my books in one draft on a first-time final basis. I focus on getting the story right the first time so that I don't have to worry about revision. That said, I make a "final pass" through the story, looking for any last-minute typos and plot holes that need to be fixed. This is a brisk run through the book, and it doesn't take much time (usually a day or two in addition to all of my other responsibilities), but it does require time, which eats away at my writing time. Because this doesn't take too long, I have been willing to sacrifice a little writing time to get books to my editor promptly. I usually try to make up for any deficiencies in my quota over the next few days.

There's also the bottleneck of publishing. It takes time to format and publish a book too. I also am willing to sacrifice a little writing time to publish new books because, obviously, that is one of the best things I can do to further my career. But it does create a bottleneck.

When you write at pulp speed, you must keep things moving at a steady clip. You've got to keep your projects moving forward every day. Otherwise, you will fall off the wagon. And once you fall off, the math gets brutal.

I am turning to short stories to help me regulate my flow. Short stories are helpful because if I'm not ready to write the next book, I can write a short story. For example, if I want to write a book that will require some research, I can't just dive into it, but I have to keep things moving somehow. I can write short stories while researching this book and maintain my word count.

Writing one million words in a year is an amazing accomplishment and one that I look forward to celebrating and sustaining for many years to come.

MORE IMPROVEMENTS TO MY
EDITING WORKFLOW

I received edits for several books this quarter after making enhancements to my dictation and editing workflow. While the results were outstanding, I noticed a few things I wasn't happy about.

For starters, introducing a voice recorder into my workflow exploded my word counts and improved my transcription accuracy, but I did notice an uptick in errors flagged by my editor. Many of these issues were silly issues that would have never existed if I had typed the book, like confused homonyms or nonsensical words.

Now, I review my manuscripts very carefully before sending them to my editor, but I can't catch everything. That's why I use a copyeditor and proofreader!

I kept asking myself if I could do better. I truly believe that no tools on the market can help me further reduce my errors. I find it to be an interesting contradiction of our time that there are AI tools that can write compelling chapters in books with no typos, yet the best AI editors on the market still don't know the difference between the words "two" and "too." I don't understand that.

Anyway, I found myself revisiting Grammarly Premium. I wanted to see if it could help me catch more dictation-related errors.

Grammarly Premium has come a long way. Not only did it help me catch more dictation-related errors, but it also helped me catch more errors.

The only problem? It also produced more false positives. However, if I waded through the results, I liked what I saw.

So, I purchased Grammarly Premium and am now using that to help me produce cleaner manuscripts.

Next, I took advantage of Microsoft Word's Read Aloud feature, which reads your text to you. I have found this to be a vital way of spotting dictation-related errors because I can often hear problems that my eyes miss. For example, if I edit exclusively by staring at a computer screen, my eyes get tired, and I will eventually start to miss things. However, if I stare at the screen while also listening to the text, I find many more errors that become harder to miss. My ears do a lot of the heavy lifting, allowing me to edit for longer before getting tired.

Also, I have found that Read Aloud helps me get through chapters faster because it helps me move at a quick, measured pace. I discovered that it takes me three minutes on average to review a page while listening to Read Aloud. I have no idea how long it would take me if I were editing manually, but I suspect it would be longer than three minutes. This gives me a predictable workflow. I know that it will take me three minutes per page to edit. When you consider that I already produce clean text through my dictation methods, and I already use tools like Word's Editor, Grammarly, ProWritingAid, and PerfectIt to clean the text even further, Read Aloud helps me regulate my editing speed.

Anyway, I continue to refine my editing workflow to achieve world-class writing and editing speeds.

DOING THE RAY BRADBURY
CHALLENGE RETROACTIVELY

I've always wanted to do the Ray Bradbury Challenge. Well, *both* Ray Bradbury challenges.

Ray Bradbury was the writer who inspired me to sit down at the keyboard and become a professional writer. He was a once-in-a-civilization talent. If I can even be as half as successful as he was, I will be somebody.

Ray Bradbury offered two challenges to new writers to help them improve their craft and further their careers.

The first challenge, which is deceptively difficult, is to read one short story, one poem, and one essay every day for 365 days. This will fill your creative well and keep you inspired.

The *concept* of the first challenge is simple, but the devil is in the details. For example, how do you find a short story, poem, and essay to read every day? Believe it or not, that requires a lot of planning. Do you read the works of one author per category, or do you randomize them?

Anyway, the first challenge is not hard, but it is time-consuming.

The second challenge is the most famous. In that challenge, Bradbury recommends writing one short story per week for a year. This will result in 52 short stories. To paraphrase Ray Bradbury, you can write 52 short stories, but it is impossible to write 52 bad short stories. They can't be all bad. And the really good ones might just change your career.

I've always had the second challenge in my sights. This quarter, I began writing more short stories professionally. My goal is to try to get stories published in professional magazines. This requires organization, discipline, and a whole lot of effort.

I wrote two short stories in one week and had a couple of ideas:

- What if I did the Ray Bradbury Challenge?
- What if, instead of doing a short story per week, I focused on 52 short stories in a year? This would free me from the weekly requirement, but I would still be required to write 52 short stories in a year.
- What if I started the Bradbury challenge *now* instead of waiting for January 1?

I was intrigued.

So, I'm doing the Ray Bradbury Challenge now. Will I be successful? I have no idea. However, the way I see it, if I fail, I will still have a lot of short stories to show for it, and some of those stories might even be accepted by a magazine.

In other words, I have absolutely nothing to lose.

GETTING BACK INTO SHORT STORIES

Last quarter, a mentor challenged me to reconsider writing short stories. As I discussed in the previous volume, I love short stories, but I have found it mentally difficult to write them in recent years because I am so focused on novels. My mentor challenged me to break that mindset.

Here's how I did it.

First, I adopted the Lester Dent plot formula method of telling stories. This step-by-step method does an excellent job of helping you hit all the elements you need to write an engaging short story that magazine editors will buy.

Dent was a pulp writer. I consider myself to be styled after the pulp writers. It's how I see the world, so I've always gravitated toward this method. I've used the Dent method in the past, but this time, I wanted to truly master it. Every story I have written this year has followed the method almost to a T. When I deviated from it, I had a good reason to do so.

The Lester Dent plot formula assumes a 6,000-word short story. You take it and divide the story into 1,500-word increments. Each increment has a beat, resulting in a steady cadence that readers have come to expect over the years.

Next, I read a lot of short stories.

Then, I developed a system to help me get organized with my short stories. If I do the Ray Bradbury Challenge, it means that I am going to have dozens of short stories. If I'm going to do all that work, it doesn't make sense for those stories to sit on my computer, so I have to push them out to magazines. Therein lies the trouble.

Using the Master Publishing File spreadsheet I created last year to help me track my intellectual property, I added a tab for short stories. This way, I could inventory my short stories and record the title, length, genre, and associated keywords with the story, such as love, coming-of-age, the 1970s, and more—helpful when reviewing anthologies with themes, for example. This gave me a good sense of what I had in my portfolio currently, and how to build my portfolio strategically with future stories.

Next, after I inventoried my work and built a scalable way to capture future work quickly, I added another tab on my Master Publishing File spreadsheet that listed the title of the story and magazine information. For example, if I submit a story to Magazine X, then I need to keep a record of that. I don't care about dates, but I do need to know *where* I have sent stories. In my experience, tracking dates is depressing and not at all worth doing, so I'm not going to do it.

I also captured how long it takes for the pro markets to return one of my stories. Most decide on stories within 30 to 90 days.

Also, there are dozens of magazines that I could submit a story to if I wanted. I counted at least 50. Some are professional markets; some are semipro; others don't pay anything.

While I want to gather as many readers as I can, I had to decide on how to proceed here. On the one hand, you want to send stories out to as many magazines as possible; on the other hand, sending your story to *every* magazine will take *years* until you know whether it is accepted or rejected. During that time, your story is "locked up," and you can't do anything with it.

If you publish a story, you can no longer publish it in a magazine, as magazines don't reprint self-published work.

Like I said, it's a delicate balance.

Here are the criteria I landed on:

1. I will only submit my stories to professional (read: paying) magazine markets that accept science fiction and fantasy stories. If I happen to write something in another genre, I will consider other magazines on a case-by-case basis.

2. The average paying market takes between 30 and 90 days to make a decision. I will allow a story to surf the markets for at least one year or until it receives an acceptance, whichever is less.

3. If a story is accepted, I will diary one year and attempt to get the story reprinted in *another* magazine that accepts reprints to maximize my copyright licensing. The story will also go into my next short story collection, since the rights will have reverted to me within a short time period.

4. If a story is not accepted (or if one year expires from the first day of submission), I will publish it in my next short story collection.

We'll see how this goes. At the time of this writing, I have five stories out for magazine consideration. I'm intrigued by what it will look like if I complete the Ray Bradbury Challenge and have dozens of stories floating around out there.

I'm going to find out whether Ray Bradbury's advice was right!

WRITING FLASH FICTION AND MICROFICTION

I want to be a great practitioner of the fiction craft.

Fiction means many things:

- novels
- novellas
- short stories
- flash fiction
- microfiction

Generally, a novel is considered anything greater than 40,000 words, and microfiction is anything less than 100 words. You can even subdivide microfiction further, but I think that's a bit much.

That said, if I want to consider myself a practitioner of fiction, I should be a practitioner of *fiction*. This means writing it in every form. Doing so gives me perspective, improves my imagination, and helps me hone skills that I would never otherwise hone if I were just writing novels.

That's why I've been thinking a lot lately about diversifying my portfolio with short fiction. The great thing about short fiction is that you can write it quickly (especially in my case), and it is a great marketing tool. It is a wonderful way to introduce new readers to your work. It doesn't cost anything except the time you take to write it. If you write quickly like I do, we're talking a matter of hours. If you sell a 5,000-word short story to a magazine at a professional rate of eight cents per word, you will make $400. Hell, you might publish a novel and not make anywhere near that. You'd have to sell approximately 115 copies of a novel to make that much money at $4.99 with a 70 percent sales commission.

The math is lucrative with short fiction, but you must be willing to do the work and be organized.

When I was in New York City earlier this year, I met Ran Walker, a fellow author who specializes in flash and microfiction. Ran has a sizable bibliography of published works in magazines, and he frequently speaks on this art form. I chatted with him about his approach and filed his advice for when I needed it someday. It appears that day has arrived.

Flash fiction is simple to write, but that doesn't make it easy. If I do the math, I could be a pretty prolific flash fiction writer if I wanted to be. When I walk my dog, I dictate at least 500 words every session. I walk my dog at least three times a day, sometimes more if I want good exercise. That's 1,500 words per day, or the equivalent of a flash fiction piece. In one day.

That's just the time I spend walking my dog. When I factor in the time I spend driving, doing chores like dishes and laundry, and the good ol' time I spend in front of the computer typing, I could probably write two to three flash fiction pieces in a single day if I was inspired, with plenty of room left over.

What would my career look like if I built a solid body of novels and novellas, short stories, flash fiction, and microfiction? How much flash fiction and microfiction would I need to write to be considered prolific?

It's hard to know for sure, but I think the answer is *at least* 100 pieces. I don't know any speculative fiction writers who have written that much. Therefore, that is a good number to shoot for—100 pieces with an average of 700 words per piece would be approximately 70,000 words, which is a long novel.

Sure, I could do that.

As I think about ways to accomplish my goal of one million words (minimum) in 2023, I consider flash fiction and microfiction to be two more tools in my toolbox.

COLLABORATION 2.0

While at the annual Writer's Digest Conference in New York City, I had the opportunity to meet and spend time with Matty Dalrymple, fellow author and podcast host of the "Indy Author Podcast." I have been on Matty's show many times, and it was great to meet her in person.

We got along famously, and we did a recap of the event on a subsequent episode of her podcast after returning home. The topic was how to get the most out of in-person speaking events, and we both talked about our experiences as professional public speakers. After the show, I made an offhand remark that the topic we discussed would make a great book. She asked if I was interested in collaborating on one. I said yes.

Over the next 24 hours, we developed a plan to write a book on how authors can master public speaking. The concept focused on the business and logistic sides of speaking rather than the rhetorical part.

Matty and I are on the same page regarding how we see writing and business, so the first thing we did was draft a contract between us that clearly outlined the responsibilities of each party, who would publish the book, how royalties would be split, and so on. We agreed to split the royalties through Draft2Digital's Payment Split service, which makes everything easier. We also built in contingencies for what happens when one of us dies or becomes incapacitated. A key provision of the contract explicitly indicated that, in the event of death or incapacitation of one of the parties, the other automatically has the right to unpublish the book and republish under their own publishing company. This will help considerably with retailer conversations.

I used some other lessons I picked up in *The Author Estate Handbook*, plus some more great ideas from Matty. The result was a contract that ensured we were in agreement before beginning. After all, this is a permanent business endeavor. It's not something to embark on lightly.

We executed the contract through an online contract signing service.

We outlined the book using Google Sheets, with each person taking their share of chapters.

We also did extensive market research, determining where the book fit in the market, who our target readers were, and how to attract them. Two heads were definitely better than one.

We decided on the style of the book and how it would be written—with a blended author voice that reflected both Matty's and mine.

We coauthored the book in Google Docs, developing a system for writing and suggesting comments.

The book is still in production, and I look forward to discussing it further in the next volume of this series, but it feels good to collaborate with someone again. It is so much easier now than it was in 2016. The tools have gotten much better.

THE ULTIMATE WRITING CHALLENGE

I've been thinking about ways to push my writing productivity to the next level.

In the writing community, there is no shortage of "challenges." These challenges are designed to help writers reach the next level of their careers.

That got me thinking about a challenge for intermediate and advanced writers that would turn them into a writer's writer.

I present "The Ultimate Writing Challenge." It's four challenges in one, and you must do all of them in one year.

CHALLENGE #1: WRITE ONE MILLION WORDS

I've talked enough about writing one million words in this series, but to recap, it means you must write at least 2,750 words per day, 19,236 words per week, and 84,000 words per month. This is a lot of words.

CHALLENGE #2: WRITE 12 NOVELS

In other words, write one novel per month, or, do the NaNoW-riMo challenge each month.

Every November, writers worldwide try to write a novel in 30 days. For 99 percent of these writers, it is an annual event. With the Ultimate Writing Challenge, every month is NaNoWriMo!

CHALLENGE #3: WRITE 52 SHORT STORIES

The great writer Ray Bradbury recommended writing 52 short stories in a year because he believed that it was impossible to write 52 bad short stories in a row. They can't be all bad. I agree.

Add in the Ray Bradbury Challenge in addition to NaNo-WriMo, and you have a compelling and difficult goal.

The next and final part of the challenge is the real doozy...

CHALLENGE #4: ADHERE TO HEINLEIN'S RULES

Robert Heinlein was a golden-age science fiction writer who laid out five simple business rules for writers. The rules are:

1. You must write.
2. You must finish what you write.
3. You must not rewrite, except to editorial demand.
4. You must put your work on the market.
5. You must keep your work on the market until sold.

Writing and finishing your work is not a big deal for most writers once they have a few novels under their belt, but the last three rules are brutal.

First, I believe Heinlein's rule about revising is a good one:

don't rewrite your work unless the editor tells you to. If you write novels and submit them to traditional publishers, then you shouldn't rewrite them unless an editor recommends it. If you write short stories and submit them to magazines, you should not rewrite unless the magazine editor requires it. In short, you must learn to write your books in one draft, and cleanly. This is the place in Heinlein's Rules that most writers check out.

And we haven't even gotten to publishing yet!

If we adjust Heinlein's Rules to reflect the era of indie publishing, we could say this:

- For novels, you must self-publish them or always keep them out for consideration by publishers and agents.
- If you write short stories, you must send them to magazines until sold and/or self-publish them.

For short stories, you could do a hybrid, submitting your stories to markets for a limited period of time (say one year) and then self-publishing if you receive no acceptances.

Whatever you do, you must keep your work out there so that a rights buyer can license it or readers can buy it.

The Heinlein's Rules part of this challenge makes it almost impossible for most people.

BRINGING IT ALL TOGETHER

To recap the Ultimate Writing Challenge, you must:

1. Write one million words in one year.
2. Write 12 novels
3. Write 52 short stories
4. Adhere to Heinlein's rules

Boy, is this a tough challenge, but consider the benefits.

In just one year, you will have written more novels and short stories than almost all writers working currently. To quantify this, you will write and publish at least 64 pieces of intellectual property (novels and short stories). That's a big deal.

Quality-wise, I can't guarantee that you will be a better writer, but I'm pretty sure that you will be. All you have to do is compare your first short story and novel to your last. I think the difference would be astounding.

Next, if you receive an acceptance in a short story magazine or publish a book that takes off, that will be its own reward. You will level up.

Those are just a few of the benefits I can think of. Complete the Ultimate Writing Challenge, and you will be well on your way to becoming a world-class writer in no time.

LESSONS IN SETTING

Earlier this year, I entered the Writers of the Future contest. It is a free contest that writers can enter for cash prizes and potential entry into the *Writers of the Future* anthology. Many household science fiction and fantasy writers that you know and love were previous contest winners, such as Patrick Rothfuss. The contest is a proving ground for burgeoning speculative fiction writers.

I have nothing to lose from submitting, so I send a story to the contest each quarter. My very first entry earned me a Silver Honorable Mention, which is one step away from Semifinalist, which means that I could have possibly been featured in the anthology. In other words, it's the highest level achievable without winning. Pretty cool and pretty encouraging.

I sent the story to one of my mentors for feedback. This person has been a judge in major contests and understands the psychology of someone reviewing slush piles. I asked him where the story potentially went wrong and what I could work on for the next story. (Please note: I asked him for feedback on the story, not so that I could fix it, but so that I could fix the problem in my next story. I don't believe in revising or rewriting.)

My mentor told me I had a great opening, but my setting wasn't strong enough. To paraphrase him, he told me it felt like my characters were in a white room talking and taking action, but the reader couldn't see the actions unfold because the setting was weak.

That was hard advice to hear because I have taken great strides over the past few years to make sure that I describe settings through the eyes of my viewpoint character, and in the five senses. I believe that I am doing this well most of the time, but this time, I didn't. It made me rethink how I approach this writing tactic. It also made me recommit to it so that I never make this mistake again. Honestly, the advice was a bit embarrassing and humbling.

When I want to learn anything new, I study the mega bestsellers: John Grisham, Nora Roberts, James Patterson, and so on. I studied ten openings by three authors, writing down the commonalities of each. I only paid attention to how the authors did their settings. It was eye-opening. I discovered with all three authors that they practice a technique best described as "winding up" the setting.

For example, they will start a chapter almost exclusively with setting through the eyes of the viewpoint character, described in the five senses. If you look at the first 500 words of the story and color-code the sections where setting is described, you will see a common pattern. First, you will notice that the descriptions of setting are most dense at the beginning of the chapter and become less frequent as the opening continues. This is when the author is "winding up" the setting. They give the reader tons of information to help them see the story and characters. Once the reader has enough information, the author backs off a little, describing the setting less frequently (but still describing the setting).

This begs two questions:

1. How much does it take to "wind up" a setting?
2. How much is enough (and by proxy, how much is too little and too much?)

When I study the mega bestsellers, I like to color-code the text. I will highlight the words associated with the technique I'm studying. This allows me to see their techniques better.

Here are my observations:

- All three mega bestsellers wound up their settings within the first 500 words of a chapter. In each of these chapters, setting descriptions accounted for between 50 and 75 percent of all words on the page.
- Immediately after the first 500 words, the setting became approximately 10 to 20 percent of all words on the page.
- The author began winding up again whenever there was a new setting, new chapter or section break, or turn of events.

In other words, the authors wound up the setting, let it go until they felt the readers needed more information, and once the wind-up ran out, they began the process again.

I committed to following this same technique in my stories. Hopefully, I will never receive feedback on poor settings again.

WRITING AN IDEA WHILE IT'S HOT

I set myself up for trouble this quarter. I did something I knew I shouldn't have done, but I did it anyway because I thought I could overcome it. I started a short story before I knew I had to take a writing break.

My wife was scheduled to go out of town on Tuesday. I started a short story on Monday night. Big mistake.

The story started off fine enough. I had a good sense of the character, setting, and plot. However, I truly had to take time away from my writing while my wife was out of town because I had to care for my daughter, pets, and house.

Here's what happened:

- I wrote the first 1,000 words of the story.
- I took a five-day break, and when I returned to the writing desk, I had lost the energy for the story.
- It took me almost two weeks to finish the damn story.
- I eventually found the energy, and I'm happy with how the story turned out, all things considered, but it took way too long.

Here's what I should have done: I shouldn't have written the story. I should have found some other project to commit words to that wouldn't have resulted in a loss of energy. Doing so would have allowed me to step away from my writing and return with a clean slate.

Instead, I got a great idea and wrote it, thinking that I could overcome this when I should have known better.

Oh well. You live and you learn. I still followed Heinlein's Rules. I started the story. I finished it. And I submitted it to literary magazines. That's what matters. But if I want to write one million words per year, I can't afford to make these types of mistakes again.

BECOME A TECHNOLOGY
AND DATA-DRIVEN WRITER

BUILDING A WORD COUNT TRACKER

In my quest to write one million words each year, I need a tool to help me stay organized. Otherwise, I won't know how many words I've written and how many words I need to write to achieve my goal.

Here's the problem: most specialized writing apps allow you to track your words per project by day, week, and month. That's great, but no writing app I know of (other than Atticus) allows you to track your word counts across multiple projects. For example, if I divide my daily word count between Project A and Project B, in most writing apps, I have to check my statistics in each project individually and then add them together. That's no good.

Instead, I need a global word count tracker that tracks these numbers. This is important because I sometimes work on more than one project in a day, especially if I finish one book and launch into another right away. Often, I will finish a book and start a new one on the same day. Not being able to get a word count on all the projects I've worked on every day is inefficient.

Instead, I relied on good old Microsoft Excel.

I developed a tracker in Microsoft Excel that tells me in

real-time how many words I've written, how many I have left ago, and some other metrics to help me understand how I am performing.

First, I have a plan of 1,252,000 words between August 28, 2022, and August 28, 2023. Because I didn't start my year on January 1, the plan number is a little weird.

Next, I keep track of my surplus and deficit. For example, if I need to write 2,750 words per day, if I write 3,000 words, I have a surplus of 250 words for the day; if I write 2,000 words, I have a deficit of 750 words. If I'm ahead, I technically need to write fewer words the next day to stay on track. If I'm behind, I will need to write more words to catch up. Since my quota is 2,750 words per day, a day's productivity is worth that much. I wrote a formula to express how many "days" ahead or behind I am. The tracker also shows me my average word count.

At the end of each day, I update the tracker and check my progress. So far, I am operating at a good surplus this year. I am approximately 30,000 words ahead of schedule at the time of this writing, representing somewhere around 13 days ahead. That's a great place to be in case I get sick or need to take some time off. I can miss up to 13 days and still hit my plan for the year! That's the power of knowing your numbers.

That said, I don't want to rest on my laurels. Every day I can, I write more than 2,750 words. Sometimes, I only write a few hundred extra words. Other times, I write several thousand extra words. Building a strong surplus helped me weather this challenge.

The word count tracker has become an indispensable tool to help me achieve my goals.

LESSONS IN COVER DESIGN THIS QUARTER

I have finally put my money where my mouth is. I made substantial progress in designing my own book covers this quarter. In fact, I made such significant progress that I am astounded by how far I have come.

First, I got into the MidJourney beta. MidJourney is an AI art generator that allows you to type a prompt and, within seconds, receive amazing art that looks as if an artist drew it. MidJourney is just one of several AI art generation apps; others include DALL-e, Stable Diffusion, and Wombo.

In experimenting with the app, I was amazed at how easy it was to use. In fact, it really is as easy as typing in what you want and getting amazing results. If you want a picture of a model wearing a leather jacket, then type that in and be prepared to be amazed. If you want a science fiction landscape in the style of a certain artist, then all you have to do is use the right keywords. This has democratized art and made it so that anyone can generate art as long as they can type. I believe this is truly a watershed moment for the Internet.

Second, I have begun working with a mentor who is quite

adept at cover design. He has offered to help me learn the tools of the trade. I promptly took him up on that offer.

Third, I invested in several cover design courses. The first course was focused on the concept of cover design. It also taught me how to think about art and some additional considerations to get quality art every time. Part of this course also taught me how to design my own covers for the first time.

I have some Photoshop experience, but I am I no means proficient at it. To rectify this, I took a book cover Photoshop course from Neo Stock. It taught me how to do some basic compositing, which is a critical design skill.

I also took a cover design course from Udemy that gave me additional context and tools to think about when designing covers.

And of course, I watched several hours' worth of YouTube videos covering different tools and techniques. These supplemented items from the courses.

Am I a professional cover designer? No, but I have a knowledge base I can leverage in 2023. This journey will consist of many steps, and I'm proud to say that I took those first critical steps this quarter.

EXPERIMENTS WITH AI-GENERATED ART

I've written in previous volumes my fascination with artificial intelligence-generated art. I discussed the program DALL-e, which represents a new wave of art creation. This quarter, I had the pleasure of experimenting with MidJourney, which is a competitor to DALL-e.

MidJourney is a program that takes your text and turns it into art. You type in what you want to see, and the AI generates a compelling image. These are called "prompts."

Examples of prompts include:

- a dog dressed as Napoleon in the style of an oil painting
- an angry crystal dragon in a shimmering quartz cave
- a cyberpunk pirate
- and more.

You can type in virtually anything. You will get amazing results if you craft the prompt correctly.

The most compelling part of MidJourney is that there is a seemingly endless number of attributes that you can apply to your art. For example, if I want to create a portrait in the style of the great artist John Singer Sargent, I can just type that in. If I don't like that and I want a portrait in the style of modern artist Chuck Close, I can just swap out the names. I can also tell the AI to generate a photorealistic portrait and even tell it what type of camera and lens to use. The choices are staggering and only limited to your imagination.

MidJourney also does textures. If I want to create a bleached oak floorboard texture, I can do that and even tell MidJourney how wide the floorboards should be.

MidJourney also paints landscapes, so if I want a rustic countryside in the style of a 90s anime, I can do that too.

As I said, the options are endless.

There is now a vibrant community of people creating art with AI art generators who have never picked up a pencil to draw in their lives (me being one of them). This is revolutionary, and I don't think people truly realize how seismic these programs are.

Millions of people worldwide have concepts in their heads but will never be able to draw or paint them. They're not artists by heart. If they're creative, they often don't have the funds to pay an artist, or, they may have difficulty finding the right artist for the vision in their head. For the artist they do hire, they have to worry about the artists meeting their deadlines, communicating effectively, and other issues that come up throughout the artistic process, such as delays.

AI-generated art has now removed those barriers. Now, anyone can come up with a concept and render it in seconds. Case in point: I taught my daughter how to use MidJourney, and within 30 minutes, we had both creative art that would have cost us tens of thousands of dollars to make if we had commissioned someone.

This is a big deal. Make no mistake—these programs are

enjoying a lot of hype right now. The hype will die down as people get bored with it or find another fad to chase, but the technology is here to stay. The art world will never be the same.

Decades from now, people will look back and draw a sharp line through history: everything before 2022 and everything after.

I think this is good, but I understand why artists are afraid and concerned about their livelihoods. AI art is perhaps the most salient example of artificial intelligence taking away someone's job.

In previous volumes, I discussed the impacts of artificial intelligence audiobooks, which has narrators understandably concerned. However, in the conversation about that medium, no one *seriously* thinks that AI audiobooks will completely displace narrators. It will affect them, sure, but there will always be a need for well-narrated audio. The technology has a long way to go before it replaces someone like Scott Brick.

I've also talked about artificial intelligence-assisted writing apps like Sudowrite. Sudowrite uses the GPT-3 model (at the time of this writing), generating short bursts of text based on a small sample of your writing. While I expect this technology to advance rapidly over the next decade, I also don't believe that anyone *seriously* believes that Sudowrite will put writers out of a job. At least right now.

I cannot confidently say that about AI art. Here's the problem: it generates art within seconds that would take an artist months to generate.

It also generates art that may also be physically impossible to create. For example, say that you want to create a piece in the style of Dadaism. This art style is based on cutting out pieces of paper and styling them. While an artist can accomplish this digitally, it would take them a lot of time. It takes an AI seconds.

Everything is just a few keystrokes away...If you want an

acrylic painting, type it in, and the AI will convert the image. If you change your mind and want a skeuomorphic style, the AI will change it. There's just no competing against the AI's speed.

There are some failings with the technology that are likely to be short term. First, there's not much control over how models and buildings look. If you type in a church, the AI will determine what the church will look like. You can assign certain descriptors to it, but you can't tailor the design much from what you see. This is also true of models and colors.

Next, you can't design images with any consistency. You can use the same keywords and prompts, but each image will look different in its own way. Therefore, you can't create a consistent gallery of images. In my mind, this is the poison pill for the technology right now. I have every suspicion that this will not be the case in a few years.

Next, the AI doesn't provide layered photo files, so what you see is what you get. At some point, I'm betting you'll be able to download Photoshop files of your art, which will take this to a completely different level.

Also, the technology isn't perfect. Sometimes it doesn't get faces right. It has a difficult time rendering fingers, for example. It also doesn't do well with feet. But these are challenges that will dissipate over time.

I feel like the *Indie Author Confidential* series so far has spotlighted different industries whose occupation is at risk due to AI advancements. That's unfortunate, but there's very little we can do about it.

As a writer, my only solace in AI art is that, for the time being, the act of being a writer is still pretty secure. Even if someone could type in a few sentences and get a novel generated in a few seconds, AI advancement is not sophisticated enough to generate text that is grammatically correct, sufficiently creative, or coherent at the moment. Right now, it reads like enlightened gibberish.

Will that change? Absolutely, but the biggest thing we have going for us is that someone can't just generate a book and then sell it. They have to read it first and make sure that it makes sense. That takes time. It's also drastically different from AI art, which can be consumed in seconds. Again, we have this going for us.

As I watch MidJourney and DALL-e evolve, I'm making a few observations about how the industry is shifting:

- The technology is democratizing art. People who were never artists can now be amazing ones.
- A community is springing up to help non-artists create effective prompts for the AI. This is called "prompt crafting." I predict that non-artists will be willing to pay money for good prompts written by artists and non-artists alike.
- Non-artists don't want to go through the trouble of learning the nuances of prompt crafting, so they will rely on other people to do it, creating a new cottage industry where you can hire someone on a site like Fiverr or Upwork and tell them what you need so they can generate the prompts for you.
- The prompts aren't perfect, so many people will hire artists to touch up and fix issues generated by the AI.
- This is transforming artistry from a creative profession into a service profession.

Those are just a few of the observations. From that, I can draw the following conclusions:

- Learning AI art and how to generate effective art with prompts will be critical. You will be able to use this art in every area of your writing business (book covers, blog articles, etc.).
- Understanding how to manipulate photos in Photoshop, Affinity Designer, or other similar software is now an essential skill for authors.
- This is the future of stock photos.
- This is the future of book covers.
- Authors will soon be hiring designers not to create their book covers, but to correct covers generated by AIs.
- Cover designers will also begin using AI technology in their designs, saving them time, effort, and money. There will be a big difference between designers who design the traditional way and designers who use AI and clean up the generations. How will you know which caliber of designer you're dealing with? Should you pay the same price for an AI designer as a traditional designer? This is going to shake up the market and create additional pricing tiers. Or, at least, it should. This is much-needed, because, as I have been saying for the last two years in this series, the price of cover design is out of control.

I have never been more excited about a technology than I have with AI art. When I first discovered it last year, I was intrigued. When I followed up on it, I was fascinated. Now that I can try for myself, I am enthralled. I highly suggest you check it out because this will be a portent for things to come.

MORE MATH BEHIND COVER DESIGN

It's time to do some more math on cover design. With the advent of AI art being a viable path now, the game has changed. As I keep saying (almost to the point of nauseum), the costs of cover designs continue to rise, and they will one day be unaffordable for the average author (one could argue that they already are). This is a shame because self-publishing is about democratizing this profession—the glory of it is that anyone, anywhere can self-publish a book with low cost and low effort compared to a traditional publisher. That glory is diminishing more every day, and the future will belong to those authors who can insulate themselves from this coming threat.

Let's do some math.

HIRING A DESIGNER

We'll use the same scenario for all the examples I'm going to give in this chapter.

We're going to assume that you publish four books per year, and each cover costs $600, representing the current average costs of three major cover designers I've been following. (If I were doing this exercise in 2018, I could have used $300 as a benchmark. That goes to show you just how expensive it is getting.)

We'll also assume a three-month wait for each cover.

So, to recap:

- 4 covers
- $600 per cover, or $2,400 per year
- Three-month waiting period
- Five hours of your time, or 300 minutes
- Total: $2,400 per year

Doing Your Own Covers

The costs to create 4 book covers are as follows:

- $600/year for the Adobe Creative Suite
- $100 for 100 stock images
- No waiting period
- 2 hours (120 minutes) to find art and design each cover, or 8 hours total (480 minutes)
- Total: $700 per year

DOING YOUR OWN COVERS WITH AI ART

This is a slight variation of the previous method.

- $600/year for the Adobe Creative Suite
- $600/year for an AI art service
- No waiting period
- 2 hours (120 minutes) to find art and design each cover, or 8 hours total (480 minutes)

- Total: $1,250 per year

COMPARING THE METHODS

The math becomes very clear when you compare the methods:

- Hiring a Designer: $2,400/year
- Doing Your Own Covers with AI Art: $1,250/year
- Doing Your Own Covers the Traditional Way: $700/year

You can argue the value of a designer all you want, but you can't argue with the math, especially if the quality of AI art is as good, if not better, than a designer.

AI art provides quality art at a fraction of the cost of a designer, and you can create as many covers as you want.

Remember, the $2,400 per year design costs will not be constant. Five years from now, it could very well be $4,800 or more. You might be able to afford cover designs now, but that may not be true in the future, even for affluent authors.

If the benchmark of an affluent author is $100,000 per year, then $2,400 in design costs per year represents 2.4 percent of their gross annual income. When you account for taxes at 25 percent, it becomes 3 percent. And that's being generous. And, again, at the risk of repeating myself, this is just for four books.

When design costs double again in a few years, the costs will account for almost 5 percent of a $100,000 gross annual income and almost 7 percent of net. Add in other business expenses and the costs of living, and you can see why this is an existential threat.

How does this compare to other professions that must also hire vendors to complete essential services? It's hard to know. I did some research, but it's difficult to make apples-to-apples comparisons. What I do know, however, is that having a vendor whose pricing is so variable is a business problem that a savvy businessperson would move to rectify so that they can minimize the impact of price increases or swings. No author I know is doing that.

As I said, this is unsustainable in just the short term.

BOOK PREVIEW APP

Authors need a better way to offer book previews on their websites. Amazon has offered an embedded preview tool for years; you install the code on your computer, and readers can preview and purchase your book directly from your sales page on Amazon. It's an elegant way to sell books.

I have been surprised over the last few years that other retailers haven't allowed similar functionality. This seems like something that Apple, Kobo, Barnes & Noble, and Google Play would have copied.

They haven't.

The only reliable way to offer book previews on your site is to use Amazon's tool, which is not ideal.

It would be great if there were a tool that functioned similarly to Amazon's but gave readers a call to action at the end to purchase the book from whatever retailer they buy their books from. A tool like this seems right up Draft2Digital's alley.

I've been looking for a tool that can accomplish this purpose, but I haven't found one yet, so I've been thinking about how to accomplish this manually. One idea is to upload a PDF with an attractive call to action at the end and then embed that PDF using an existing PDF viewer tool. That may be the only way to solve this problem until someone develops a better solution.

ADDITIONAL THOUGHTS ON SALES
TRACKING FOR AUTHORS

In 2020, I developed a way to automate my sales reports. I wrote about it in previous volumes of this series, but here is a recap.

As an indie author, I receive over a dozen sales reports from the book retailers I sell at, affiliate platforms, and other miscellaneous revenue streams such as Patreon, direct sales, and paid speaking engagements.

Before 2020, I had to manually calculate all the royalties for each of my books and put that data on a summary worksheet.

Once I put my data on a summary worksheet, I analyzed it for insights. This often took me several hours per month, and it was tedious. In fact, I often neglected it because it was so painful.

I developed a workflow that allowed me to apply Microsoft Excel macros to standardize the data in my sales reports and then feed that data into a database that I could use to run reports. The process eliminated the manual data entry, sped up the process of aggregating my reports, and made my life 100 percent easier. It is still the method I use today.

I have noticed a few changes in the author sales tracking

market that are worth noting. First, there has been an increase in the use of a service that tracks all your sales online through a browser extension. I won't mention the name of the company because this is not meant to be a critique of this specific company; rather, this is a critique of the method itself. This method of sales aggregation provides much of the automation that authors seek, and there is no doubt that it makes the process easier.

However, I am not a fan of browser extensions for a few reasons:

•You are effectively handing over your sales data to another company. Who knows what they are going to do with it?

•The company you give your data to could be hacked, no matter how much they swear they won't be. Just look at the statistics of cybersecurity attacks. No matter how ardently developers insist they won't be targets, the math is not in their favor.

•Having your sales data hacked and made publicly available could be devastating. I believe this data is best kept private.

This is why I am not on the browser extension sales tracking bandwagon. I believe developers approach this problem with good faith, but I haven't seen any evidence yet that such a service would not be vulnerable to cyber-attacks. Such an attack would create a massive headache. I do use one service's browser extension tool for sales tracking, but that is for Amazon only. The issue remains, and I choose to take that risk because it makes running profitable Amazon ads much easier, but it is still a risk that I probably won't engage in the long term.

In my book the *Author Income Problem*, I wrote that it is highly unlikely that someone will solve this problem for authors in a way that does not involve a moderate level of risk. As such, it is up to every author to learn how to solve this problem for themselves in a way that minimizes their time and allows them to glean insights into the nature of their book sales.

I'm still convinced that this is the case. I hoped that current sales tracker programs on the market would continue to improve, but that hasn't happened. I still believe that the best solution to this problem is one that resides locally on your hard drive and does not transmit data over the Internet. That's why I liked the concept of one such app on the market, but it is no longer supported, and it does not calculate sales data correctly. While not perfect, this method preserves your privacy while giving you flexibility and insights into your sales data.

But alas, it cannot be.

STREAM DECK REVISITED

Last year, I purchased an Elgato Stream Deck. It is a high-tech equivalent of a macro pad, a device with physical buttons that you press to perform functions on your computer without using your keyboard or mouse.

Let me illustrate why macro pads exist. For example, if you want to copy text, you can do it one of a few ways:

- Right-click and select copy.
- Use the keyboard shortcut Ctrl + C or CMD+ C.
- Use a menu in whichever program you are using, such as Edit<Copy.

Those options are perfectly fine, but they're not ideal because they require you to stop what you're doing and find the command or keys you need. Few people have the skill to do this by memory.

A macro pad provides a techy yet clever solution for this problem by giving you a one-button solution. In the example I used, I could map Ctrl+C or CMD+ C to one button so that the button controls the command. I can also add additional commands to the button so that it acts like a switch. I could set it up so that the first button press initiates the "select all" command, the second press initiates the "copy" command, and the third press initiates a "paste" command. It saves time and effort.

This technology has been around for a very long time, works extremely well, and solves productivity problems that many people have—assuming they're willing to purchase a new tool, go through the learning curve, and commit to using it.

I like the Stream Deck because it is dynamic. You can program the buttons to change depending on which app is in the foreground. Therefore, you can have one set of buttons for Chrome, another set for Photoshop, another set for PowerPoint, and so on.

I've used my Stream Deck almost exclusively for streaming for the last year. That has been a great use case, but I kept thinking I could do more with the technology.

This quarter, I finally figured out how to maximize my Stream Deck.

Since moving to Microsoft Word as my primary writing app this year, I have adopted many macros and keyboard shortcuts to help me be more productive. I use these tools, especially when I am writing short stories. I mapped many shortcuts and macros to buttons on my Stream Deck.

Here are some examples:

- I can now run my dictation macro with a button.
- I can get a word count for a string of selected text or an entire document.
- I can toggle the spellchecker.
- I can pull up a dictionary or Google.
- I can select all text, copy, and paste with a three-way switch.

- I can activate the Read Aloud function, helping me catch invisible typos.
- I can launch the macro window to select a macro to run. This normally would have required me to navigate to the Developer tab on the Ribbon and select the macro button, which was time-consuming if I was in the middle of a task.
- I can switch between apps on my Mac.
- I can activate Word's built-in Dictation feature.

And that's just Microsoft Word.

With conference call apps such as Zoom, I can mute and unmute my microphone, turn my camera on and off, share my screen, and more—with the press of a button.

In short, the Stream Deck turned out to be one of my best investments in 2021 that I am only fully realizing now.

But it gets better. I discovered that Elgato released a new product called the Stream Deck Pedal, which is a USB switch activated by your foot. It sits underneath your desk, and you use it like a guitarist would use a foot pedal. It has three programmable buttons, much like the Stream Deck, and the buttons are dynamic and change depending on which app is in the foreground.

I immediately purchased one because it has so many benefits.

For starters, when I use the Stream Deck, I like to have my right hand on my mouse and my left hand on my keyboard. This way, I can activate whichever button I need on the Stream Deck with my left hand. But sometimes, I don't like removing my left hand from the keyboard. The foot pedal serves that purpose.

Here are some examples of how I use it:

- When streaming, I use the foot pedal to advance my graphics and mute my mic if I cough. Muting my microphone with a foot pedal is a godsend.
- When editing in Microsoft Word, I can use the foot pedal to engage editing commands such as accepting track changes, initiating macros, and even formatting text.
- When editing videos and audio, I can use the foot pedal to help me achieve commands faster.
- When designing book covers in Photoshop, I can map commonly used commands to the foot pedal to use it in tandem with the Stream Deck.

I love technology because if you look hard enough and are willing to do things differently, you can find suitable solutions to your problems.

UPGRADING MY MICROPHONE

One of my biggest pain points with my studio configuration was my microphone. When I upgraded my studio in 2021, I felt that I had made a good decision in selecting my camera, desk, and other accessories. I did not, however, purchase the right microphone. That microphone was an Audio Technica AT2035, which is a great one in its own right, but it was not the right one for me.

The Audio Technica was a condenser mic, and condenser mics are extremely sensitive. They pick up everything. That's part of their charm because you can hear subtle nuances and instruments and singers' voices. However, for radio, podcasting, and broadcasting, they are terrible choices because you can hear everything. This microphone picked up everything in my background: my furnace, laptop fan, and even my next-door neighbor's thoughts.

After thorough research, I picked up a Shure SM7B dynamic microphone, which is a much better fit for my situation.

Boy, did it make a big difference. It captures my voice while ignoring most of my background. It also makes my voice sound fuller and more robust.

However, I needed to take an additional step to improve my audio quality further. I hired an audio engineer to listen to samples of my voice recorded with the new microphone and apply noise reduction, equalization, de-essing, and compression to my voice so that it sounded radio-quality. The engineer provided preset files that I could then plug into my existing applications to sweeten my voice live.

I picked up a pair of applications called Audio Hijack and Loopback that "hijack" the microphone audio at the source, apply the effects to sweeten the signal, and then reroute the sound to the application of my choice, be it Zoom, GoToMeeting, or eCamm Live. The apps work amazingly well, and the engineer did a great job. I am so much happier with my audio now, and I feel like I have leveled up in this area.

Ironically, even with my old condenser microphone, I frequently received compliments from people about the high quality of my audio, but I knew I could do better. Now, I feel like I have turned over all the stones. Because I want to eventually return to YouTube on a semi-regular schedule in 2023, this will be an important step toward doing that. I also have plans to do more online courses and speaking engagements, so this microphone is an investment that will pay for itself.

Out of all the things I have purchased in my writing career, I have never had to worry about microphones. When I purchased my first microphone—a Blue Yeti—I was worried about whether it would be worth spending the $120 required. I was wrong. The Blue Yeti blew the rinky-dinky headset I was using out of the water, giving me amazing-sounding audio overnight. Even the Audio Technica microphone paid for itself because it allowed me to record my first audiobook, which has since recouped the investment. I am positive that this Shure SM7B will do the same, if not more.

WHISPER: A WATERSHED MOMENT IN AI TRANSCRIPTION

A friend recommended that I check out Whisper narration, a new service released by OpenAI in Q3 2022. He said that I would be pleasantly surprised.

The link he sent me was a playground that promised to accurately transcribe any YouTube video; all I had to do was insert a link. I found a random, educational video with voiceover narration; I inserted the link into the tool, and waited about two minutes.

The result almost made me spit out my tea. It was astounding, and I don't use that word lightly.

The narration was not only accurate, but it was punctuated. All the commas and periods were in exactly the right places. To say it was grammatically correct was an understatement. While there were a few errors here and there, it looked virtually no different from if I had sat at my computer and typed exactly what the narrator said.

It appears that AI has reached yet another watershed moment that will have implications for authors, though most won't realize it for some time.

It's no secret that I use dictation skillfully to write my books.

Fortunately, my computer is powerful enough to run Parallels, which is a virtual machine application that allows me to run Windows on my computer side-by-side next to Mac applications. Because of this, I have Dragon Professional Individual, the preeminent dictation software that, at the time of this writing, is only available on Windows operating systems. So, I get the best of both worlds.

However, many of my Mac friends aren't so lucky. Nuance Software used to make a version of Dragon for Macs, but it was always an inferior version, and it has been discontinued with no plans to revive it soon. When you also consider that Microsoft now owns Nuance Software (acquired in 2021), then you can see why the situation is especially dire for Mac users. Dragon has a mobile version called Dragon Anywhere, but it has significant downsides and is not as accurate.

So, the result has been that Mac users have not had a real dictation solution since Dragon for Mac was discontinued. Sure, there are services like Google Voice Typing, but it's not Dragon. Not by a long shot.

Also, while dictation features on phones have improved significantly in recent years, they also don't offer the functionality that Dragon does. If you're lucky enough to own a Google Pixel phone, that phone does have a transcription feature that I have heard rivals Dragon, but Google Pixel phones only represent a small market share. And if you're a Mac user, you may not own a Google phone or even want one.

That brings us back to OpenAI's Whisper narration model. Like all AI applications, it can be integrated into other applications using the Python programming language.

This means that:

1. Future uses of AI applications will not depend on operating systems because Python is universal (at least as I understand it).
2. A developer could, in theory, *very easily* develop a simple application that allows you to upload dictated audio files locally on your machine and get amazing transcription results in the same amount of time that it would take Dragon to transcribe audio (if not faster).
3. All of this can be accomplished *today*, with very little programming knowledge and expertise.

I could hire a programmer on a site like Upwork tomorrow and pay them to develop an application that utilizes the Whisper API to create a Mac application that followed the following steps:

1. Get dictated audio from a specified folder or allow the user to select a file or batch of files.
2. Run those files through the Whisper API.
3. Display the output in a text file and save that file in the same directory as the audio (or a directory of the user's choosing).

And that's it. Now, the user doesn't need Dragon at all. Oh, and did I mention that the Whisper API is free (for now)? I have some concerns about that, to be sure, but I also think that Mac authors can take advantage of this leap forward in technology to finally achieve dictation if they have previously been unable to do so.

There is another very good reason for migrating to the Whisper platform. As I mentioned previously, Microsoft has acquired Nuance Software, and the fate of Dragon is in question. Microsoft has introduced a dictation feature into its Office suite. I've tested it, and it is pretty good. Not quite as good as Dragon, but still very good. You don't have to do too many mental gymnastics to predict that Microsoft will eventually retire Dragon and integrate it into Microsoft Office. If that happens, Mac users are especially screwed. Or maybe not, but knowing the rivalry between Microsoft and Apple, they're probably screwed. Windows has always had the superior versions of Microsoft Office applications, and I don't see that changing anytime soon.

The worst part about the Microsoft Office suite at this time is that it doesn't offer transcription. There is a podcast/interview transcription feature, but it inserts awkward timestamps into your text. One day, Microsoft will probably get smart and integrate Dragon's transcription technology into its dictation suite. When that happens, goodbye Dragon.

The end of Dragon may not be so bad; after all, most authors are already using Microsoft Word in some capacity anyway, even if they use a dedicated writing app like Scrivener. However, there is a doomsday scenario in which Dragon is no longer available, and users cannot access the same level of dictation and transcription quality that they're used to.

Whisper solves this problem. I think it is a smart strategy for me to develop an operating system-agnostic method of transcription that will allow me to avoid becoming a victim of Microsoft's whims. It's just a good business strategy. I refuse to be one of those authors who gets hit with a sledgehammer and can no longer continue my preferred way of working. Not gonna happen.

Therefore, I have committed to developing a personal Mac-based application powered by Whisper to give myself options. Also, I consider moving to Whisper a technological enhancement because of the punctuation. It's possible in the future that

I may not need to speak Dragonese. If that happens, then the speed of my dictation will improve by somewhere between 20 and 30 percent, and so will the accuracy of my transcription. Imagine never having to speak a comma or period again and rarely having to fix them. That's incredible.

There is another, less visible watershed moment here that I think will also positively impact authors. One of the biggest problems with Natural Language Processing (NLP) is that it struggles with the grammatical structure of English. I wrote in previous volumes that it would be nice if I could develop an application that could police commas and punctuation. Sadly, the technology cannot do that. If it could, Microsoft Word's Editor and Grammarly would do a much better job of ensuring users adhere to proper comma usage. In my mind, there's no good reason why Grammarly still confuses the words "to" and "too."

I don't know how the team at OpenAI did it, but they seem to have figured out this punctuation and grammatical structure problem. After all, all the commas are in the right places and used correctly!

Whatever they did, I see this potentially coming to apps like Grammarly in the future. In fact, I potentially see Grammarly becoming a legacy app. We will look back on the days when we thought tools like Grammarly and ProWritingAid were state-of-the-art. What's coming is going to make them look like child's play.

If you think about it, we have artificial intelligence writing apps that recommend grammatically correct, sometimes useful text that is getting more useful every day. We also have artificial intelligence transcription. What we don't *truly* have yet is artificial intelligence editing. Grammarly is the best we have right now; frankly, while it's good, it could be much better.

The day that an artificial intelligence editor arrives, that will be a game changer. If it comes through an API, that will be even better.

I don't believe that this technology can or should replace a human editor. But a human editor's time is best spent fixing things that a computer can't detect, like advanced grammar and story issues. I believe advancements in AI editing will allow editors to work faster and focus on the things that really matter —not policing Oxford commas and comma splices.

I am very excited about the future of AI transcription. I believe this is a watershed moment, and I think more watershed moments will come.

THE POWER OF DIGITAL HIGHLIGHTERS

I like to joke that I went to college at the wrong time and that I also went to college at the right time.

I went to college at the right time because the Internet was not as prominent in the lives of college students as it is today. While I had a laptop computer and used digital applications extensively to write papers and take care of my everyday college responsibilities, life between 2006 and 2010 was still very manual. E-books as we know them didn't exist; if you wanted a book, you had to go to the library. And in those days, the library still had the Dewey Decimal system. You couldn't look things up like you can today, so you had to find the book you were looking for and actually page through it to figure out what was relevant.

I am old enough to remember when you had to do citations manually, and professors policed your Works Cited page to ensure you got them right. Now, I'm 100 percent positive that a college student can use a program to generate their Works Cited page before turning it in to a professor.

I like to think that going to college when I did benefited me because I still have an appreciation and affection for the print medium. Though I don't read paperback books often anymore, I understand them and understand people who prefer them. I also understand the reluctance to give up the tactile sensation that paper provides.

My college years were also a time before smartphones. The iPhone wasn't introduced until I was a junior in college. In those days, if you wanted to do something with someone, you had to *do something with someone.* You had to call them on the phone. If you wanted to plan your day, you had to plan your day with a detective pad, your brain, or a physical planner. Sure, kids use planners today, but they have so many more options.

I also like to think that I went to college at the wrong time because I have such an affinity for technology that I would have been dangerous as a college student with some of the tools that are out there today.

Exhibit number one: digital notebooks like Evernote, Microsoft OneNote, and Bear. I was an early adopter of Evernote when it hit the market around 2010. Unfortunately, I had already graduated from college, but if I had been in college, I would have used the hell out of Evernote. It would have made everything so much easier. I could have had notebooks for each of my classes, used the Evernote Web Clipper to do research for projects and essays, and so much more. It could have been my college yearbook that, because Evernote is still around today, would still be accessible for me to review all these years later. That's a beautiful thing.

Exhibit number two: digital smart pens. The LiveScribe pen came out also in 2010, right around the time I graduated. It was a smart pen that used special paper to turn everything you wrote into a digital counterpart. It also had a microphone on it so that you could record your lectures while taking notes. Even cooler, you could tap a section of your notes and play back the audio that was recorded while you were writing that note.

Seriously, smart pens were such cool technology, and it's a shame that they didn't take off more than they did. As a college student, I probably would have owned several of them.

Exhibit number three: Rocketbooks. These are a variation on smart pens. They are smart notebooks requiring special gel pens that serve the same purpose. You can turn anything you write into a digital note for better safekeeping.

Trust me that there are many other technologies that I would have used in college to become the best version of myself. But the technology I want to talk about now is one that would have truly been a game changer: digital highlighters.

A digital highlighter is a handheld device with a scanner that you can use to scan text directly into a computer within seconds. Imagine reading a book, highlighting a section, and the text you highlighted popping up on your computer seconds later, with the ability to listen to it as well. You could highlight text directly into Microsoft Word or Evernote. This would've saved me so much time.

A digital highlighter solves one of the problems I have had recently: studying mega bestsellers effectively.

While traveling, I stumbled upon a reading library in a hotel with several novels from authors that I love. At the time, I was studying openings, and I was interested in reviewing at least 100 openings from mega bestsellers to see how I could improve my skill in this area. A digital highlighter would have been amazing to have because I could have taken a book off the shelf, scanned the first two or three pages directly into my phone, and had that text available to review later.

If I want to do something like that today without a digital highlighter, I have to sit down in front of my computer and type the opening of the book. Or, I have to take a picture of the first few pages, run those pictures through an OCR application to turn the image into text (which is not always accurate), or—and this is a bridge too far that I would not cross—I would have to find an EPUB version of the book, find a way to get it onto my device, and then copy the text that way. When you consider that DRM protects most traditionally published books, that means I would have to break the DRM. I'm no fan of DRM, and I don't use it in my books, but I don't believe in circumventing the technology. Plus, it's a violation of book retailers' terms of service.

So, there is no easy way to study the works of other authors at this point without some effort. A digital highlighter can help solve that problem. At the time of this writing, they are pricey at $149, but I think the investment could be worth it one day just for the time you would save. Imagine going to the library, picking a random book off the shelf from a mega bestseller, scanning a random two or three pages, and then taking it home to analyze potential techniques. Of course, I believe you should read a book before studying it, but sometimes you don't need to.

I like digital highlighters a lot, and I will probably purchase one in the future.

THE CASE FOR A WRITING
COMPUTER NOT CONNECTED TO
THE INTERNET

I have heard many successful writers advocate for a writing computer that is not connected to the Internet. Jonathan Franzen recommended this in a magazine article interview once, and it struck me as a bit eccentric, and I rejected the idea outright at the time.

Prolific author Dean Wesley Smith has also recommended writing on a computer that is not connected to the Internet. His rationale is that it is a useful trick to get into the "writing" mindset quickly. After all, if you have a dedicated writing computer, you will also have a dedicated writing desk, which means that when you sit down at the desk and fire up that computer, you will be ready to write because you will condition your brain over time to transition into creative mode. When Jonathan Franzen said it, I was young and naive and didn't understand why anyone would do this, but when I heard Dean say it, I was a working writer and understood the wisdom behind it.

During a YouTube video interview with Stephen King, I also heard John Grisham express a similar concern about having a dedicated writing computer. Grisham's rationale was completely different: he recommended it for security purposes. Since he is one of the best-selling authors in the world, he is terrified of someone hacking his computer and stealing his manuscripts and other valuable data. That to me is perhaps the best reason to have a dedicated writing computer not connected to the Internet, but then again, we are all not John Grisham.

Cybersecurity attacks against businesses are on the rise, though. I've said this for a while: the data clearly shows that small businesses are the biggest targets for cybersecurity attacks such as hacking, malware, and ransom attacks. This is because small businesses do not have the resources or technical expertise to protect their networks. It is out of sight and out of mind because small business owners have a million other things to do.

I've also said this for a while: authors are small businesses. It's just a matter of time before the self-publishing sector gets hit with a string of cybersecurity attacks that will destroy everyone's innocence and naivety. We are currently living in a golden era, the equivalent of living in a small town and being able to leave your door unlocked at night without any fear of getting burglarized. I would dare say that the technical times we live in as authors are Edenic. It won't be this way forever, and it pays to start investing in your cybersecurity today. I even dedicated an entire online course that is criminally under-viewed called "Writing in Hard Times" which attempts to help authors think about this vulnerability so they can take the meaningful first steps in protecting their data, platforms, and readers. However, this is still out of sight and out of mind for most authors because they don't think something like this could ever happen to them. In fact, I bet the thought hasn't even crossed many people's minds. But the threat is very real.

Back to Grisham. I think John Grisham has the best rationale for maintaining a writing computer that exists in a vacuum. I don't know for sure how John Grisham operates, but here is my best guess:

- John writes his novels and new material on this dedicated computer. He never connects it to the Internet, and if I were a betting man, I would guess that he has had the network card physically removed so that connecting to the Internet is not even possible. As his computer ages, he just purchases a new one.

- When he finishes a manuscript, he downloads it onto a password-protected USB thumb drive—make that two thumb drives. He then ships the drive from a non-obvious address to his publisher in New York via certified mail, with insurance. He requires a signature before the package can be delivered.

- He keeps a copy on a separate thumb drive for himself; he probably maintains a separate database and/or network of hard drives containing *all* of his work. These hard drives have never been connected to the Internet, are password-protected, and are set up in a way that only he and his heirs understand. If he is as paranoid as I think he is, he probably has his manuscripts both at his home and at another off-site location just in case anything were to happen.

- When his publisher receives the manuscript, they either have very lax controls or follow strict protocols themselves (I would bet on the former). If it's the former, then his editors also work on computers not connected to the Internet. The only time the manuscript comes online is when it is formatted and ready for the printer, which is often many months before the publication date, but this creates a tight seal so that the manuscript does not leak. But I'm just speculating on how the publisher operates.

- Rinse and repeat.

Of course, I'm just playing a guessing game here. I don't know about Grisham's security protocols, but if I were him, those would be the protocols I would follow.

So, have I come around to a dedicated writing computer? Not quite.

For a tech-savvy author like me, the concept is brilliant in theory but poses several practical problems.

First, I am not John Grisham. While I am certainly a target for attacks just like anyone else, I doubt anyone will go out of their way to make that happen. Therefore, the need for a dedicated writing computer is minimal because the risk is minimal. If I won a prestigious award or started selling at a higher level, then the calculus would change.

Also, it's just inconvenient. It means you have to have two computers and two writing desks. That's no good. I have space but would rather not clutter it with multiple desks.

The logistics also pose a challenge, given that I work with all of my editors and freelancers online. Unless my editor was willing to operate within the constraints that I outlined above, it would be impractical, increase my editing costs, and also drastically increase the production times for my books. There would be no way to have complete privacy over the book. As much as we like to think there is such a thing as privacy in today's digital age, it is a mere illusion.

So, this isn't practical for me at this time, but it's something I reserve the right to think about more deeply in the future as my career and needs change. It's also something I recommend other authors consider as well.

That said, I do like the wisdom of Dean Wesley Smith's advice, and I do believe it would be a useful trick if one could figure out the logistic problems I discussed in this chapter.

HOTEL LIBRARIES AND LITTLE FREE LIBRARIES

While traveling this quarter, I stumbled upon a reading library in a hotel. It was a massive bookcase filled with hardcovers by all the big-name authors. There was a mix of thrillers, suspense, and romance.

I kicked myself that I forgot to bring one of my books. If I had, I would have left it in the reading library. I have been meaning to do this, but I always forget to grab a few of my paperback books before I walk out the door to hit the road.

You never know who is going to be interested in reading your book. Assuming that you have a professional cover, book description on the back cover, and thorough editing, I see no reason why your book can't sit on the same shelf as James Patterson or Clive Cussler. The reading library I stumbled upon had a shortage of science fiction and fantasy, and it would have been a great opportunity for me to diversify that shelf!

But alas, maybe one of these days, I will get this right.

Another thing I noticed about reading libraries is that it is probably best to leave a hardcover on these types of bookshelves. I should travel with a few paperbacks and hardbacks, just in case. If most of the books on the shelves are hardcovers, then I will leave a hardcover. If most books are paperbacks, then I will leave a paperback. I think it's important to blend in. When in Rome...

I have also learned to appreciate the power of Little Free Libraries. These are libraries that people can construct and put in their front yards. Pedestrians and passersby can look at the library, take a book, and leave a book. They are a wonderful thing, and I have seen a proliferation of these Little Free Libraries in my city of Des Moines, Iowa. Again, as I write this chapter, I am kicking myself because I still have not taken advantage of this opportunity. It would cost me very little to, for example, print 50 authors copies of my books, spend an afternoon driving around, and inserting them in every Little Free Library that I can find. Sure, I have to pay for author's copies and shipping, but what do I have to lose?

In my upcoming book on marketing, I dedicated an entire chapter to hotel libraries and Little Free Libraries. I will post it here.

───

I don't know if this is true everywhere, but over the last decade, I have seen a proliferation of Little Free Libraries, which are simple wooden shelves that people build in their front yards that house books. Passersby can see what's in the library, take a book, and even leave a book.

In my neighborhood, Little Free Libraries are on every corner. You can bet that I leave my books in these libraries. Why not?

While writing this chapter, I did a quick web search and discovered 25 Little Free Libraries in my zip code alone.

Another free library you should consider is the library at your local hotel or coffee shop. They frequently have shelves where you can grab free books and leave them. Leave a copy of your book on the shelf before you check out from the hotel. Even better, autograph it!

But, you really, really, *really* need to make sure that you have a great cover that looks professional and would fit in with other books in your genre. Otherwise, no one will touch your book, and the staff will probably throw it out.

You can also find these free libraries in your local coffee shops and other small business establishments, so don't disregard them.

LOOKING FORWARD

DEALING WITH A PRODUCTIVITY SLUMP

I experienced my first productivity downturn with my million-word challenge.

I wrote about this in a previous chapter where I discussed the importance of writing a short story while the idea is hot. But that was only part of the story.

My wife traveled out of town, and I was on double-parent duty for a week. My daughter had many activities going on, and I truly had to take a week off writing. I thought maybe I could achieve 25 percent or 50 percent of my quota, but that didn't happen. That in and of itself wasn't a big deal because I could still consume content and progress in other areas of my writing business. For example, I got a lot of reading done and cleared my inbox down to zero. I also fixed some issues with one of my book's sales pages. So the week wasn't a complete loss.

However, I found it extremely difficult to ramp back up to 2,750 words per day. In fact, it took another week and a half before I returned to my previous productivity levels. And even then, my word counts were often right at my quota.

I found myself frequently asking why this was. I also found, strangely, that the drive to write fiction just wasn't there.

I've been doing this long enough to know how to handle it. I would have been anxious about returning to the writing desk early in my career. I would have been anxious at the fact that I was missing my daily word count and potentially falling behind on the challenge, especially when I had worked so hard to build a surplus.

However, experience has taught me a few things. First, there are three root causes of writer's block:

1. anxiety/fear
2. lack of inspiration/boredom
3. personal circumstances

At the same time, I had water in my basement due to a leak from an old water softener unit. The leak was significant enough that it caused mold, and I had to file a claim to have part of my drywall ripped out and replaced. That was also causing some unconscious stress.

And finally, two immediate family members had health scares during that week.

So, in short, the stress of double-parent duty, homeowner woes, and family issues really put a damper on my productivity. My creative voice seized up, and it took a week and a half before it determined that it was safe to write again. It also didn't help that I wrote a story that I got stuck in the middle of—all these things culminated in a perfect storm.

Once I finished the story and got used to writing at pulp speed again, I was back into my regular routine, no problem. But it took a while.

This experience taught me the importance of building surpluses whenever I can. My rule of ABC—always be adding surplus—saved me from falling behind on the challenge. Even with a loss of writing days, I was still ahead for the year. The productivity downturn brought me close to zero, and now I must begin the process anew of building a surplus so that I can be prepared for the next time this happens.

As a writer, I go through seasons of abundance, seasons of winter, and seasons where things are pretty steady. The trick is understanding where I am and how to address each season.

If I'm in a season of abundance, I bank as many extra words as possible and prepare for winter.

If I'm in a season of winter, then I do the best I can, wait it out, and hope for the best.

If I'm in a season of steadiness, I just keep going.

That's the life of a writer. You just have to keep going.

DEALING WITH ECONOMIC DOWNTURNS

I've heard a lot of talk from writers terrified about their careers. It started during my travels to writing conferences this year. I spoke with one writer who told me that her Facebook ads were no longer working, and her income had dropped by over 50 percent. She made a living from her writing and didn't know how she would continue. This author was attending the conference in hopes of finding a new set of strategies that she could use to improve her income.

At another conference, someone mentioned offhand that authors were seeing their sales drop. I noted it, but because it wasn't true for me at the time, I didn't pay much attention to it.

Then, I heard more prominent authors lament the drop in sales. Kristine Kathryn Rusch even wrote a blog post about it, and the popular Six-Figure Authors Podcast came out of a hiatus to address the issue. Then I started really paying attention.

First, I got the data about my sales. My sales numbers are slightly up this year, but certain segments are down. It's no different from any prior years. The sad reality about being an author is that some years you're up, and some years you're down. There often isn't a rhyme or reason to it, but there are clues.

At the time of this writing, we are in a unique and challenging profit environment. The war in Ukraine is driving instability and inflation. Greedy corporations are also taking advantage of the pandemic and unfairly raising their profit, contributing to inflation.

And, of course, we have—wait for it—record inflation, which means that people have to pay more for everything, including food, fuel, energy, and rent. All readers are faced with pricing pressures in almost every area of their lives, so it's no surprise that they're spending more money on essential services and less on entertainment.

Also, in the United States, this is a midterm election year, possibly the most covered midterm in recent memory. Usually, people don't pay much attention to midterm elections. This year, almost everyone paid attention. When people are focused on politics, they aren't reading books.

So, when I thought about it, it wasn't surprising that book sales are down across the board for many authors. What was clear to me (and not clear to many of the authors lamenting this) was that sales will be back up. They always come back up. That's just the cyclical nature of the book business. The best thing that we can do is make smart long-term choices, wait out the economic "winters," and take advantage of the good times when they come.

If the book business weren't cyclical, then most authors wouldn't have careers. As long as authors continue to publish books, find readers, and do the right things even when times are hard, I don't doubt that most will continue to have careers.

This is why I have focused so much on cutting my costs, investing in automation and technology, and diversifying my income so that I am less susceptible to economic swings. I can definitely say that my strategy so far has been successful. If it weren't, I would be one of those people complaining about my sales dropping.

Here are some of the techniques I have used to insulate myself and protect my business from the ravages of inflation:

- **Don't overpay for services**. While I am a big fan of paying the right people to do a job, I don't overpay. This is critical in an unregulated market where anyone can charge whatever they want for a service.

- **Learn how to do your own book covers**. You probably knew I was going to say that, but investing the time to learn cover design will cut your costs by at least 50 percent, therefore improving your profit. This is especially helpful if the book production process is expensive for you and your sales do not completely pay for the production costs of your books.

- **Consider raising your prices, but do understand what inflation is**. Inflation is when everyone raises their prices and wages at the same time. Therefore, if you increase the price of your books, you're only contributing to the problem! That said, I understand why some authors would be tempted to do this, but in today's current environment, you can only raise the prices of your books so high. Besides, this industry is one of the few bastions where readers are complaining about increased book prices. We as authors can take advantage of that by keeping our books priced the way they are until the current inflation environment subsides.

- **Diversify, diversify, diversify**. If you're all-in with Kindle Unlimited, now's the time to start planning your escape strategy. Establishing a plan to diversify is still a smart strategy even if revenue streams do not immediately pay off. For example, if you don't have direct sales set up on your website, now is a good time to do that.
- **Cut your costs**. If you don't need it, cut it. Operate on the leanest budget that you can and carry it into the good times with you. This will ensure that you will protect your profit even if your sales decrease.

Economic downturns are not easy, but they are not forever. We will all get through this, just as we got through the last ones. The trick is to be proactive and be patient.

DESIGNING NEW BUSINESS CARDS

I found myself at a writing conference without business cards. You would think I would know better, but alas.

It has been a few years since I ordered business cards. A few things have changed. First, they have gotten more expensive, but we won't talk about that.

I ordered middle-of-the-road business cards—not the cheap ones, but not the most expensive ones either. I wanted something that presented nicely and didn't go over the top.

I settled on VistaPrint, which had the best card design experience. I didn't want to hire someone to design my cards because I will be doing a rebrand in the next few years anyway, and I will have new business cards designed at that time. I just needed something to last me for a few years. VistaPrint served that purpose at an affordable cost.

My very first business cards were poor at best. They had my name, phone number, email address, and website, but the print was too tiny, and the cards themselves were so small that they weren't effective. This time, I went with a colorful but simple design, and I opted for a QR code business card instead. This type of business card has a QR code that goes wherever you want—your website, a social media profile—you name it.

Psychologically, I like the idea of a QR business code because it is a subliminal pull. With a regular business card, the person you give it to has to remember you well enough and care about your conversation enough to go to their computer or phone and visit your website. It sounds simple enough, but it's actually a big ask. Think about all the people you meet throughout a conference. You must capitalize on someone's memory pretty thoroughly for them to follow up with you after meeting them. That rarely happens.

A QR code business card solves this problem because it reduces friction. Almost everyone is within two feet of their phone at all times, and if you use compelling copy next to your QR code, you're going to intrigue them enough to take action. And if you can get them to do that, you can increase your community, connections, and income.

So, that's why I went with a QR code business card.

I also include my face on business cards. I do this because most people will not remember faces after conferences either. When you put your face front and center on the business card, they have no choice but to remember your face. Combined with a QR code, you have an effective lead machine.

Now that I have ordered business cards like a proper author and businessperson, I have plenty to hand out and tuck in the back of my books.

THE RETURN TO MICROSOFT WORD

I wrote in a previous volume about my return to Microsoft Word as my primary writing tool. It gives me no pleasure, but Word is the best writing app to accommodate my dictation needs.

Here is my current workflow and how I am using Word to achieve my goal of writing one million words in a year.

As I have written previously, I dictate my words into a voice recorder and connect the recorder to my computer, using Dragon's Auto Transcribe Folder Agent to transcribe my voice into text. After transcription, I load the words into Microsoft Word and run my proprietary dictation macro, which cleans up the text and does the majority of the editing for me so that I only have to focus on a few stray errors. I then use Microsoft Editor, Grammarly Premium, ProWritingAid, and PerfectIt to clean up the text.

Next, I use Word's Read Aloud feature to listen to the dictated text at about 1.5 speed. When I listen to dictated text, I find common issues like dropped articles and missing words a lot easier and faster. I did some timing tests, and it took me approximately five minutes to review 500 words. Therefore,

Read Aloud keeps me on a guided track and gives me a realistic expectation of how long it will take to edit my stories.

When I have finished the story, I rerun Editor, Grammarly, ProWritingAid, and PerfectIt for good measure. Then, I observe Heinlein's Rules and ship the story off to my editor.

Microsoft Word is the best tool to help me achieve my current goals. I never thought I would be here, but sometimes fate has a way of being funny.

No other writing app on the market offers the tools I mentioned. Therefore, I will use Microsoft Word as my primary writing app for the foreseeable future. At the end of the day, all I care about is quality and quantity. I am not above using any tool that will help me achieve my goals. This is why I invest so much time in technology to be nimble.

TRAVELING TO SAUDI ARABIA

This quarter, I received a once-in-a-lifetime opportunity to travel to Saudi Arabia. I was invited to speak at the Jeddah International Book Fair, one of the largest publishing conferences in the region, with over 70,000 attendees and over 400 publishers. The theme for the event was science fiction and fantasy, and the organizers placed special emphasis on self-publishing, which is picking up steam in the Middle East.

At first, I wasn't sure if the invitation was legit. It was.

You don't hear much about Saudi Arabia. It only recently opened to foreigners. Whatever you do hear about the country on the news is not pleasant. Ultimately, I'm not here to talk about politics. I just want to help writers, wherever they are in the world.

I accepted the invitation and found myself on a frenetic pace to prepare for overseas travel. After all, I had never been to the Middle East or North Africa before, so I had to get a battery of vaccines. I also had to buy some new luggage and travel supplies. Most importantly, I had to research Middle Eastern customs, taboos, and things to watch out for while traveling. I was to be a guest in Saudi Arabia, so I fully intended to abide by the country's laws. After intense preparation and self-education about Saudi Arabia and Islam, the day finally came to step on the plane and leave the United States for the first time since the pandemic.

Twenty-three hours later, I landed in Jeddah with no contacts other than the person who was supposed to pick me up. I truly threw myself into the experience.

Despite Arabic being the official language of Saudi Arabia, almost all the signs are in English. Many people in the airports, hotels, and restaurants speak good English. The customs agent noticed that my birthplace was in Missouri. He asked me where, and I told him St. Louis. Turns out he spent four years in Illinois in college and visited St. Louis a lot when he lived in the United States. Crazy coincidence. He handed me my passport and told me to enjoy my time in Saudi Arabia.

When I arrived, the first thing I immediately noticed was all the men walking around in white thobes and the women walking around in black abayas. Some women had their faces covered, and you could see only their eyes. By my clothes alone, I was easily pegged as a foreigner.

Getting around wasn't hard. The conference sent me a shuttle from the airport to the hotel. Uber also works well in Saudi Arabia, and many of the location names are in English, so they're easy to find on the app.

I stayed at the Crowne Plaza Jeddah Al Salaam, a newer hotel in the northern part of Jeddah. It was like any modern hotel, but a little more advanced. One thing I noticed was that there were employees everywhere. You never see bellhops anymore in American hotels unless they're upscale. Here, there were at least three in the lobby. Several employees in the gym made sure the equipment was clean and the floor was dry.

Staying at this hotel was like staying at a hotel decades ago in the states. The service was excellent.

The hotel also provided complimentary meals for the speakers. The restaurant was quite large, and had beautiful white and blue Islamic tiles on the floor, with buffet-style options. There were at least ten different stations of food, serving everything from fruit, pastries, hot food from all over the world, western food like hamburgers and hot dogs, and soups and salads. The waiters served soda in bottles. Large flatscreen televisions played the World Cup games, which was happening in Qatar while I was traveling.

I met several other speakers from the United States, Canada, and Jamaica, and we stuck together. I didn't know any of the speakers previously, but I had done my homework, looking them up and watching YouTube video interviews they had done. I brushed up on my knowledge of their areas of expertise, which made for easy conversations.

A curious detail about the trip that I anticipated but took the other speakers off-guard was Arab hospitality, that was also matched by what could best be described as "hands-off." The organizers did an amazing job getting us to our destination and helping us be comfortable, but beyond that, they did nothing else. Therefore, it was up to the speakers to determine how they wanted to spend their time in the country. This was frustrating to some.

As for me, I expected it, so I made an itinerary once it was clear that there wouldn't be any planned events for the speakers other than the conference.

Places I visited included:

- the "corniches," beachfront trails along the Red Sea that locals love to visit
- the Red Sea Mall, a megamall with every shop and brand you can think of

- Al Balad, or the old city where the buildings are made of coral and sand
- The Tomb of Eve (yes, *that* Eve)
- Al Baik, a fast food franchise that sells fried chicken seasoned with saffron and turmeric
- Al Tayebat, a giant museum that could best be described as "the Smithsonian of Saudi Arabia."
- And more!

I made the most of my time and had a blast, even though I didn't speak the language. I had learned a few Arabic phrases, and those worked wonders. Simple things like "hello" and "thank you" go a long way.

I found the people to be extremely warm, hospitable, and friendly. Foreigners still aren't amazingly common, so many were curious. Many people went out of their way to say hello and to ask where I was from. They also went out of their way to help. The hospitality reminded me of the friendliness I had received in Costa Rica and Nicaragua. It's a type of kindness that you don't generally see in the United States.

And then there was the main event itself: the Digital Publishing Conference. The entire program was in Arabic, but the event provided headsets that let you listen to a real-time translator. That translator was one hard-working guy, let me tell you. Whenever someone spoke Arabic, all the English speakers put their headsets on as the translator spoke English. Whenever someone spoke in English, all the English speakers put their headsets down, and the Arabic speakers put their headsets on as the translator switched immediately to translating into Arabic. It was truly a sight to behold.

I also had to wear the headset on stage. I sat on a panel with four people who all spoke excellent English, but they spoke in Arabic for the panel since most people in the audience didn't speak English. On the panel, we talked about self-publishing in the Middle East and North Africa, and I learned a great deal about how distribution is handled in the region, what tools authors have available to them, and the process they follow to publish. It was an eye-opening hour for me.

In many ways, publishing in the Middle East reminds me of how things were in the west ten years ago. Self-publishing was accepted but not encouraged. Most people still chased the glory of traditional publishing. Yet, the authors who chose to self-publish were winning in a big way, especially those who focused on acting like traditional publishers and producing books with excellent covers, good writing, and editing, and good packaging such as book descriptions and prices.

Anecdotally, I heard from a few people that there are self-published authors in Saudi Arabia who are wiping the floor with traditional publishers, and that made me smile. Unfortunately, I didn't get to meet any of those authors. I would have paid money to talk to them.

The event organizers did a great job, and I enjoyed myself at the conference. Suddenly, it was time to go home.

My return flight was through Dallas, and (wait for it) I got stuck there. Unfortunately, a tornado near the Dallas-Fort Worth airport wreaked havoc on travel. I had to spend the night in a nearby suburb.

When I finally returned home, I felt as if I had woken up from a fever dream. I traveled to the Middle East, got to experience a part of the world that very few people have seen until this point, and immersed myself in a culture that I enjoyed. Sometimes I still don't believe I traveled there.

I'm grateful for the experience and will never forget it.

KICKSTARTER LESSONS

This year, I was part of a successful Kickstarter that funded in 36 hours. It was a short story anthology.

Kickstarter has been on my list of marketing tactics to explore for quite some time, but I haven't yet had the opportunity to get around to it. I paid careful attention to how the organizer structured the campaign, and I am recording some of the lessons I learned that I could apply to my Kickstarter campaigns when I am ready to start running them for my books.

- The organizers started planning well in advance--around eight months.
- They communicated early and often about their marketing plans and sought ideas from the contributors.
- All the stories were finished and edited before they even considered sending the Kickstarter campaign live.
- They went into the campaign with a solid list of potential stretch goals, just in case.

- They leveraged the network of all the authors contributing to the anthology. Each author shared the campaign with their respective audiences immediately when the campaign went live. Momentum is everything with Kickstarters.
- They studied other successful campaigns to figure out what was working.
- They were thoughtful about everything throughout the process.
- They made a funny, catchy introductory video. Most Kickstarter campaigns do not fund without one.
- They delivered the goals on time and within budget.

While the Kickstarter did not raise much money, it raised a ton of money compared to the original goal. It was an astonishing success that taught me a lot about navigating this emerging platform.

AUDIO COMMENTARY REVISITED

I wrote about audio commentary in a previous volume of this series. In short, I used to love audio commentary features on DVDs, and it is malpractice that streaming sites like Netflix and Hulu have not re-adapted it for the streaming era. Commentary represents millions of hours of valuable content that even casual fans love.

Anyway, before I launch into an assault on streaming platforms' misjudgment, I want to talk about how an author could "hack" the audio commentary process for their books.

I took part in a Kickstarter campaign this year that successfully funded. It was a short story anthology that I contributed to. One of the stretch goals was audio commentary. The anthology editor told me to pick at least three places in the short story where I could expound on what inspired those sections, much like a director talks about a section in a movie commentary and how it inspired them or what went on behind the scenes.

To paraphrase his directions, he said, "Think of it as if the reader could tap the section in your story and listen to what inspired it."

That got me thinking about how I could commandeer this

idea for my books. It's really quite simple, and I'm surprised I didn't think of it sooner.

Here's how it would work: I could record high-quality audio commentary and host it on a website with links that do not change. I could then link it to text that inspired the commentary. If the reader wants to hear it, they can simply tap on the link. Or, to make this a little less obtrusive, I could hide the link in a footnote and set the expectation on the copyright page and the author's note so that the reader can tap the footnotes to listen to the commentary.

For paperback readers, I could simply print a QR code in the back of the book that takes them to a playlist with commentary. I would just need to be intentional about naming the files and announcing the chapter and section at the beginning of the recordings so that readers know where they are.

Furthermore, I could release a limited edition or special edition of my books with this feature enabled, in addition to other things like AI art inspired by the series, a video interview with me talking about the book, and other bonuses. Hell, this is the kind of content you could put in an omnibus. I always struggle when thinking about what to add to those to make the higher price point more attractive. This would be a great way to get people to buy omnibuses.

The only problem is figuring out the hosting situation. I think I could use a service like Google Drive or Dropbox, but I would have to look at the fine print. It's one thing if you're selling a few copies of your novel here and there; it's another thing entirely if your book becomes a bestseller. That would drive traffic to your files, and a hosting service might not like that. However you addressed this issue, you would need to ensure without a doubt that readers could access the files at all times and that there would be no surprises. Perhaps a podcast hosting provider such as Libsyn would be a smart way to host this content safely and permanently, but the downside is that you would have to pay for it, which is a non-starter if you are not selling that many books.

And, of course, there is the untapped functionality of EPUB 3, something I'd like to explore soon.

This is the most sophisticated way around the audio commentary problem I can think of. As I wrote this chapter, I found myself getting very excited about the prospects of this workaround.

WRITING WHILE TRAVELING

In a previous chapter, I discussed my struggles with writing while my wife was out of town. Several weeks later, we took a family trip to Chicago. I was back to my regular productivity routine, hitting and exceeding my quota on most days.

Now, suddenly, I was faced with a new challenge: how could I continue being productive while on the road? I feel like I'm always asking this question, and it feels like the answer changes every time I address it. What made this particular trip unique is that:

1. My surplus was anemic due to the productivity downturn I described in a previous chapter.
2. I had a lot more control over what to write, and I had a unique opportunity to choose my project before the trip because I was writing primarily short stories and nonfiction. This would have been a completely different chapter if I had been in the middle of a novel (or wanted to start one).

We left on Thursday and came home on Sunday. That

meant I needed to write a total of 11,000 words while on the road, or I needed to make up for any lost words before I left or when I returned.

First, I built up my surplus as high as possible between Sunday and Wednesday. Fortunately, I left for Chicago with a surplus for the week. That meant I started the trip slightly ahead of schedule and could afford to slip a little in case I didn't hit my quota on some days.

Next, I chose a nonfiction book as my primary project while on the road. While I didn't like that too much because I wanted to focus on fiction, nonfiction is a lot easier to write and requires less friction to get started. Therefore, I could achieve higher word counts on the days I traveled simply by virtue of writing nonfiction. That was a beautiful thing.

I also had another nonfiction book in reserve in case I needed to divert words to it, and, if I wrote an exceptional amount, I also had a fiction short story teed up to start, but if I started the short story, I made sure that I didn't start it until at least Sunday morning. This way, I wouldn't start the story and have to stop it in the middle, like I did with my productivity downturn. If there's anything I've learned, it's that if you start a story, your primary goal should be to finish it as soon as possible with no delays. Otherwise, finishing the story takes twice as long and twice as much effort.

Next, I used every opportunity to write on my phone. My wife and I alternated driving, and the drive from Des Moines to Chicago is approximately five hours. I spent my two and a half hours in the passenger seat writing. I did this even though it only amounted to a few hundred words both ways. When you're on the road, a few hundred words goes a long way.

Next, I made sure that my email inbox was at zero before I left. I find that when I zero out my inbox, the "zero effect" lasts for approximately two days before emails with action items start rolling in. What's in your email inbox is what's on your mind. Since there was nothing in my email inbox, I could focus on writing.

I also brought my voice recorder with me and used some down time in the evenings to take a walk and dictate.

Lastly, I made sure to rest when I got home. I didn't immediately run down to my writing computer even though I had a deficit. By getting rest, I was able to take a long nap and wake up refreshed. This helped me make a dent in my deficit, and I ultimately met my quota for the week even though I spent more than half of it away from home.

So, that's what it's like to write while traveling when you want to achieve one million words per year.

SELF-SUFFICIENT SELF-PUBLISHING

As I did my planning for 2023, I realized that I was moving toward a destination that I hadn't yet been able to articulate for myself. As I looked at my accomplishments for the last three years and I now look ahead to the next few years, I realized that I am moving toward something that I call "self-sufficient self-publishing."

I define self-sufficient self-publishing as follows: the ability to run a profitable publishing business without overreliance on others.

As the global economy heads into an economic downturn and the future looks uncertain, this will be more important than ever. It is the answer to continuing to publish on your terms without undue financial stress. In other words, it is the ultimate freedom as an author and artist.

I believe it's critically important to build a publishing business that runs itself. I've discussed ad nauseum my commitment to technology and data to make that happen, but there is much more to it than that.

Creativity

As writers, we often feel that we need the opinions and validation of others. We frequently tie our self-worth to the performance of our books, but that is a terrible idea. Before even going into some of the more mechanical aspects of self-sufficient self-publishing, I want to stress that one must also become emotionally self-sufficient with their writing. They must not succumb to self-doubt, comparisonitis, and unnecessary anxiety. Otherwise, self-sufficient self-publishing will never become a reality because they will be too dependent emotionally on others.

This means doing the emotional work to fortify your mind, body, and spirit so that you can continue writing no matter what happens in your life. Life happens to us all, but a writer is someone who writes, even when life strikes.

Writing Books

Learning how to write quality stories as quickly as possible is a career-defining trait for any writer. The more you publish, the more potential money you will make. The math of publishing is simple enough, but many people choose to play checkers when the real game is chess. It's not about quantity versus quality. It's about quality *and* quantity. That's the challenge, and the writer who can figure that out will tap into a bonanza.

Of course, this requires the convergence of craft, marketing, and business, but I believe that it is possible. I see no reason why it can't be. I see more people giving excuses about why they can't achieve world-class quality instead of actually figuring out if there is a way for them to achieve both. I believe we should change the conversation and the lens through which we look at what it means to be a writer.

What if you could publish the books in your mind quicker? How many books would that be? What if you did the very best you could on all those stories? What if readers proved they didn't care about quantity versus quality, and they--this never happens--they actually got mad at you because you had too many books?

I'd call that a good problem. Readers love challenges like that, especially when you operate at a consistent quality.

Editing Your Books

Here's where the rubber meets the road. To publish a book, you need to have it edited. An editor is someone whom you rely on to publish a book.

At a minimum, you must ensure that you always have access to an editor, no matter what happens. If you must wait many months to get on an editor's calendar, then you are hamstringing your writing output.

Therefore, you owe it to yourself to learn how to create manuscripts that are as clean as possible to reduce your editing costs. Fortunately, editors are easy to find, easy to work with, and generally don't have long waits, but if that were ever to change--that's what you need to be thinking about.

Economic times change. Just because you can find an editor easy today doesn't mean that you will be able to find one easily tomorrow. All I'm proposing is that you learn how to exercise sanity in these moments of mania. That sanity comes from long-term thinking, smart planning, and prudent decision-making.

For example, if my current editor became unavailable temporarily or permanently, I would take the following steps:

- If possible, I would look to editors I've worked with in the past to see if they are available.
- If my previous editors are unavailable within my price range, I will look for another editor on the

common channels where authors find editors like Reedsy, Upwork, and word of mouth.

If there were a disaster and I could not find the right person, I would call the head of the English department at my alma mater, tell them to send me their brightest English major, and I would pay them a fair fee to read my manuscripts and comment on them. I would instruct them to look for basic spelling and grammar errors. Nothing more, nothing less. Sure, this person wouldn't be a professional, but there are tens of thousands of college students out there who need money and experience. Even with liberal arts programs in shambles, I am confident I would have no problem finding someone to work on my books.

If such a scenario were to occur, and I had to rely on a college student for editing, then the burden of ensuring clean manuscripts would especially be on me. Therefore, it would be in my best interest to ensure that my manuscripts are as error-free as possible before they ever went to the college student.

Why not do that now, when times are good? Clean manuscripts are clean manuscripts, and clean manuscripts are a smart idea no matter who you are as a writer. This is why I have spent so much time implementing automation and technology into my workflow to clean up my text as much as possible. It's why I spent so much time on my dictation macros, because they are the clearest path to cleanliness.

But there's also another snake in the grass here that I need to be wary of: Dragon software. As I wrote in a previous chapter, Microsoft acquired Nuance Software. As I write this chapter, the tech industry is going through an economic bust, with tens of thousands of layoffs that look to be surpassing the dotcom boom in the years 2000 and 2001. The optimist in me says that everything will work out and I will continue to be able to use

Dragon as I do today; the pessimist in me says that there are some red lights flashing that I need to pay attention to:

- For Mac users, the only way to run Dragon is on a virtual machine using Parallels or Bootcamp. The new Apple Silicon chips do not support virtual machines, so while Parallels works on Apple Silicon Macs, it doesn't work well right now. That may not ever change due to the direction Apple is headed. Therefore, assuming that Dragon will continue working on a Windows virtual machine is not a safe bet.
- When companies get acquired, their products get retired. If Microsoft integrates the Dragon technology into its Microsoft Office platform, it will change. Some of those changes will be positive, and some of them will be negative, but there will always be an impact. Sometimes users come out ahead; most often, they do not.
- If Dragon became unavailable tomorrow, there would be no viable alternatives except for Whisper. But only the most tech-savvy people can use Whisper right now.

So why not learn how to use Whisper now? Why not reduce my dependence on Dragon so that I won't be nearly as impacted when the fateful day comes and Microsoft makes a product deprecation announcement?

Many authors use Dragon for dictation and transcription; if it went away tomorrow, there would be mania.

Book Cover Design

Perhaps the biggest expense that authors have is book cover design. I've talked about my gripes with book cover designers enough that I don't need to rehash them here. Suffice it to say that we rely on cover designers too much. In fact, we rely on them so much that we are at their whims.

Self-sufficient self-publishing means you can create high-quality, professional covers without needing a cover designer. Or, if you need a cover designer, you don't need them as often.

Here's the doomsday scenario: due to a massive economic downturn or a change in the industry, cover designers become unavailable, and the shortage is even worse than it is now, driving the rates way up. New authors will be priced out of publishing entirely, and mid-list authors will have to cut their production because they cannot afford to publish at the same pace they are used to. Only the most affluent authors will be able to afford rapid-release publishing. That's a scary landscape. Both authors *and* readers lose.

A self-sufficient self-publisher, while they may not be among the most affluent, would not be impacted at all by a cover designer shortage because they can design their own covers. They can do more with less. So, though a self-sufficient publisher may not be affluent, they would have more opportunities to grab market share and readers because everyone else won't publish nearly as much.

So, why not start learning cover design now?

Bringing It All Together

A self-sufficient self-publisher can continue writing and publishing rain or shine because:

- They do not rely emotionally on the opinions of others and therefore work independently.

- They publish independently.
- The methods by which they work are independent and not overly reliant on industry changes or the whims of tech giants.
- They produce manuscripts that are so clean that they could technically publish them without editing.
- They create their own covers or pay significantly less than others to get better results.
- Their profit margins are astronomically higher compared to other authors with similar experience levels, and they reinvest their profit back into the business in good times so that they can thrive in hard times when everyone else is suffering.

As I did my planning, that's what I realized I was heading toward—self-sufficient self-publishing. I'm fortunate enough that my writing business is profitable, but even if it weren't, I could continue publishing at the same pace and building my platform. In other words, I will keep charging forward as long and as fast as possible, no matter what is happening around me. That's critical.

MY THOUGHTS ON THE METAVERSE

I have been studying virtual reality and augmented reality a lot this quarter after I experienced what they can do. The technology has come a long way over the last few years, and people are exhibiting shortsighted behavior when it comes to the metaverse.

Say what you want about virtual reality. Yes, the headsets look gimmicky and inconvenient to wear for long periods. However, virtual reality *headsets* were never the point. The point was always augmented reality. Today's headsets are no different from the chunky cathode ray tube computer monitors that existed in the 1990s and early 2000s. It's the same thing. The technology will eventually become more like glasses, and when it does, it will take off. Most people are too shortsighted to understand this.

Also, say what you want about Mark Zuckerberg. I have my gripes with him, and I'm no fan of Facebook. However, I do believe his vision is clear, and it is correct.

We should also acknowledge another fact: Zuckerberg was simply the first to recognize where society is going, and because he is one of the richest men in the world, he has a disproportionate influence on where we will go. I have some problems with that, as I am not someone who is going to simp to the billionaire class. I'm under no illusions about the seemingly altruistic initiatives of billionaires, but I am also not in the realm of politics or policymaking, and, because the future is what it is, we've all got to survive as best we can. That means thinking ahead and adapting to new technology and working methods. Otherwise, we will be left behind. This is a particular danger for writers, for whom developers may not support as well as other professions and an increasingly technological future where people will need to pay for services and subscriptions.

I've said for a while that the future will be what we make it, and no one will do anything for us; if we want something, we have to be the stewards of our fates. And if the world is headed toward a metaverse, we must learn how to make it work for us rather than focusing on things we don't like and resisting the technology. You can see how well that worked out for people who decried the Internet and smartphones. Hint: it didn't work out so well.

I have my problems with the metaverse too. I've read *Snow Crash* and *Ready Player One* like everyone else, and if Mark Zuckerberg ever asked me for constructive criticism, I would tell him that his biggest problem when he unveiled his vision of the metaverse is that he didn't address these books, and that he didn't explain that he was trying to create positive versions of the technology detailed in those books. The result was that people subconsciously assumed that Zuckerberg was trying to take us to a bleak, dismal reality where we have no agency or cause for optimism. I don't think that's what Zuckerberg had in mind.

Instead, the headlines around Meta's metaverse were negative due to this association.

Whether Zuckerberg realizes his vision or not, the metaverse will be here to stay.

The core philosophy of the metaverse, virtual reality, and augmented reality seems to be this: let's take everything that people do in real life and make it better in the metaverse. That's where the use cases are right now.

For example, if you work from home using a tiny little laptop, why not use virtual or augmented reality to spawn as many screens as you need? Instead of two-dimensional Zoom calls, why not meet your colleagues in a realistic 3D work room where you have a full-body avatar that tracks your eye and facial expressions? This way, you can talk and interact with your colleagues as if you were in the same room, even though you may be halfway around the world. Sure, it's not the real thing, but it's the closest we can get to human interaction. Avatars look cartoonish right now, but in a few years, you will be able to create an avatar of your real body.

For gaming, why not become the character you're playing? The metaverse takes the term "first-person shooter" to a whole new level. The future of video games is in the first-person. (This saddens me because I never was a first-person videogame kind of guy. I prefer third-person experiences, but how cool would it be to play a game like *Final Fantasy* where *you* are the protagonist?)

If you want to hang out with friends who don't live near you, why not spawn your avatars in a virtual environment so that you can do things like go to the movies, go bowling, sit around and chat while having a coffee, and so on? Otherwise, you'd have to travel to get to them.

Need to learn how to drive? Do it with augmented reality. How about archery? Or shooting a gun? Or any other tactile function where it may not always be possible to physically attend?

The future of events is virtual as well. I predict that in the very near future, I will be conducting speaking engagements as an avatar to participants who reside in a virtual room. They will be able to ask me questions, and I will be able to interact with them as if we were in the same room.

The future of schools is also virtual. Especially colleges. Think about it. College is so damn expensive these days. Instead of flying halfway across the country to a school where you have to pay excessive room and board, many students can simply be "digital commuters." The colleges of the future may not even have a single real estate footprint. Sure, nothing beats the actual experience of living in a dormitory, but legacy colleges where you attend physically will probably be bastions of the rich.

I even think there is a use case for digital sports. With special equipment and headsets, it's not out of the realm of possibility that we could have something like a virtual Olympics.

And we haven't even gotten to augmented reality yet.

Imagine walking down the street and seeing your text messages pop up in your peripheral vision. Or, as already exists, imagine walking down the street and seeing turn-by-turn directions appear in front of you.

Anyway, I can see the future of the metaverse very clearly, and I have decided to become an early adopter. The term "writer of the future" will encompass the metaverse. Here are some use cases across every phase of publishing that I think the metaverse could potentially touch, allowing us to do our best work faster and more efficiently.

Creativity. With a pair of augmented glasses, imagine being inspired in the moment and turning your glasses to record mode (we will ignore the potential problems that this could cause, as it did with Google Glass in the mid-2010s). Let's say you walk into a bakery that inspires you. Record the experience exactly as you see it through your own eyes, and you can narrate it as well, as if you were recording it with a high-quality DSLR. The augmented glasses could potentially scan the entire area, and you could replay the event virtually, going back to review particular spots of the recording that you want to remember. What did that painting on the north wall look like again? What was the music playing over the loudspeakers when you entered? What was the guy at the front counter bellyaching about? This would take the term "replay" to a whole new level.

When you want to capture ideas today, you do it in two dimensions. In the future, you will be able to capture your ideas in three dimensions.

Also, you will be able to create your own custom digital workrooms. Let's say that you live in a tiny studio apartment, and you don't really have a writing space, so to speak. No problem. You can design (or hire someone to design) the perfect writing space. It would be your home away from home, especially if you don't want to spend a ton of money on coffee at coffee shops or if your writing space just isn't that pleasant to look at in the first place.

And it's not just a visual trick. You could also have a whiteboard that syncs wirelessly with your digital notebook software, so you could draw, take notes, outline your novel, and so much more without needing paper for physical space.

For the right people, this will be a game changer. I bet that there would even be solutions for people who are neurodivergent or have disabilities. These peaceful, serene writing spaces might be the best way for them to work.

Writing And Editing. This is a tougher vision because I'm not quite sure how it will shake out, but I do think that the way we write will change.

Writing is writing, and editing is editing, and I don't think the fundamental activities of each will change that dramatically. I think we will be able to do more faster with augmented reality.

As you're writing and you come across the need to research something, your virtual environment would change. The lights in the room would come back on, multiple screens would return--one with a web browser, maybe one with a dictionary--and you would be free to carry on your research until it's time to start writing again, in which case the room will go into a do not disturb mode again. When you're editing, the words could become the room, with your entire manuscript wrapped around you like a big circle. You could walk between the pages, and augmented reality would make the typos lift off the page so you could see them more easily. Combined with artificial intelligence, you could simply touch a section, speak to edit it, and watch the words magically transform before your very eyes.

Formatting. When it's time to format your book, you can use a previewer to hold a sample device in your hands and test out the e-book version. Imagine holding an actual e-reader, testing the operating system, and proofing your book. This could work the same way with paperbacks.

Marketing. Marketing is so two-dimensional these days. When it's time for you to market your books with virtual reality, you will be able to interact with your readers through your avatar. After all, readers buy from authors they know, like, and trust; if they have met your avatar and like you, they will be more likely to look you up in the future.

Imagine doing book readings, author interviews, and even speaking engagements and writing conferences as a virtual avatar in a virtual convention center.

This could also be interesting with augmented reality. If you attend an in-person event and meet people, imagine information bars that pop up over their heads. Let's say you're getting coffee at a concession station, and you start a conversation with a fellow author you've never met before. In theory, both of you could opt into an application where you put in your information, such as the types of books you write, where you live, and other interests that could be great icebreakers. The information bar would display the information that is most relevant to your conversation. You would skip the small talk and jump into real conversation. For example, your coffee mate might also write in the same subgenre as science fiction as you do. You might even see the cover of their latest book. In plain reality, you could be standing next to a bestseller and not even know it. In augmented reality, you'll never be caught off-guard.

Imagine a system where people can opt into public profiles, and when someone passes you on the street, you get their information. Yes, I know this is a little big brother-ish, but I'm looking at the optimistic side of things. In this fashion, augmented reality could help people make deeper and more meaningful connections in a world where we seem to be losing the ability to do that.

New Experiences. While I'm not a big fan of this use case, it's not out of the realm of possibility that authors could partner with developers to create their own virtual reality experiences. Mystery authors will have an amazing opportunity here. Imagine a series of mystery books where you are the protagonist and must solve a murder. In your virtual avatar, you will traverse a city and visit all sorts of locales to solve that murder. You might even have to find a bad guy or two. Good God, would this make for amazing virtual reality experiences, especially if the genesis is a best-selling series of books!

Science fiction and fantasy authors will have a great time with this too because they can create entire worlds, new races of characters, and all sorts of quests and missions that readers can go on and feel like they are truly in an immersive experience.

Nonfiction authors can also benefit from this. Imagine selling access to a course or service that you attend virtually. For example, if I'm a nutritionist, I could hold a seminar with a thousand people in a packed virtual auditorium and teach a class there—no more 2D Zoom calls. The same is true with anyone who offers a consulting service.

Those are just a few use cases I can think of that could positively impact writers. As I said, I'm excited about the future. It may not happen as soon as we want, but it can also happen sooner than anyone expected. Regardless, I'll be prepared, and I'll be right out front.

MASTERING THE FUNDAMENTALS

In 2021, I wrote that 2022 was the final year to get my fundamentals right. Here's why I wrote that.

Given the impending future that is on the way (and in some respects, here now), it'd be awfully easy to want to protect the publishing status quo. There's something simple and quaint about writing books, uploading them, doing some marketing, and enjoying the benefit of your hard work. Why mess around with blockchains, AI, Web 3.0, and other technology that has a deep learning curve and requires a skill set many authors currently do not have?

That's what I think will happen. It's human nature. Therefore, I must resist that nature and try to see the potential in any new technology despite criticisms, however valid those criticisms are.

I believe 2022 is the last full year to get my fundamentals in order. Change is coming, and I want to be ready when it arrives so I can take advantage of it...repeatedly. When December 31st, 2022 arrives, I will stand ready to finally become the writer of the future—the result of several years of planning.

Wow, was I right. It's December 26, 2022 as I write this, and I'm five days away from that deadline.

What fundamentals did I work on?

Sound business fundamentals and a good tax strategy. I had a profitable writing year and am set up to do quite well with my taxes. Check.

Being a writing machine, writing more books than the average author per year with less effort. This year, I wrote 12 books and published 10.

Creating manuscripts with fewer errors than the average author's. Based on my data, my average copy-edits for my novels this year were 1 edit per 673 words. In 2018, my average was 1 edit per 346 words. I nearly doubled my quality in this area, and I continue to improve.

Turning the art of publishing into a science by creating high-quality, well-packaged books on day one. With my final book this year, *Be a Writing Machine* 2, I released the e-book, trade paperback, large print, and audiobook editions on day one. That's the first time I've succeeded in accomplishing this task, and I now have the tools and workflow to do this with every book I publish. Not every book will get all editions, but the point stands.

Maximized distribution, meaning the books are available to buy everywhere humanly possible. This is true of my catalog now that I am finally distributing it through IngramSpark.

Maximized formats, meaning the books are available in as many formats as I can manage. Check.

A reliable and sizable community of people willing to buy my books on day one. Check.

A good, up-to-date website that gets the right

book to the right reader at the right time. Semi-check, though I plan to create a new website sometime in the next one to two years.

The ability to track expenses using automation. Check.

The ability to track book sales using automation. Check.

The ability to use data to make informed decisions about the business. I've talked about this enough.

Reducing costs wherever possible to keep the business lean and ready for anything. I've learned to do my own covers, which will go a long way toward satisfying this fundamental.

Supreme organization skills. Check.

An estate plan that takes care of my family. Check, evidenced by writing *The Author Estate Handbook* and *The Author Heir Handbook*.

Chaining all of these elements together with technology to increase my efficiency and deliver more value to my readers. Check.

In short, I have delivered on the major fundamentals of being an author. By improving my quality and quantity, production workflow, and utilizing data and technology, I am extremely well-positioned to take advantage of everything that 2023 has to offer.

With the rise of AI art, new chatbot and AI writing technology, rising cover art costs, and so much more, I feel good about navigating this new shifting landscape we're entering. Whether I succeed or not is another story, but at least little will catch me by surprise.

Since I am no longer focused on the fundamentals, the theme for next year is this: taking advantage of hidden opportunities that others are missing because they are stuck in the status quo. I do not expect these opportunities to bear fruit in 2023 or even 2024, but they will lay the groundwork for long-term advantages. So, in other words, the things I will be doing may look like failures. Some will be, but the wins will be big wins.

Here's to 2023.

Q4 PROGRESS REPORT

2022 is now over. It was a good year but not a great year. That said, I made a ton of progress toward my goals.

BECOME A WORLD-CLASS CONTENT CREATOR

To achieve my goal of becoming a world-class content creator, I will focus on the following tactical priorities:

- Demonstrate a commitment to learning the craft of storytelling and teaching
- Demonstrate a commitment to outstanding quality AND quantity

Examples of day-to-day activities that will help me carry out my tactical priorities include:

- Keep learning through online courses and workshops taught by professional writers who are further down the path I want to write
- Reading
- Developing mentorships
- Finding new ways to increase my daily word counts
- Mastering different writing methods
- Documenting my process of becoming a successful writer in the *Indie Author Confidential* series
- Cleaning up my platform to ensure a consistent quality reader experience

What did I do to become a world-class content creator during Q4 2022?

1. I deepened the relationship with my mentor acquired in Q3.
2. I have read (and studied the craft in) 35 books.
3. I am still on track to publish 100 books by end of 2023.

BECOME A TECHNOLOGY AND DATA-DRIVEN WRITER

To achieve my goal of becoming a technology and data-driven writer, I will focus on the following tactical priorities:

- Use technology to make the business more efficient
- Use data to get insights

Examples of day-to-day activities that will help me carry out my tactical priorities include:

- Developing a tax plan

- Developing an estate plan assisted with technology
- Learning how to design my own covers
- Hiring a personal assistant for small tasks where it makes sense
- Developing a metadata database for my work
- Improving my readers' experience on my website
- Implementing direct sales for my fiction

What did I do to become a more technology and data-driven writer during Q4 2022?

1. I began ramping up my testing of AI apps to improve my workflow and processes.
2. I began learning how to design my own book covers.

HIGHLIGHTS

There were many highlights this year, but here are a few.

Become a World-Class Content Creator:

- I ended the year with 81 books published. While reaching 100 will be a stretch, it's not impossible.
- I exploded my dictation word counts with voice recorder dictation.
- I started writing short fiction again, sending my work out to magazines.
- I am now officially an international public speaker.

Become a Technology and Data-Driven Writer:

- I produced cleaner manuscripts with enhancements to my dictation macros.
- I created a sophisticated word count tracker.
- I upgraded my microphone and audio setup, resulting in higher quality video and audio for my YouTube channel and media interviews.

Become the Writer of the Future:

- I branched into AI audio, publishing my first titles in the medium.
- I began exploring how to leverage AI to transform my writing career.

As I said, this was a challenging year. My wife received a devastating long COVID diagnosis, and I had to have a major surgery this year. Those things definitely set me back, but I still have a lot to show for this year.

MY 2023 STRATEGIC PRIORITIES

2022 gave me clarity.

2020 was about survival and staying focused. 2021 was about building on success. I started 2022 with the aim of creating stability and a new normal. That happened in some respects, but in others, I got what I wished for in unexpected ways.

To say that my life was upended in 2022 is an understatement. Yet it taught me a lot about resilience, and it made me grateful.

You see, I've spent so much time automating and focusing on the things that matter. Even though 2022 wasn't as great as I hoped, I was still able to keep producing books and make record profit—all while facing tough personal issues.

If I hadn't spent the last ten years leading up to this year, it could have been devastating for me. But it wasn't, and I live to write another day.

Last year, I reduced my number of strategic priorities from five to three. That worked very well.

In 2023, I will maintain my three strategic priorities, but I will be changing how much time I allocate to them. Currently, I spend equal time on content creation, technology and data, and looking forward. In 2023, I will be reallocating my time so that 50 of my time is spent looking forward and the remaining time is divided between content creation and technology and data.

Why?

I still need to publish 100 books of course, but that is secondary to making a big pivot. As I wrote last year, I believe that 2022 is the last year to get my fundamentals right because things are changing in a big way. I need to be prepared to pivot in 2023, and to do that, I have to spend a significant amount of time learning new skills, particularly with AI. I anticipate that my first half of 2023 will be very quiet production-wise. That's okay because I'll make up for it with the knowledge I'll learn.

2023 is about leaning into the paradigm shift that's coming. I'm as ready as I will ever be. I'm extremely prolific, have a profitable writing business, and have made key investments that are beginning to pay off. Now it's time to figure out what's next: what the future of writing will look like.

I don't know what 2023 will have in store for me, but I'm looking forward to finding out.

MEET M.L. RONN

Science fiction and fantasy on the wild side!

M.L. Ronn (Michael La Ronn) is the author of many science fiction and fantasy novels including *The Good Necromancer*, *Android X,* and *The Last Dragon Lord* series.

In 2012, a life-threatening illness made him realize that storytelling was his #1 passion. He's devoted his life to writing ever since, making up whatever story makes him fall out of his chair laughing the hardest. Every day.

Learn more about Michael
www.authorlevelup.com (for writers)
www.michaellaronn.com (fiction)

MORE BOOKS BY M.L. RONN

Books for Writers

Indie Author Confidential (Series)
 How to Write Your First Novel
 Be a Writing Machine
 Mental Models for Writers
 The Indie Writer's Encyclopedia
 The Indie Author Atlas
 The Indie Author Bestiary
 The Reader's Bill of Rights
 The Self-Publishing Compendium
 150 Self-Publishing Questions Answered
 Authors, Steal This Book
 The Indie Author Strategy Guide
 How to Dictate a Book
 Advanced Author Editing
 Keep Your Books Selling
 The Author Estate Handbook
 The Author Heir Handbook

Interactive Fiction: How to Engage Readers and Push the Boundaries of Story Telling

Indie Poet Rock Star

Indie Poet Formatting

2016 Indie Author State of the Union

More Books for Writers:

www.authorlevelup.com/books

Fiction:

www.michaellaronn.com/books